JOAN

JOAN

The Remarkable Life of
JOAN LEIGH FERMOR

SIMON FENWICK

MACMILLAN

First published 2017 by Macmillan
an imprint of Pan Macmillan
20 New Wharf Road, London N1 9RR
Associated companies throughout the world
www.panmacmillan.com

ISBN 978-1-5098-4869-0

1 3 5 7 9 8 6 4 2

A CIP catalogue record for this book is available from the British Library.

Typeset in Electra LT Std 11.25/16 pt by
Palimpsest Book Production Limited, Falkirk, Stirlingshire

Printed and bound by CPI Group (UK) Ltd, Croydon, CR0 4YY

Visit **www.panmacmillan.com** to read more about all our books
and to buy them. You will also find features, author interviews and
news of any author events, and you can sign up for e-newsletters
so that you're always first to hear about our new releases.

Contents

List of Illustrations

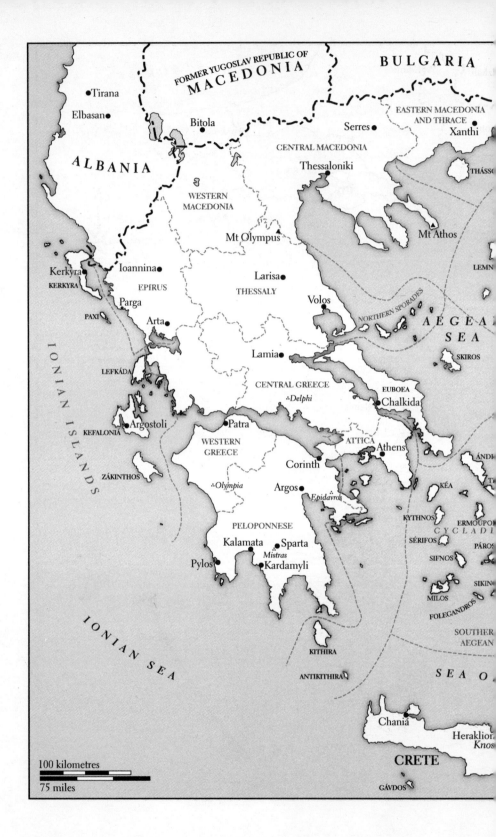

Introduction

Joan Leigh Fermor's life encompassed much of the twentieth century and the very beginning of the twenty-first. Born Joan Eyres Monsell in London in 1912 she was brought up on her family's estate in Dumbleton in Gloucestershire. She died aged ninety-one in 2003 in a house which she and her husband Patrick – 'Paddy' – Leigh Fermor built outside the village of Kardamyli in the southern Peloponnese. Joan's mother was an heiress and her father, who was of Anglo-Irish descent, was a highly successful politician during the inter-war years. Whatever assumptions her parents had about the life their daughter might lead – or thought she ought to lead – Joan's life turned out to be very different.

Joan's formal education was slight: such matters were thought unimportant. All a girl of her class was obliged to do was find an eligible suitor. When Joan's first lover, a young would-be writer called Alan Pryce-Jones, was found to have little money and doubtful prospects, he was soon sent packing. Pryce-Jones, though, was an incurably sociable young man and he moved in literary and bohemian circles; however brief their relationship, it changed her life. Through Alan, Joan met fashionable figures of the 1930s: the likes of John Betjeman, Cyril Connolly, Maurice Bowra, Brian Howard, Evelyn Waugh and Osbert Lancaster. They became her friends and Joan, who was beautiful, witty and fun, proved herself equal to their company. Throughout the 1930s Joan featured in the society pages of newspapers and magazines because of her clothes, because she went to the opera or the ballet or dined at the Ritz, or because she travelled to Russia with Robert Byron, or with Tom Driberg to New York.

In the 1930s Joan became interested in photography, which was a respectable means of earning a small income independent from her family allowance. She started to take pictures of her young intellectual friends. Betjeman was one, and it was he who suggested that she specialize in photographing architecture, an enthusiasm shared by them both. After the outbreak of World War II, she also took photographs of buildings destroyed by the bombing. In 1939 Joan married her first husband, John Rayner. Brought up in Dulwich, Rayner was a journalist. As features editor of the *Daily Express* and an influential figure in the world of newspapers, he had redesigned its layout when the *Express* was the biggest-selling newspaper in the country. However his marriage to Joan did not last: they had different ideas about the importance of marital fidelity.

In order to escape from the marriage Joan trained as a cryptographer and in 1942 she went to work abroad. In Cairo in late 1944 she met a young war hero called Paddy Leigh Fermor. They fell in love. Although Paddy and Joan were a couple for the rest of their lives they were frequently apart. Joan often stayed by herself in London or Gloucestershire and continued a highly sociable existence while Paddy went away to write – usually abroad. They loved Greece and everything Greek. In the 1960s they were at last in a position to buy a plot of land in Greece and at Kardamyli they built a house on the very edge of the Mediterranean. Joan taught herself the language by reading Greek translations of Agatha Christie novels.

Joan made it possible for Paddy to write, the only thing he ever seriously wanted to do. Although Paddy became famous for his military adventures, these were, in a sense, achieved by accident: he was the right man in the right place at the right time. But as one of his close friends said of him, a man who was forever losing his mackintosh was not suited to be a regular soldier. Joan supported Paddy both emotionally and financially, enabling him to become one of the finest travel writers of the twentieth century. That said, Joan is scarcely mentioned in any of his books. In *The Traveller's Tree*, Paddy's first, he makes a few references, including a description of her taking three films of photographs in a cemetery on the island of Guadeloupe. Some of Joan's pictures of monasteries in Anatolia are used to illustrate *A Time to Keep Silence*; and *Mani* (which is dedicated to Joan) and *Roumeli*, both of which are about Greece, include more of her work. The letters in *Three Letters from the Andes* were originally written to Joan. And this is all. Yet although diffident about her achievements, and deeply private, Joan was very far from being an anonymous figure.

In 1990 the academic and university administrator Noel Annan published a book called *Our Age: Portrait of a Generation*. Some four hundred and fifty pages long, *Our Age* is a tour de force, a sweeping history of British intellectual and political life during the course of the twentieth century. Annan begins by imagining who Maurice Bowra, the most famous Oxford don of the day, would claim to have made the times significant: 'to be a genuine member of Our Age it was not enough to be well-born, or well-known, or pleasure-loving. Nor was it enough to be a scholar. He liked people to be quick, intelligent and to delight in general ideas.' Among them he would have included Joan: she was, Annan wrote, a 'life-enhancer'.[1] Joan, who was perhaps surprised to find herself mentioned at all, wrote to Lord Annan to thank him. 'Dearest Joan,' he replied, 'how sweet of you to write about the book. I was so determined that you should feature on the first page.'[2]

This is a book about someone who enhanced many lives.

*

Paddy Leigh Fermor died in June 2011, eight years after Joan. I am an archivist, and was asked by the executors of the Leigh Fermor estate if I would go to Greece to sort out Paddy's papers before they were returned to England. A month later, I flew out to Kardamyli. What I remember most vividly about my arrival at the house where Paddy and Joan had lived for forty years was the scent of the jasmine that grew within the interior courtyard. That first evening I went down to the beach below the house to take my first swim; the sea was warm – I swam a lot that summer. Paddy's archive was substantial and quite chaotic; I spent two months sorting, listing and packing the papers, and by the time I finished I had filled nineteen large cardboard cartons with Paddy's records. I also filled nine black plastic sacks with rubbish – broken pens, bits of cardboard, newspapers, half a pornographic novel without a cover (I never found the other half), and all manner of general detritus. Eventually, after I had left, the archives were shipped back to the UK. In 2012 the archive was purchased by the National Library of Scotland in Edinburgh with a grant from the John R. Murray Charitable Trust.

If Paddy was a hoarder, Joan was the very opposite. Although the Dumbleton estate records still exist (in Gloucestershire Records Office), there are few Eyres Monsell family papers among them. In 1959, during the sale of Dumbleton Hall, Joan wrote to Paddy about her mother who was 'getting desperately ill just in the middle of moving, refusing to give up, rushing up and downstairs sorting out 80 years of rubbish.'[3] It is likely that this 'rubbish' included any family archives – which is all the more disappointing, since Joan had interesting and significant ancestors. Joan's personal archive was also very small. Only two or three paper items survive from before the 1940s: a couple of letters from John and Penelope Betjeman; a typed account by Joan of a tour by horse and trap around Ireland; and a 1936 pocket diary. Even these probably survived as much by accident as intention. Later, Joan kept other items, including Paddy's letters to her, but far more ended up in the waste paper basket or the fire-grate. Fortunately for a biographer, some of Joan's friends did keep her letters, and there are references to Joan in the biographies, autobiographies and published letters and diaries of her contemporaries, including those of John Betjeman, Maurice Bowra, Robert Byron, Cyril Connolly, James Lees-Milne, Nancy Mitford, Frances Partridge, Evelyn Waugh and, of course, Paddy. Also, importantly but untidily, there are about 3,000 photographs in Joan's collection; these too are now in the National Library of Scotland.

Although so much has been written about Paddy Leigh Fermor's life, no one had ever researched Joan's own history and so little had been written about her long relationship with Paddy. And so it was suggested that Joan too might be a worthwhile subject for a book. In writing this book, I would like to thank Paddy's god-daughter Olivia Stewart for her help at the start of the project, and the Paddy and Joan Leigh Fermor Arts Fund for making funds available for the original research.

In addition I am grateful to the following for their help in many and varying ways: Professor Stuart Ball; Elpida Beloyannis; Nick Casey; the late Susan Casey; Ian Collins; David Fenwick; Rev Dr John Fenwick; Diana FitzGeorge-Balfour; Jonathan Gathorne-Hardy; Philippa Jellicoe; James Kenward; Robert and Bridget Kenward; Lord Kinross; Martin Mitchell; Richard and Ruth Olney; Michael O'Sullivan; Professor James Pettifer; Antonia Phillips; David Pryce-Jones; Jonathan Reeves; Hamish Robinson; Father Julian Shurgold; Julianne Simpson; Sam Trounson; Jochen Voigt; Rita Walker; Alix Waterhouse; Chris White.

I have received hospitality from many people, but I must mention in particular Janetta Parladé and the late Jaime Parladé and Heulyn Rayner in Spain, Olivia Stewart in Italy, and Catriona and Mark Wilson in Edinburgh – all of whom I stayed with during the course of my researches.

I am indebted to Charles Arnold for his initial enthusiasm. He introduced me to my agent Michael Alcock of Johnson and Alcock, to whom I wish to express my gratitude for his patience and equanimity; I also thank my editor at Macmillan, Georgina Morley.

JOAN

David McClay, Graham Stewart and Helen Symington at the National Library of Scotland were always immensely helpful, enthusiastic and remarkably forbearing in my all-too-many requests for their assistance. I am grateful too for access and archival help from James Cox at Gonville and Caius College, Cambridge; Judith Curthoys at Christ Church, Oxford; Cliff Davies at Wadham College, Oxford; Adrian Glew at Tate Archives, London; Eleanor Hoare at Eton College; Julian Reid at Merton College, Oxford; Mary Ellen Budney at the Beinecke Rare Books and Manuscript Library, Yale University; John Frederick at Special Collections, University of Victoria, British Columbia; Pam Hackbart-Dean at the Lawrence Durrell papers, Special Collections Research Center, Morris Library, Southern Illinois University, Carbondale; Gayle Richardson at the Huntington Library, California. This book also owes much to the staff and resources of the London Library.

I am grateful to the Literary Executors of the Sir Patrick Leigh Fermor Estate for permission to quote from his papers; and to the Executors of the Joan Leigh Fermor Estate for permission to use both her photographs and archives. The photographs have been supplied by the National Library of Scotland.

Most of all I have to thank Joey Casey who has been a constant support and frequent companion in London, Gloucestershire, Scotland and Transylvania. Without her encouragement and friendship, and the many meals and bottles of wine enjoyed together, this book would have been much less of a pleasure to write. Both she and Ian Collins have read this book in draft form, but any errors I have failed to spot are of course my own fault.

This book is dedicated to my late parents. It is because of the encouragement I received from them during my childhood and youth that I have wanted to read books and tell stories.

London, June 2017

1

The Eyres and the Monsells

Every year Joan Leigh Fermor came back to England from her home in Greece three times – for Christmas, in the summer and in the spring, when the Dumbleton woods were thick with bluebells and the sound of cuckoos. A village of whitewashed cottages and red-brick houses on the border of Gloucestershire and Worcestershire, Dumbleton was always a home to Joan. 'One sunny walk in the woods was perfection, the trees all different greens & pale browns, their skeletons still showing, & carpets & carpets of bluebells & white garlic.'¹ It was May 1962 and Joan was writing to Paddy, her lover and partner although not yet her husband. Her childhood and early life had been spent in Dumbleton Hall, a large, rather ungainly mansion built in 1830 for the agriculturalist Henry Holland and sold by his descendants to Joan's family, the Eyres, fifty years later. The Eyres had considerably extended the Hall, and its great wealth of bedrooms made it the perfect place for childhood games of hide and seek. When Joan was born, in 1912, her family, the Eyres Monsells, owned most of Dumbleton and its surrounding land. The hedgerows were full of partridges. In 1928, when Joan was sixteen, the Great Western Railway began the construction of a steam train called Dumbleton Hall in its workshops in Swindon.*

---

* The train still runs on the Torbay and Dartmouth Railway.

1

Hymns composed by Joan's great-grandfather are still sung in the parish church of St Peter's. Her family monuments remain within the walls of the church and their family graves are in the churchyard. After the Hall was sold, Joan's brother Graham moved to a house on the edge of the village, so Dumbleton remained Joan's home in England.

Shortly after Joan first arrived in Athens in September 1945, to work at the embassy, she decided that – if she could get some land somewhere – she wanted to live in Greece. She felt guilty over the break-up of her first marriage and Greece suddenly seemed to represent a freedom from her past. Paddy, whom she had met less than a year earlier, already knew and loved the country and was more than willing to agree. England of course had its hold but, as Paddy said, a damp, green, summer's day in Dumbleton was much like living in a lettuce.[2] The attractions of a dry country were somewhat greater, particularly one where the cicadas whirred in the olive trees all summer long, where the people settled the world's problems over endless cups of Turkish coffee in cafes and enjoyed a passion for sitting up late eating and drinking and singing whenever the slightest excuse cropped up.[3] As it turned out, it was some years before Paddy found that piece of land for a house near Kardamyli, a remote village by the sea in the southern Peloponnese. It was Joan who paid for the house by selling her personal jewellery and using her family inheritance. But it seemed a price worth paying for a house that enabled Joan and Paddy to divide their lives across two countries and two cultures.

The money – of which there was a great deal – came from Joan's mother's side. Sybil Eyres Monsell was an heiress. Sybil's great-grandfather, Samuel Eyres, was a mill owner from Armley, on the outskirts of Leeds. He made his fortune from manufacturing worsted, the hard-wearing woollen cloth that was a staple of Victorian wardrobes. On his death in 1868, his obituary in the *Leeds Times* read:

A Leeds Millionaire has departed this life during the past week. Mr. Samuel Eyres had for a number of years been the principal member of the well known firm of William Eyres and Sons, woollen manufacturers of Leeds and Armley, and the career of his house has been almost exceptionally successful. This was partly owing to the business application of the deceased, and partly to the extreme penuriousness which marked his personal expenditure, and which characterized all his business transactions in which he was engaged . . . We do not find that he ever took an active share in either politics or social questions, his peculiar bent and disposition being to acquire wealth, which he succeeded in accumulating to the extent, it is rumoured, of above a million and a half.[4]

Not only, as the notice suggests, was Samuel Eyres both a skinflint and a miser, but he was famous for it. Asked why, when he travelled by train, he always sat on the wooden benches of the third-class carriages when he could easily afford the cushioned seats in first class, he retorted: 'Because there's no fourth class!' As a result of his hard work and his miserliness Sam Eyres died, in twenty-first-century terms, a multimillionaire. In his will Eyres left £1,000 a year for his daughter Anne and £500 to Anne's husband, the Reverend Samuel Kettlewell, vicar of Woodhouse in Leeds. The greater part of the fortune was left in trust to Anne's two children by Kettlewell, eleven-year-old Henry and nine-year-old Charles.

Anne died only a few months after her father. Her widower promptly left Woodhouse, claiming that it was a rough area and that the vicarage was damp. Furthermore, he was unwell and the boys were delicate, and it was not appropriate that they should 'meet with associates other than such I should like them to have'.[5] Kettlewell resigned his incumbency, moved south, married again and devoted the rest of his life to writing about Thomas à Kempis from his new home at 26 Lancaster Gate in London. Meanwhile, the income from the wealth was accumulating at a rate of some £50,000 a year, which was invested by the trustees in a mixture of land and property, including the Grand Hotel, Scarborough. The first part of the Dumbleton estate, including the Hall, was bought at auction by the trustees in 1875. According to the sale particulars, the estate was 'one of the most compact and remarkable freehold properties in England':

> It comprises a substantial, stone-built mansion containing accommodation for a Family of Distinction, seated on rising ground, surrounded by charming pleasure grounds, ornamental plantations and a well-timbered park, in addition [there] are several first-class farms, with superior residences and good homesteads, corn mill, brickyard, numerous small occupations and cottages, including the whole of the village of Dumbleton and the well-arranged schools, with teacher's residence embracing altogether an area of 2,182 acres, 0 roods and 35 perches.

The purchaser of the estate also became Lord of the Manors of Dumbleton and Didcot and had the right to appoint the rector of Dumbleton.

At the age of twenty-one, Henry and Charles each came into their considerable fortunes. Henry, who had attended Harrow and Trinity College, Cambridge, from which he graduated with a poor third as a Bachelor of Law, had changed his name by Royal Licence from Kettlewell to Eyres. In October 1880 he married his second cousin Caroline Sharp, the daughter of a wealthy Yorkshire landowner, at St Bartholomew's Church, Armley, 'in the presence of a large and fashionable company'.[6] In gratitude Henry presented the church with an enormous Schulze organ at a cost of £20,000. He had already given his fiancée a diamond tiara, which she wore in her hair with real flowers, and a pearl necklace; afterwards the bride left for her ill-starred honeymoon on the continent in a travelling dress of ruby satin, trimmed with plush, with bonnet to match. In their absence, additions and improvements were being made to their new house in Upper Grosvenor Street. By the spring of the following year Henry and Caroline – always known as 'Carrie' – had reached Rome, but during their stay at the Hotel Constanzi they fell ill with malaria. Instead of being ordered to return north, the local medical attendant suggested they convalesce in Naples. Unfortunately, both went down with typhoid fever. Carrie, who was now pregnant, recovered, but Henry died on 6 April at the age of only twenty-three.

Charles Kettlewell was tall and good-looking, but he was also weak-willed and suggestible. Because he was still a minor when his grandfather died – and presumably because of the amount of money involved – the courts appointed a guardian; his mother was dead but rather than appoint his father for some reason they chose a certain Captain F. Bowyer Bowyer-Lane. Captain Bowyer-Lane lost no time in taking young Charles off to 'see life', which meant the captain travelling around Europe while obtaining large sums of money from his ward. In Vienna, Bowyer-Lane was already the lover of a Hungarian woman called Lina Stern – a former mistress of the emperor's son, Crown Prince Rudolf – whom he subsequently married. At the age of nineteen, Kettlewell was soon introduced to Lina's sister Ernestine. Ernestine herself was only about seventeen when Bowyer-Lane induced them to marry. In later court actions she was described as a 'High Class Viennese Prostitute', and in the decades to come there were to be many complicated court proceedings relating to Charles's activities.

JOAN

After coming into his inheritance in 1880 Charles commissioned a 420-foot schooner, the *Marchesa,* from a shipyard on the Clyde. He wished to make a voyage which would be more than a pleasure trip – it would have a serious anthropological, biological and geological purpose, and to that end he invited Francis Guillemard, a twenty-nine-year-old doctor and naturalist, on board with him. Guillemard, who wrote an account of the voyage in his unpublished autobiography, had already travelled extensively and worked in South Africa during the First Boer War after taking his MD. He also knew that he had to get Kettlewell away from Bowyer-Lane, a man he called 'one of the most finished scoundrels [he] ever came across'. Now that Bowyer-Lane was Charles's brother-in-law he had access to Charles's £40,000 a year. Charles, however, seemed afraid of his former guardian and anxious to get away from him; Bowyer-Lane was a very bad sailor, and indeed hated the sea.

The *Marchesa* was very well appointed within and without, having curtains, brass lamps and fringed cloths on the tables. At last, in January 1882, she set sail from Cowes with thirty people on board. Kettlewell, who was accompanied by his wife Ernestine, was captain, but in name only; Lt Richmond ffolliott Powell and Guillemard were, in effect, the only officers on board. After a voyage through the Mediterranean via Sicily and a stop in Ismailia, Egypt, for a spot of quail shooting, they docked in Socotra and the Maldives before the *Marchesa* reached Colombo in Ceylon in April. In Ceylon, Charles immediately bought a half interest in a tea plantation. From Ceylon, the schooner proceeded via Singapore to Formosa and the Liu-kiu Islands, 250 miles east-north-east of Formosa, which Guillemard found 'approaching one's ideas of a terrestrial paradise'. They left 'laden with the mingled memories of ruined castles and the waving of innumerable fans', with a south-west breeze wafting them to Japan. The stop there was brief; the *Marchesa* left Yokohama for Kamchatka at the end of July. Guillemard was enraptured:

Ah! Those mornings of the far north! Does not the current of our blood, thickened by the fogs of a London November, or languidly pulsating under the sweltering heat of a tropic sun, quicken at the very thought of them? Do we not all feel young again as we recall the sound of our footsteps ringing on the frozen ground, and picture the wondrous beauty of the combination of pine-tree, sunlight and snow.[7]

Charles, 'who had little in the way of camp lore and backwoodmanship', managed to get lost just as night was falling and had to be rescued by some of the crew, who climbed up the almost perpendicular cliff of a fjord in the dark with lanterns to get at him.

They stayed two months in Kamchatka and did not return to Japan until the beginning of October. Four months' travel on a return trip to Japan was followed by six weeks cruising in Chinese waters. Leaving Hong Kong at the end of March 1883, some weeks were devoted to exploring the islands of the Sulu Archipelago in the Philippines, during which time Charles bought, or thought he had bought, one of the islands. After the Philippines, they proceeded to North Borneo, which was at the time still the territory of the North Borneo Company. The *Marchesa* started its homeward voyage, returning to Singapore to take in stores. On another visit to Ceylon, Charles spent £20,000 on a second tea plantation at Deltota in the centre of the island, eighteen months after he had bought his first.

Although many of the zoological specimens – including the gem of the collection, the Twelve-Wired Bird of Paradise – were to die on the journey, the schooner was always full of wildlife:

In the early morning our Dorei Bay cassowary [. . .] was as playful as a puppy. His favourite diversion was to get up a sham-fight with a ventilator, dancing around it in the approved pugilistic style, now feinting, now getting in a right and left. The blows were delivered by kicking out in front, and appeared to be almost ineffective, and quite unlike the really formidable method of attack adopted by the ostrich. The decorum of our service on Sundays was often considerably disturbed by his appearance among the congregation, engaged in a lively skirmish with a kangaroo – an amusement which invariably drew a select gathering of our dingo 'Banguey', various dogs, and a tame pig to see fair play.[8]

The schooner docked in Southampton on Easter Monday, 14 April 1884. The voyage had taken just over two years. Those animals and birds which survived were handed over to the Zoological Society of London, and the skins of those which had died and been preserved by Guillemard were presented to the Cambridge Zoological Museum. At the end of the voyage, Guillemard, despite all the problems of making notes on board ship when surrounded by bird cages, spent two more years writing *The Cruise of the Marchesa to Kamschatka & New Guinea: with notices of Formosa, Liu-Kiu and the Malay Archipelago*, which was eventually published in 1886 and dedicated to Charles for 'one of the pleasantest of many pleasant cruises'.

The Cruise of the Marchesa is a fascinating account of a late-nineteenth-century voyage of scientific discovery, but Guillemard's references to the ship's human inhabitants are very discreet. He must have been aware, though, of much else that was happening. In August 1884, only four months after their return home, a deed of separation was drawn up between Charles and Ernestine. Two law cases subsequently ensued: Kettlewell v Kettlewell and Lane, and Kettlewell v Kettlewell. Charles petitioned against Ernestine on account of her adultery with Captain Bowyer-Lane. Ernestine and Captain Lane counter-filed, naming countless adulteries with prostitutes and blaming Charles for her venereal disease, which Charles himself had contracted in Japan. In October 1882, on landing at Yokohama, Ernestine claimed Charles had gone up country for several weeks: 'After his return she had reason to complain of legal cruelty. They lived together for some time in Bryanston Square, where he neglected her very much, and absented himself from their house for days and nights. There was no truth in her husband's charges against her and Bowyer-Lane. Corroborative evidence of the legal cruelty was then given.' Charles Kettlewell's petition was dismissed in favour of Mrs Kettlewell and Bowyer-Lane, and on Ernestine's petitions the judge pronounced a decree nisi with costs and awarded a £3000 annuity.

In 1885, as if intent on using his money to buy his way into respectable society, Kettlewell became a governor of St Bartholomew's Hospital. In July that year, the Prince of Wales and three princesses went down by special train to Swanley in Kent in order to open the Kettlewell Convalescent Home. The home had been erected by Charles as a memorial to his brother Henry, and was for the use of the patients of St Bartholomew's. The brothers' father, the Rev. Samuel Kettlewell, said a short prayer at the opening.

Charles died in Aachen in Germany in February 1909, at the age of forty-nine. The will he had made took five years to discover, but in any event there were no assets. Over the previous twenty-eight years he had run through the whole of his vast fortune and was technically bankrupt. His financial and legal affairs were totally chaotic and his funeral expenses were paid by family trustees. Carrie bought her brother-in-law's great collection of stuffed birds and presented them to Leeds Museum. Years later, Guillemard was asked to identify the birds but all his careful numberings and identification notes had been lost. In 1910, a hunt started for the property on 'the Island of Sooloo' which Charles had bought during the cruise of the *Marchesa*. It was never found. The Ceylon plantations were finally sold by the trustees in 1932 for enough profit to pay off his borrowings from the estate and the sums due to Charles's last wife, Mabel. Within Joan's family, Charles Kettlewell was always known as 'the Wicked Uncle'.

Henry's early death meant that he was never able to squander the Eyres family inheritance in the manner of his brother although his widow Carrie was willing to make her own, more modest, financial speculations. Carrie returned to Dumbleton and her late husband's posthumous daughter was born on 21 August 1881. Caroline Mary Sybil Eyres was christened at St Peter's Church, where her grieving mother, Carrie, had installed a new east window in the chancel, 'To the Glory of God and in loving memory of Henry William Eyres'. The infant Sybil appears as an angel at the feet of Christ in the bottom of the central light. Over the next few years, Carrie oversaw the remodelling of Dumbleton Hall. The north wing of the house was very much enlarged – out of all proportion to the original building – in order to provide staff accommodation and service bedrooms. A *porte-cochère*, the very height of fashion in the 1890s, especially for railway stations and grand hotels, was added at the front door and a new conservatory adjoined the southern side of the house and extended into the garden. The original three-storey house was built by George Stanley Repton, the son of the landscape gardener Humphry Repton. It was sizeable if undistinguished; Repton's buildings invariably looked better in the imagination than they do in reality. The trustees had had a lake dug in the grounds and a boathouse built beside it. Dumbleton village was improved, too, with a new village hall, a new dairy and a laundry, as well as a group of four cottages which, after Sybil said that they looked more like palaces than estate workers' houses, became known as 'The Palaces'.

The Hall was home not only to Carrie and Sybil, but also to Carrie's mother Maria Sharp, her thirty-nine-year-old brother

Arthur Henry 'Harry' Sharp and Harry's seven-year-old daughter Maud. Harry, although only in his thirties, was a widower and a retired barrister. Carrie also invited her nephew Eddie Watt and his best friend Ewart Grogan to stay. Both had been Cambridge under-graduates until Grogan was sent down for rowdiness. Grogan's own mother was dead so 'Aunt Carrie' took him under her wing and he became part of the family. When a revolt broke out in Matabele-land, which had recently been invaded by Cecil Rhodes, Grogan set out for southern Africa and signed up as a trooper in the Matabele Mounted Police. Inevitably, the Ndebeles' spears were no match for the Maxim machine gun, and thousands of the natives were killed, after which Grogan became part of Rhodes's personal bodyguard for a time. Grogan drifted into Portuguese East Africa in search of game, where he nearly died of blackwater fever and a burst liver abscess. After accidentally killing a Portuguese man in a brawl in a bar over a girl, he left Africa in a hurry and returned to Dumbleton Hall.

Carrie decided that Grogan needed to marry and saw Eddie's sister, her niece Gertrude Watt, as the ideal wife. Having recovered his strength, Grogan went out to New Zealand with Eddie to meet his family, who were some of the wealthiest landowners and sheep ranchers in the country. As Carrie had hoped, Ewart Grogan and Gertrude were taken with one another and more than willing to marry, but Gertrude's stepfather considered Grogan a charming fortune hunter and told him he had to 'prove himself' first. On his return to England he went to stay again at Dumbleton. Aware of Cecil Rhodes's vision of a railway and telegraph stretching the length of Africa – an Africa preferably under British rule – Grogan decided that he would be the first man to trek from Cape Town to Cairo, despite his friends in the Foreign Office warning him that to strike due north for the Nile from Lake Tanganyika would be sui-cidal. Carrie not only offered to finance the whole expedition, but encouraged her brother Harry Sharp to join it. Harry was, as Grogan put it, 'bored with the dismal day to day life of the ultra rich'.[9]

Together they ordered mountains of supplies and equipment, including rifles and ammunition and Worcestershire sauce, 'without which life, or rather native cooking, is intolerable'. They read all available books and went to see 'old Africa hands';[10] they underwent a crash course in map-making from Mr Coles, the Map Curator of the Royal Geographical Society. Finally, at the end of January 1898, Grogan and Harry set sail for Beira in Mozambique; Grogan reckoned that he had already completed the Cape Town to Beira leg on his first trip to the continent. In order to acclimatize themselves on arrival, Harry and Grogan went on a hunting expedition to the extremities of the Gorongoza plain, where they encountered blue wildebeest and buffalo, one of which charged Harry. He stood his ground as if receiving a cavalry charge, and shot it dead at three yards. After three months of acclimatization they returned to Beira, with the trophies they collected helping to defray the costs of the expedition. They had also completed a rite of passage; big-game hunters were idolized in Europe and America as 'real men'.

Grogan and Harry Sharp made their way separately to Lake Tanganyika, where they met at M'towa, the principal station on the Congolese side of the lake. Sharp had pressed on in an attempt to escape the fevers which had afflicted him even more than Grogan. At the start of the journey he had been portly, but had become skeletal by the time Grogan met him at M'towa. His life had been saved by an itinerant doctor, who had nursed him back to relative health before himself succumbing to the fever and dying within days. When Sharp could be moved, the expedition crossed the lake to Ujiji on the German side of the lake – the meeting place of Stanley and Livingstone. At dawn on 12 April 1899, Sharp, Grogan, five Watongas bearing the Union Jack, ten armed Asiskas and 150 porters marched out of Ujiji, accompanied by an escort of German soldiers, each carrying on average a load of sixty pounds. They headed north-west into the Rift Valley lakes, through areas not previously visited by white men, carrying out mapping and survey work and shooting game on the way. As was the custom of explorers, they gave names to the mountains they encountered, and the first of the volcanic mountains of Rwanda they called Mount Sybil, after the daughter of their benefactress. An enormous flat-topped volcano became Mount Sharp and a peak to the east, of an estimated height of 13,000 feet, was named Mount Eyres, after Carrie herself. Here, in the foothills of the volcanoes, they survived attacks by cannibals as they passed along a trail lined not only with bodies but with grinning skulls, skeletons and pools of dried blood. Many of the porters deserted, and there were thefts by natives, encounters with lions and hyenas and yet more bouts of fever.

At Fort Portal in Uganda, Harry decided to go home. He was ten years older than Grogan and over the past months his health had suffered considerably. He had also received an urgent telegraph message saying that there were pressing family affairs at home. He set off with a hundred bearers carrying the unwanted stores and crates of trophies for England. On his return, the drawing room at Dumbleton Hall became adorned with lion skins, huge elephant tusks were hung on either side of the tall double doors leading from the outer to the inner hall and the staircase walls were covered in buffalo and antelope heads.

Grogan achieved his goal of reaching Cairo. By the time he got back to England in March 1900 he was a celebrity, and was met by a barrage of newspaper correspondents. Britain was by now in the midst of the Second Boer War; this great journey was a patriotic good-news story from a continent that was providing very few of them at the time. The Royal Geographical Society invited Grogan to address them; at twenty-five he was the youngest man ever to do so. Carrie Eyres invited him back to Dumbleton Hall to write *From the Cape to Cairo*, his account of his adventure. On its publication, the book met with considerable success. Queen Victoria summoned Grogan to Balmoral, where he presented her with one of the Union Jacks he had carried with him across the length of Africa.

In October 1900, Grogan finally married Gertrude, three years after they had last seen one another. Most of the rest of Grogan's life was spent in Kenya, where he accumulated about half a million acres of land. He was also politically active and, after his election as first President of the Colonialists' Association, became a thorn in the flesh of government authority. Ewart Grogan died in 1967 at the age of ninety-two, having outlived Harry Sharp by more than sixty years. Harry had died aged forty-six in 1905, never having recovered his health after his African adventure.

In May 1900, at the age of eighteen, Sybil Eyres was presented at court by her mother, and just over two years later she came of age. She was slight and very short-sighted, but she was now also very rich. In thanks, she paid for work to be completed on the tower of St Bartholomew's Church in Armley. A local newspaper reported Sybil's visit to see the work in progress:

> What a 'fine bonny lass' she looked. There were some on that day who thought it wasn't safe for 'Miss Sybil' to go climbing about in the new tower. But 'Nay' said the others, 'she's going to marry a sailor and it'll be a bit of practice for her.'[11]

The sailor was Lieutenant Bolton Meredith Monsell, the only surviving son of five children. His four younger sisters all adored and spoilt him. Known to family and friends as 'Bobby', he was tall, immensely good-looking and sociable, as well as charming and amusing. ('We didn't see much of that side of him,'[12] Joan commented.) In December 1904, he and Sybil were married by the

Rector of Dumbleton at St Paul's Church, Knightsbridge. Her Uncle Harry Sharp gave her away. The reception was held at the couple's new London home in Belgrave Square, and afterwards the bride and groom left for a honeymoon in the New Forest. They joined their names together and henceforth would be known as Eyres Monsell.*

The Eyres brought money to the marriage but the Monsells brought an ancient heritage. A Philip Maunsell served under William the Conqueror and received confiscated English lands as a reward. In the sixteenth century, John Mounsell was a merchant of Weymouth and Melcombe Regis in Dorset and his second son, John, became a prominent London merchant. In a bid to join the gentry, John purchased land in County Limerick in 1612 and the family eventually became prominent members of the Anglo-Irish ascendancy.

Bolton's grandfather, J. S. B. Monsell, was a clergyman and a prolific hymn-writer – his three hundred hymns include 'Fight the Good Fight' and 'Oh Worship the Lord in the Beauty of Holiness'. His son, Bolton James Monsell, was an army officer who joined the police service in 1886 and became Chief Constable of the Metropolitan Police. In turn, this Bolton's son – Bolton – was a very socially aware and highly ambitious young man. From leaving Stubbington House, his preparatory school in Fareham, he had spent nearly all his early life at sea. In 1894, he entered HMS *Britannia* as a cadet, went to sea as a midshipman two years later and from 1903 he specialized as a Torpedo Lieutenant. Sybil was a very considerable catch for such a lowly officer – albeit one with a name – and his

---

* Patrick Leigh Fermor, loving pedantries, made notes on Joan's father for his entry in the *New Oxford Dictionary of National Biography*: 'If the name was ever written with a hyphen, it appears to have been dropped in practice, as it is absent in Burke, *Who's Who*, and *Debrett's Handbook*, and though the two names are written together neither Graham or your sisters have ever used the hyphenated form.'

marriage to an heiress enabled him to buy himself out of the navy and embark upon a political career.

Graham, Bolton and Sybil's only son, was born in November 1905, and Diana, their first daughter, in 1907. In January 1910 Bolton was elected Conservative MP for the constituency of Evesham and the following year, at the suggestion of Bonar Law, he was appointed a whip. On 5 February 1912, his second daughter was born in London and christened Joan Elizabeth. Joan's younger sister, Patricia, was born in 1918. All resembled one another physically and temperamentally: the Eyres Monsell children were tall and slim and shared the same high cheek bones; all seemed reserved, and all in varying degrees were private and apparently aloof. Sybil was so painfully stiff and shy that she used to invite the wife of her husband's political agent, Bertram Cartland, to her own house parties in order to break the ice.* From their mother the children inherited both their shyness and the short-sightedness for which Sybil carried a lorgnette. Physically however they took after the Monsells.

As an adult, Joan never spoke about her family, saying only, vaguely, that she had nothing in common with them (her adored brother Graham was the exception). This was not quite true. Her father was a sailor and on both sides there were travellers, explorers and writers. It is understandable why she might have wanted to share her life with someone who shared these longings.

---

* Bertram Cartland and his wife, Polly, were the parents of the romantic novelist Barbara Cartland.

2

Growing Up

According to the census return of 2 and 3 April 1911, Dumbleton Hall had fifty rooms including kitchens (sculleries, closets and bathrooms were not counted). Bolton and Sybil were at home that weekend, along with ten indoor members of staff – one of whom was designated the 'electric light assistant'. Their two children, Graham and Diana, were at the family's London home in Belgrave Square, which was next door to the Austro-Hungarian embassy. To look after them in London they had a children's nurse, a nursery maid and a Swiss governess, Mlle Fanny Gree. In London there were also eight other members of staff. Graham was five, Diana three.

At Dumbleton, the young Eyres Monsells were brought up in the nurseries on the attic floor above the main bedrooms, which was where the staff also lived. When she was young, Joan spent more time with the maids and the nursery staff than with her parents, and later said she really only loved her nanny. The children's mother and father were not seen until teatime, when, after having been spruced up and made presentable, Joan and the others were taken down into the drawing room. Bolton's sisters, who lived in London, also had children; there were eleven cousins in all and the Eyres Monsell, Watkins, Christian and Daniell children spent much of their time together. There is a photograph of eight of the cousins taken at Sandbanks in Dorset, where all the children used to stay in the summer with the Watkins grandmother. The children are arranged in descending order of height, from Diana on the left. Joan is the fifth along, aged about six. Her gaze at the camera is suspicious and resentful – even at so young an age she never liked having her picture taken.

Dumbleton was ideal for the young; there were all those bedrooms full of toys, there was a rocking horse in the conservatory, a fourteen-acre garden, a swimming pool (which was invariably covered in green weed), woods, and a lake with a boat and an island on which the older children could maroon the younger ones. Graham and Diana had a game they called 'The Charge'. The main herbaceous borders at Dumbleton were on a steep hill, and the aim was to descend as fast as possible using every mode of transport, with or without brakes, to propel themselves and (willingly or not) their visitors and little sisters down the hill and over the path without crashing into the railings or falling into the lake. This game, needless to say, was a cause of many accidents, tears and much sticking plaster.

At Christmastime, the big rooms in the Hall were decorated with holly and mistletoe; there were great blazing logs in open fireplaces, and splendid meals at which the children sat down together at one table. At breakfast on Christmas morning the presents were all piled on each plate. There was also dancing, a village Christmas tree, church and carols and visits to the well-scrubbed dairy to drink cream. The Dumbleton Dixies gave a performance in the village hall and the cousins blackened their faces, danced and played what instruments they could find. Gino Watkins, a young cousin, and Smith, the genial chauffeur, sang 'I'm Alabama Bound' till the strings broke on Smith's ukulele.

One day in August 1914, while Bolton was playing tennis on the lawn at Dumbleton during a house party, a footman approached with a telegram. The game stopped and the guests rapidly dispersed. Great Britain, its empire and colonies were at war. Bolton returned to active duty in the navy as a Lieutenant Commander. In 1915, he was in command of a monitor (a small battleship) at Gallipoli; afterwards he became a liaison officer between the army and navy in Egypt and was awarded the Order of the Nile for his service. His wife had her own wartime maritime drama on her way to meet him in Egypt: in December 1915, Sybil was on board a Japanese liner, the *Yasaka Maru*, in the Mediterranean, when the ship was hit by a torpedo. She wrote an account of the submarine attack from Shepheard's Hotel in Cairo, which was later published in the *Upton Times*. Sybil, who always cared about what she wore, appeared to be as much concerned with clothes as anything else:

> Now I will tell you about the shipwreck! It happened at about 2.45 in the afternoon. I was dressed in my old brown tweed and my little purple velvet hat as we did not expect to get in till after dinner and I was going to make myself respectable later. I had just gone down to my cabin and I was discussing one or two things with Cameron [her lady's maid], when there came this violent bang which shook the whole ship. Cameron remarked, 'There now, there's that submarine' and started putting things hastily into her bag! I got down the lifebelts and put one on and my big coat [. . .] Just when the bang came I don't think I felt frightened; it was just a sort of hopeless feeling that everything one possessed must be lost.[1]

The lifeboat, which had about twenty-five people in it, was rescued the next day by a small French tug. Everyone was hauled over the sides by two men, arriving on board head first, and there were only old oil cans to sit on.

People of course were dressed anyhow, half of them hadn't any hats on. One woman was changing her dress, so just had a fur coat on top of her petticoat, and there were several women with small babies and no nurse or anyone with them. It must have been awful for them.

At the end of the war, Sybil was awarded the CBE for her war work as a donor and administrator for King Edward VII's Hospital for Officers in Grosvenor Crescent. Bolton and Sybil's busy wartime lives meant that they were even more absent than they would otherwise have been from their children's lives. There was just over six years between Joan and her brother and the young girl had become close to her sibling – perhaps she found in him a substitute masculine figure for her absent father. When Graham was absent at his preparatory school at Bexhill-on-Sea she must have felt it keenly. Joan meanwhile, like her sister Diana, was educated at home.

After leaving Bexhill-on-Sea, Graham entered Eton College in September 1919, two months before his fourteenth birthday. He was beginning to make his way in the world. On his first day and in the same house – Corner House – Graham found a new friend in Alan Pryce-Jones, the much-indulged son of a colonel in the Coldstream Guards. They were both young aesthetes in the making, and their friendship was intimate and life-long. Pryce-Jones later wrote how Graham had 'early developed the art of rejecting unnecessary ties of thoughtless friendship and devoted himself whole-heartedly and generously to the very few chosen'.[2] Corner House overlooked the rat-infested graveyard of Eton Chapel and had been in use as a boys' boarding house since 1596. It was not a pleasant environment:

A narrow staircase with uneven wooden treads worn shiny, smooth and razor-edged by generations of boys led up to three boys' passages. There was little uniformity about either the passage or the boys' rooms. In parts the passages were so narrow that two people could pass only by turning sideways [. . .] the appearance of the boys' side was mournful to a degree; in fact taken as a whole it was like a slum tenement, with two dingy bathrooms with concrete floors at the end of the middle passages for the use of forty-one boys.[3]

Pryce-Jones recalled Aymer Whitworth – their housemaster and Classics 'beak' – as a rather austere man, but to Alec Dunglass (who later became Alec Douglas-Home), Whitworth had a great understanding of human nature, and of the young male going through 'the dark tunnel of adolescence'.

A generation of star pupils – Harold Acton, Cyril Connolly, Brian Howard, Eric Blair (George Orwell), Anthony Powell – had just left Eton, but among Graham's contemporaries were Henry Yorke (Henry Green), A. J. Ayer, Ian Fleming, Peter Watson – who later funded Connolly's *Horizon* – James Lees-Milne, Hamish Erskine – an early, fruitless obsession of Nancy Mitford – and Nancy's brother, Tom Mitford. School days passed in a regular rhythm from divisions (lessons) at 7.30 a.m. until 5.45 p.m., followed by a long period of prep. Each day there was also compulsory chapel attendance and two periods of PE or military drill. The day ended at 9.15 p.m.

At Lent 1921, Graham was recorded as being in OTC (Officer Training Corps) No. 1 Squad. Aged fifteen, he was already five foot nine and physically robust. The free life he enjoyed on the Dumbleton estate had suited him. He had learnt to ski in Switzerland and he played tennis avidly. Graham's school fellows Jim Lees-Milne and Tom Mitford were near neighbours, and – together with his sister Diana – regular opponents at tennis matches. Lees-Milne disliked Graham and found his behaviour terrifying.

At children's tennis tournaments he used to bash his racquet over my head so that I looked like a clown peering through a broken drum, and once at Wickhamford* he let out my father's parrot so that it flew away, and [he] drove the car out of the motor house into a ditch.[4]

Probably Graham, who never wavered in his sexual inclinations, was already active in other ways. A discreet homosexuality was as much a part of the Eton environment as arts and games. In this exclusively male atmosphere, love affairs flourished. The prettier young boys became a substitute for girls – prefects sent fags on bogus errands so that others could ogle them. Boys who did not excel at games retreated into femininity. 'We were feminine,' wrote Henry Yorke, 'not from perversion [. . .] but from a lack of any other kind of self-expression [. . .] we screamed and shrieked rather than laughed and took a sly revenge rather than having it out with boxing gloves.'[5] Peter Watson, 'a slow-speaking, irresistibly beguiling young man', enticed Alan Pryce-Jones up to his room. He led him to his bookcase, where he extracted a little bottle from behind the Latin dictionaries which he 'unscrewed in ecstasy, murmuring, "Smell this: it is called *Quelques Fleurs*."'[6] And Jim Lees-Milne's relationship with Tom Mitford went well beyond tennis:

> On Sunday eves before Chapel at five, when the toll of the bell betokened that all boys must be in their pews, he and I would, standing on the last landing of the entrance steps, out of sight of the masters in the ante-chapel and all the boys inside, passionately embrace, lips to lips, body pressed to body, each feeling the opposite fibre of the other.[7]

---

* Wickhamford Manor was Lees-Milne's childhood home.

Shortly after he had turned seventeen in November 1922, and without completing the school year, Graham left Eton. In August 1923 he entered the Royal Military College at Sandhurst and stayed until the end of 1924. With a service background of his own, Bolton doubtless considered that the army regime – of drill, physical training, lectures on leadership and strategy – would help make a man of his only son. He must already have been aware of Graham's artistic interests and, quite possibly, his sexual preferences. How amenable Graham was to all this it is difficult to say, but it is unlikely that he would have been strong enough to resist his father's wishes. In January 1925, Graham was commissioned into the Royal Dragoons where, ironically, there were aspects which might have appealed to him. A Guards officer was, first of all, a gentleman, and the life was not necessarily unsuited to an aesthete and a dandy. Graham was a tall and handsome young man and his expensive and close-fitting uniform would have suited him very well. Regiments like the Royal Dragoons were largely composed of men from the great public schools and great families, usually with large independent incomes. They considered themselves outside middle-class morality in matters of profligacy and sexuality, and still maintained a connection with the world of Beau Brummell.[8] Homosexual encounters would also have been easily available on the fringes of this social circle. There were plentiful working-class rent boys and soldiers from the lower ranks of the Guards regiments who would be willing to provide sexual services, and could be paid to keep their silence.

Graham should have been happy in such a milieu, if he was to be happy anywhere. But by November, just ten months after his commission, his army career, for whatever reason, was finished.

Graham had spent the summer before he left Sandhurst in the French Alps with his cousin Gino Watkins. Gino was two years younger than Graham and was about to go to Cambridge. He had travelled out alone, sleeping quite happily on the wooden seat of a third-class carriage, and had met Graham at Chamonix. They spent their time together climbing in the mountains until Graham returned to England. Gino was fair-haired, blue-eyed, sleek and lithe; 'an elegant and unserious young man, confident in his popularity among acquaintances or his charm of manners among strangers to ensure his enjoyment of the game of life'.[9] Such an air of insouciance was something Graham could never possess.

The Watkins family were very much the poor relations of the Eyres Monsells. Unfortunately Gino's father, Colonel Henry George Watkins of the Coldstream Guards, 'possessed an uncanny ability to spot a dud investment from a long distance'. Finding himself embarrassed by his lack of money – for to do things in London was very expensive and not to do them was dull – he left his wife Jennie and went to live in Switzerland. When Gino was only twenty, his mother quietly said goodbye to her three children and their old nanny, then caught a train to Eastbourne, where she hired a taxi to take her to the cliff at Beachy Head. She was never seen again.

That same year Gino organized his first expedition to Spitsbergen, as a result of which he was made a Fellow of the Royal Geographical Society even though he was officially under age. He was famous. His last expedition – undertaken in order to establish an air route between England and Winnipeg – was Gino's crowning achievement. 'If a man wants anything badly enough, he can get absolutely anything,' he said. The RGS awarded him its Polar Medal, its first for sixty years. He was, however, diffident about these achievements, as Gino's biographer and frequent companion on his expeditions recalled:

Gino was lent a small, simply furnished room on the second storey of the Royal Geographical Society – a room which was to become very intimately connected with him later on. There, during nearly two months, he and I sat at a trestle-table drawn up to the open window. One morning Gino brought a Japanese fan which he had looted from a dance the night before. He leaned back, fanning himself and gazing out of the window whenever he stopped to recall some incident of a journey of which the survey notes reminded him; and he always kept the fan beside him 'so that,' he said, 'I can always give the right impression if anyone very tough and hearty comes to see me.'[10]

Unable because of the Great Depression to raise funds for an Antarctic expedition, he went back to Greenland to continue the British Air Route expedition. He spent the Christmas of 1931 at Dumbleton, where he read two or three books a day, helped with the village Christmas tree, and walked as far as the dairy to drink cream as he had done as a child; he also met Stanley Baldwin at a lunch party. He gave a polar-bear skin rug to the Eyres Monsells as his present. The following August, Gino went out alone in his kayak one day to hunt for seals to feed his party. Later two of his companions found his kayak floating upside down upon the water, the paddle floating about 150 yards away and his trousers on an ice floe. 'He was always appropriate, and it was right that none should see him dead.'[11]

Joan's extended family of aunts and uncles and cousins were close and spent a great deal of time with one another. In their company even Sybil felt at ease. There are a lot of photographs of family gatherings, both formal and informal. When anything happened, everyone cared. A memorial plaque was raised to Gino in Dumbleton church. In an odd coda to this story, some years after both his mother and Gino had drowned, Gino's brother Tony shot himself in a swimming pool. There was a strain of eccentricity in that branch of the family.

*

Immediately on leaving the army Graham went on a scientific and big-game shooting expedition in central Africa with Major F. G. Jackson. In going to Africa, Graham would at least have avoided his father. Jackson, who was sixty-five at the outset of these travels, was an explorer and imperialist in the manner of Cecil Rhodes. He had made significant polar expeditions in the 1890s serving in both the Boer and First World Wars. His travels with Graham were motivated more by a love of adventure and the opportunities for big-game hunting they presented than any genuine scientific or imperial endeavour – and Graham's parents were paying for them. Graham and Jackson began their journey at Beira in Mozambique and travelled westwards across the continent. At Nyansa in Rwanda, the king gave an exhibition of sports in their honour: spear throwing, archery and high jump. In Jackson's published account of their travels, *The Lure of Unknown Lands*, there is a photograph showing a Watusi tribesman leaping over Graham – who was six foot three and wearing a double-crowned hat – with space to spare.

After seven months without news, at Stanleyville on the Congo they found letters from England and comparatively recent newspapers. They stayed ten days in Stanleyville before taking a paddle steamer to Kinshasa, and from there a train to Matadi and a steamer for Europe. They had walked nearly 1,700 miles from the Indian Ocean to the Atlantic.

The expedition over, Graham arrived in Oxford in October 1927 to study history at Merton College. If Bolton and Sybil had hoped the rigours of their son's African adventure would curb his 'artistic' tendencies, they were to be disappointed. Although obliged to write essays and attend lectures, Graham was not the most assiduous of scholars. Indeed, after the disciplines of Eton and the Guards, it was probably at Oxford that Graham felt himself sufficiently liberated from his father to enjoy himself fully. Shortly after his arrival at

Merton he celebrated his twenty-second birthday, and took the opportunity to be as eccentric and as uninhibited as he dared. Only a couple of weeks after the start of his first term, on 2 November, he was fined £1 for making a noise in his room. With his looks, Graham would have stood out anywhere, but he set a fashion for wearing black polo sweaters and minute bow ties. He held tea parties wearing fancy dress and gained a reputation for being 'dashing' – the 'fastest' man in the university – and it was alleged that he took drugs. This was jazz age Oxford. Osbert Lancaster, a new friend who was also a 'figure' at Oxford and who also dressed to be noticed, set the scene:

> The student body as a whole formed an admirable chorus-line against which the principals could make their exits and their entrances. On the one hand were the hearties, grey-flannel trousers or elaborately plus-foured, draped in extravagantly long striped scarves indicative of athletic prowess; on the other the aesthetes, in high-necked pullovers or shantung ties in pastel shades from Messrs. Halls in The High, whose hair in those days passed for long and some of whom cultivated side-burns.[12]

Both Osbert and Graham were unquestionably aesthetes. Lancaster also recalled, with regard to his own lack of enthusiasm for Anglo-Saxon and Middle English studies, how his tutor 'very soon, I fancy, came to realise that to arouse, let alone maintain, my interest in the insufferable Beowulf or Sir Gawain and the Green Knight was a task well beyond his powers, and it was seldom long before we had abandoned Grendel and his mother in their gloomy mere and gone on to discuss the latest performance of *Les Biches** or the social impli-

---

* This ballet was choreographed by Bronislava Nijinska to music by Francis Poulenc, and premiered in 1924.

cations of Graham Eyres Monsell's party the previous Saturday'.[13] In his favour, Graham was acknowledged as the most accomplished pianist – jazz and classical – in the university, as well as its finest skier.

Two Oxford dons were rivals for the attentions of the undergraduates: George Kolkhorst and Maurice Bowra. Kolkhorst was known as 'the Colonel', because he was so little like one; a young Spanish don at Exeter College, he was a natural eccentric. He wore white suits and an eye glass and carried an ear trumpet 'to catch any clever remarks'. On Sunday afternoons, he held sherry and marsala parties in his gas-lit rooms in Beaumont Street, which he furnished with Japanese coats of armour and oriental figures under domes. The room smelled of dogs and chicken soup and of the mice living in the armour. Graham gravitated naturally to the Kolkhorst set, and was a regular visitor at Beaumont Street.

Maurice Bowra was the most influential don in Oxford. Although in some ways very much part of the Oxford establishment, Bowra was also an anti-institutional figure. In his autobiographical poem *Summoned by Bells*, John Betjeman remembered his 'grand contempt for pedants, traitors and pretentiousness'. Bowra was not an eccentric like Kolkhorst, but the students who gathered in his rooms found themselves both dominated and stimulated by his overwhelming and life-enhancing personality. His circle of favoured undergraduates included students who were later to become celebrated in their own right: John Betjeman, Cyril Connolly, Evelyn Waugh, Hugh Gaitskell, John Sparrow, Isaiah Berlin, Harold Acton, A. J. Ayer, Kenneth Clark and very many others. Bowra also later became an intimate of Joan. Graham must have spoken of all this to his sister and she can only have envied him for his opportunities. Joan's world at this time was still limited to the confines of school and the pony club.

While the vast majority of students no doubt got on with their work and lived quite modestly and conscientiously, less academic necessities were a concern for many. Where there were so few opportunities to meet women, homoeroticism and sentimental male friendship were considered by many as both acceptable and normal, although egregious homosexual behaviour was still an offence punishable by expulsion. 'Men who liked women were apt to get sent down,' Cyril Connolly wrote.[14] While they might later have suppressed or lost interest in their former sexual behaviour, for the time being many were caught up in the prevailing culture. Connolly himself went on to be a famous womanizer, but his early experiences were all with his own sex. John Betjeman was alleged to have had sex with W. H. Auden for £5, and he swooned over Hugh Gaitskell ('Hugh, may I stroke your bottom?' 'Oh, I suppose so, if you must.').

Whatever his social reputation, Graham's behaviour and academic work were never satisfactory. Too much of his career at Oxford was spent socializing with well-bred young men and dining at the George, a bohemian cafe-cum-restaurant at the corner of Cornmarket and George Street, whose habitués called themselves 'the Georgeoisie'. Having failed to return to classes a full month after Christmas 1927, Graham was not allowed to return to Oxford for the remainder of his second term.

When he returned to Oxford for the summer term, the student magazine, *Cherwell*, carried two drawings of Graham – one a portrait of his head and shoulders, which occupied nearly a full page and another, much smaller sketch of Graham on a ski slope. There were also a few paragraphs of gossip relating to him at which Graham took – or pretended to take – offence. *Cherwell* was edited at the time by Maurice Green, with Osbert Lancaster as his deputy.*

---

* Maurice Spurgeon Green (1906–87): journalist at the *Financial Times* and *Times*; editor of the *Daily Telegraph*, 1964–74.

Their editorship had already caused many confrontations with the university proctors, the most recent of which had resulted in a heavy fine for publishing an indecent joke about the writer Godfrey Winn.

When Graham next met Maurice Green in the George, he handed him his card 'in the approved style' and challenged him to a duel. The *Daily Mirror* and several regional newspapers took up the story, under the headline 'A Real Duel – Undergraduate Pinked at Oxford':

> Graham Eyres-Monsell [sic], son of the Conservative Chief Whip, fought in eighteenth-century costume of knickerbockers and silken hose in Dead Man's Walk, Merton. It was no mock affair, one of the duellists stated on Wednesday. [. . .] Apart from the principals and seconds, only two persons saw the duel, one being a Munich doctor who arrived at the meeting place armed in readiness with bandages and cotton wool and the other a curious passer-by who inquired if all the fuss was for films. Mr Eyres-Monsell said that when he challenged Green it was not with any seriousness. 'But one thing led to another and finally we had to fight. I never thought the affair would result as it did. It might have proved very serious. As a matter of fact I have made up my quarrel with Green and we are quite good friends.'[15]

Most of the undergraduates, including the 'Munich doctor' were members of the Oxford University Dramatic Society, and they had hired props from a theatrical costumier. A photograph appeared in the Saturday edition of *Cherwell*, together with a fictitious account of the duel. In university circles it was all regarded as a successful hoax, and three days later cheers greeted Graham and Maurice Green when they arrived for a debate at the Union.

The university authorities took matters less lightly. The principals were each fined £10 and the seconds – Osbert was Graham's

– £5. Although he succeeded in passing his preliminary exams during the summer term, in June 1928 he was fined both for smoking in hall and for holding another noisy party. He also appeared for debt in the Vice Chancellor's court. The debt had still not been paid by the following October, and the Warden's and Tutors' Committee passed a resolution that Graham be sent down unless he paid his kitchen and buttery expenses, which were known as 'battels'. They still had not been paid at the end of November, he was gated and told to pay by the following Wednesday or be sent down. Early in May 1929 he was nearly sent out of residence yet again for the non-payment of battels. Then in June the warden and tutors at Merton decided that Graham would not be allowed to continue at Merton unless he passed a scripture exam before October. He also had to return to the Vice Chancellor's court for not having paid a debt of £34 4s 9d, which he had run up at Sidney Acott's music shop in the High Street. Maurice Green became a distinguished journalist and his double-first degree was counted among the most brilliant of his generation, but after only two years Graham returned home to Dumbleton, his name was taken off the college books, and his university career came to an inglorious end.

Not long after her brother had left for Eton, Joan's sister Diana was sent to St James's School, which stood on the slopes of the Malvern Hills in Worcestershire. She hated it. The school had been founded by two sisters, Alice and Kitty Baird, in 1896. Although the Miss Bairds tried to make school life pleasant, St James's came as a considerable shock to any girl used to home comforts. The position of the house, a converted nineteenth-century mansion, was exposed, and sometimes it was bitterly cold. The bedroom annexe had three outside walls and windows to the floor. Even in winter, the windows were kept open at night, and the girls woke to find that snow had drifted into the room. The school uniform was basic – white cotton shirts, navy blue coats and skirts, and in summer the girls wore yellow straw hats with yellow knots and black velvet ribbon, which they called 'scrambled eggs'. Juniors were only allowed to wash their hair once a month – no doubt to discourage vanity – and all girls were only allowed to brush their hair three times a week.

Examinations were not regarded as being of much importance. Miss Alice, the headmistress, adopted an American system which, in her words, 'developed the spirit of enquiry and curiosity and joy in learning'. There were no rigid timetables and girls were to regard the teacher as a friend and helper. What the Miss Bairds most wanted to instil was citizenship and public service. St James's girls were to be prepared for their intended status in society; educating them for a career was of secondary importance, if considered at all. It was not until the 1960s that a girl from St James's went on to university. Such was the sense of excitement at this great achievement that the whole school was given the day off.

When Joan joined her sister at St James's she hated it every bit as much. Joan regarded her school career as hopelessly unsatisfactory, and her consequent lack of a university education was a lifelong regret. She had learnt neither Latin nor Greek, and it was a cliché among her school contemporaries, 'to think the only thing I learnt at St James's was how to curtsey.' Joan joined the Girl Guides, which was strongly encouraged (Baden Powell and his wife were close friends of Alice Baird and in July 1927 the Chief Scout and Guide paid their first visit), but perhaps the school's only lasting virtue as far as she was concerned was that it encouraged the arts. Along with a music club, a ping-pong club and a junior branch of the League of Nations, there was also a photography society at the school and it was through photography that Joan would one day find a means of liberation.

After leaving St James's, Joan attended a finishing school in Paris. The sisters of the French teacher Mlle Delpierre, a strong disciplinarian whose 'silent presence at the top of the stairs could quell a Boot-Hole riot',[16] ran the school at the Villa St James in the rue de Charles Lafitte, where older girls could improve their French accent. St James's in Malvern also had a connection with a Swiss finishing school at Beaupré outside Geneva. Here Joan learnt to ski, although, unlike Graham, never very confidently.

During the 1920s Joan grew up from a girl to a young woman. In the family photograph albums there are pictures of Joan picking lavender and paddling in streams with her family or with horses. In September 1923 she received a mention in the *Gloucestershire Echo* as runner-up as a skilful rider on a child's pony in the gymkhana at Winchcombe Carnival – the local hunt met frequently at Dumbleton for, in so many ways, hunting was at the heart of local society. Nearly seven years later, in February 1930, Joan celebrated her eighteenth birthday. In April her photograph appeared in the *Bystander*, a weekly society magazine: 'The Beautiful Second Daughter of Sir Bolton and Lady Eyres Monsell'. Joan had moved on from the pony club. She was ready to be presented to society.

3

Romance

After his ignominious departure from Oxford in 1929, Graham returned home to Dumbleton in disgrace. Following the fiasco of his brief time in the army, this second disaster was a humiliation. Graham was twenty-four and in need of a proper career, but his next plan – to go to Paris and study to become a concert pianist – was regarded by his father with distaste. In June, just as his son and heir was shamed, he had been knighted. Sir Bolton was a worldly man with regard for his position in society and the social order. He liked women and the 'smart set' and had little time for any inferiority; he did not regard being a musician as either an appropriate or a sufficiently manly profession for a gentleman.

Two of Graham's closest friends, John Betjeman and Alan Pryce-Jones, suffered similar embarrassments. Betjeman left Oxford under a cloud at Christmas 1928, when it became obvious that he was incapable of passing his forthcoming exams. C. S. Lewis, his tutor, refused to give him a good reference and he was only rescued from his lowly teaching post when Maurice Bowra and other influential friends pulled strings for him. Subsequently, he was appointed assistant editor at the *Architectural Review*, a job to which Betjeman brought a genuine interest and enthusiasm, and which paid him a salary of £300 a year. Pryce-Jones's career at Oxford was even briefer than Graham's. (Alan's mother had asked Betjeman to look after him at Oxford; Osbert Lancaster said it was like asking Satan to chaperone sin.[1]) After two terms, during which time he neither worked nor paid his bills, Pryce-Jones was sent home for breaking college regulations. His father was furious, his outrage made worse because Peter Watson had delivered Alan home in his Rolls-Royce, and greeted the Pryce-Joneses with hearty geniality before the storm broke. Alan's father told him that he was unfit even to serve in the colonies, and he would certainly not be returning to Oxford. The following morning Alan had the good luck to encounter a friend who told him that Sir John Squire, the editor of a literary monthly, the *London Mercury*, was having his hair cut in the National Liberal Club. Alan introduced himself and was taken on as an unpaid assistant editor at the magazine.

Despite a recent encounter with a French girl – which he had found disappointing – Alan was largely homosexual; he was, however, self-aware enough to know that for a charming young man, both his sexual ambivalence and his attractiveness could be a passport into social and literary success at what was to be the beginning of a lifelong literary career.

Graham, who wrote to Alan regularly, started his studies in Paris with the best of intentions: 'I work very hard: my newest piece is the 1st Intermezzo in the Brahms Op. 118, which I think is heaven, do you know these six pieces?'[2] However, while Graham may have been, as Betjeman said, a 'lovely and mad and kind old thing',[3] he was also very easily distracted, and had as little self-discipline as ever. Paris was more tolerant of homosexuality than London; men such as Proust, Gide, Cocteau and Diaghilev lived openly, without any of the fear of arrest which was a constant danger in England. The bars, nightclubs, parks and Turkish baths all offered opportunities for pick-ups. Graham wrote to Alan, who had very recently returned from South America.

JOAN

Alan dear,

I hear from Arthur to-day that you are back in London: what joy!

I had a charming letter from you a few days ago, but from somewhere so remote & improbable that it had little essence of reality. Come quickly to Paris & convince me you are still a fact.

It is incredibly late & I should be in bed, but I have had a slight misunderstanding with my boy-friend (who is divine & who is, I hope – or perhaps I don't, – asleep next door). It has set my nerves a-jangle and sleep seems out of the question just yet, so I have sat down to write to you now that you are once more accessible.

Why does one have these tiresome malentendus when probably a few words would explain everything, yet neither will commit himself to an explanation? Why, indeed, does one have these affairs at all? Just as I thought I had finished with them for always, this creature came down my reach of the river; I got out my mildewed rod & line & chose the brightest of flies, – for, after all, it was spring – and proved myself not so inexpert as I should have thought I had become.

That was a month ago, but alas, I feel it is one of those fishes which, even fried and filleted on the plate, will suddenly reconstitute itself & slip back into the cool of the river. A little further down one will find the next fly thrown & taken.

La, countess, how I do prattle & to be sure! I was delighted to hear about the nimble little alpacas: they must be a constant source of delight to the earnest student of nature.

When does your book come out? and who is publishing it? for I must begin at once to collect your first editions: I hope it will be a limited edition; one day they will say, 'Really, a Jones first edition' or 'By Jove, a 1931.'

I am getting light-headed from too many cigarettes & too many aspirins. Write to me soon, my dear, or better come in person.

Very much love, Graham.[4]

Joan wanted to visit her brother but could not think of a way without her parents knowing. She had now left school and returned home to Dumbleton. From her eighteenth birthday in February 1930 and over the following months Joan came out in society. Her name began to appear regularly in small print in the long, dense columns of the Court Circular in *The Times* and in the society pages. As was expected of upper-class young women, she attended the balls and social events, which were regarded as a means of introduction to suitable and marriageable bachelors. She went to Buckingham Palace to make one of the deep curtseys she claimed were her sole legacy from her years at St James's: it was as if her whole life had been leading up to that moment. In early June, Sir Bolton and Lady Eyres Monsell gave a dance in their London home for Joan, her sister Diana and a cousin. The garden was walled in with trellis work and rambling roses to provide extra space and its roof covered with blue material and electric lights to simulate the sky and stars. 'A realistic moon "obliged", and Chinese lanterns added to the gaiety of this pleasant supper room,'[5] prattled the *Cheltenham Chronicle*. A studio photograph was taken of Joan in her three-tiered dress, of a very virginal white and silver, holding an ostrich-feather fan in her hands. It is difficult to discern much enthusiasm in her expression for the role she was having to play. Although she was on the verge of becoming a professional photographer, she claimed that she always hated being photographed. Remarkably few pictures exist from her later years but in the 1930s she was to find it hard to resist the camera. Often she seems guarded and even awkward, but when she was at ease – animated and smiling warmly – the pictures are irresistible.

Joan found such social occasions tedious. At one ball she attended, Edward, Prince of Wales was also present. It was a time when all of the future king's clothes, social engagements and dance partners were endlessly discussed, and he was supposedly the centre of every debutante's desires. Joan just walked away. The balls were uncomfortable for at least one other reason. Joan had inherited her mother's myopia, and was so short-sighted it was difficult for her to recognize people across a crowded room – of course no young society woman of that time would be seen dead in glasses, let alone be photographed wearing them. After Joan's father was appointed First Lord of the Admiralty in November 1931 the family moved to Admiralty House. Joan used to escape by its underground passages and slip out to the parties in Bloomsbury, which were much more fun. Taking part in the London season did, however, allow Joan to meet two girls, Wilhelmine 'Billa' Cresswell and Dorothy 'Coote' Lygon, who were to remain friends for the rest of her life. Billa was the daughter of an officer in a Norfolk regiment who had been killed in action at Mons in 1914, when she was only three. Her mother's remarriage to another officer, General Sir Peter Strickland, meant that Billa's early years had been peripatetic, because of her stepfather's postings. Billa, who was plump, dark-haired, bossy and very funny, was educated privately then briefly at the Sorbonne; afterwards she became a wardrobe mistress at various London film studios. Coote Lygon was the sixth of the seven children of Earl and Lady Beauchamp of Madresfield in Worcestershire. Her father had a distinguished political career; he was made Governor of New South Wales at the age of twenty-six, before serving as Lord President of the Council in Asquith's Liberal government of 1910. He was appointed Knight of the Garter and Lord Warden of the Cinque Ports four years later, and from 1924 he had been leader of the Liberal Party in the House of Lords. While all her brothers and sisters were good-looking, Coote was plain, with a round face and thick glasses. Her dim, unmaternal mother had left her unprepared for life, and Coote was hopelessly unsophisticated. But she was sweet-natured, caring and intelligent. Her natural discretion was responsible for her nickname – her family said that she reminded them of the hymn 'God moves in mysterious ways', which they believed, wrongly, had been written by a 'Mrs Coote'.

Not every society ball turned out to be tedious however, and in the winter of 1931 Joan met Alan Pryce-Jones. A party of sixteen had gathered over a long, champagne-filled weekend for a hunt ball at the Lygon Arms in Broadway, Worcestershire. They had originally intended to stay at Dumbleton Hall, but there had been a change of plan. After dancing till five in the morning, the party were still wearing their dressing gowns when they breakfasted the following afternoon. Alan's sexuality was not wholly unambiguous. Although he quite possibly had been Graham's lover, he could be swayed – and that weekend he only had eyes for Graham's sister, Joan. Joan and he fell in love. Many years later he would write about her:

> She was very fair with huge, myopic eyes. Her voice had a delicious quaver – no, not quite a quaver, an undulation rather, in it; her talk was unexpected, funny, clear-minded. She had no time for inessentials; though she was a natural enjoyer, she was also a perfectionist whom experience had already taught to be wary. I was twenty-three when we met; she barely twenty. For the next two years we spent as much time together as we could, hampered only by family disapproval.[6]

Alan, in retrospect, saw himself as 'a very young man, full of affectation . . . too poor, too unsporting, too non-political, too unambitious except in the single realm of literature, and even then laziness and a natural triviality stood between me and fulfilment'.[7] Such diffidence was also typical. He was good-looking, dapper, and he had perfect, if affected, manners. He enjoyed gossip, and he was funny and intelligent – all of which was of interest to Joan. Alan lived in a very small flat off the King's Road which he had decorated in the bohemian fashion of the day – silver oilcloth curtains, unpainted wood furniture. On the walls, he had hung drawings by Duncan Grant and dry-points by Picasso. Everything was bought on a shoestring; he had very little money, although now that he was earning his father had at last relented and given him a small allowance. By 1931 he had started to make a literary career for himself. That year he published *The Spring Journey*, an account of his travels in Egypt and the Middle East with Bobbie Pratt Barlow, an old friend of his parents. *People in the South*, Alan's next book, was a collection of three novellas based on his trip to South America, again with Barlow, and was published the following year, albeit to lukewarm reviews from the press. Alan would leave Joan just after he met her, having already arranged to sail with Barlow to Africa.

Alan had a considerable talent for friendship. He brought John Betjeman into Joan's world, who became one of her most intimate friends. John loved nicknames: he was 'Betj', Joan was 'Dotty', Alan was 'Boggins' and Graham, as he had been at Eton, 'Groundsel'. Betjeman and Pryce-Jones first met at Magdalen when, as they passed one another going to and from the bathroom, John praised Alan's unusual, cape-like dressing gown. Ever afterwards Alan entered into Betjeman's private world, his love of literature, architecture, and the absurd: 'He did not trouble to brush his teeth or change his shirt, yet he knew very well how to cast a spell. He was all response, like a piece of litmus-paper; and to people he responded brilliantly.'[8] John was forever falling in love. In 1931, he had met Penelope Chetwode, who had just returned from India. Having written an article on cave temples in the Deccan, she took it to the *Architectural Review* for consideration, and John, although not remotely interested in Indian art, found Penelope intriguing – he was always excited by dominant women – and he agreed to publish the piece. Penelope, finding herself unexpectedly attracted to John, determined to meet him again. Penelope's parents were not impressed by her journalist suitor – they were expecting at the very least 'somebody with a pheasant shoot'. 'My daughter's got entangled with a little middle-class Dutchman,' Lady Chetwode told her friends.[9] Penelope soon found herself packed off back to India.

On Alan's return from Africa, Joan and he resumed their affair. He wrote in his diary:

> Am I in love with Joan? I suppose that question means that I am not. Or only in love with a beautiful ideal, with the perfect bathing dress, the most lovely face, the most elaborate evening-dress. She could not be more lovely; yet, could we be happy if she was as foolish as I fear she is?[10]

As First Lord of the Admiralty Sir Bolton was now in the Cabinet. The country was in the midst of the Depression, and his expectations were similar to the Chetwodes'; he thought his daughter should marry a Tory with a future in deciding the affairs of the nation – or at the very least an understanding of it. His children were turning out to be a disappointment. His eldest daughter had so far failed to find a partner, his son was a pansy apparently unfitted for any manly profession and his second daughter also surrounded herself with bohemian types. Pryce-Jones was just another bad influence. Patricia, his last hope, was still at school. But the children had begun to feature in the press and were now public property:

Graham Eyres Monsell . . . is paying a short visit to London
from Paris, where he is studying music. I hear he has greatly
impressed the last year. His debutante sister is most attractive
and also amusing. Mr Eyres Monsell is noted for his wit and his
hatred of conventional country life.[11]

Meanwhile, Lady Eyres Monsell continued with her good works. In
November 1932, just after making a radio appeal on behalf of the
Disabled Men's Handicrafts, she went to Devonport to launch a
cruiser; having already launched two battleships this was her third
boat of the year. Graham was on holiday in Boulogne. He wrote to
Alan about his make-up and his sun tan. In the 1930s a decent sun
tan was all the rage.

> *It's so long since I've seen you that I scarcely know where to*
> *begin. Perhaps with a piece of very important news: I have*
> *discovered the ultimate slap. Haggard & green I was, from – I*
> *regret to tell – having seen too much of Jeanette;* in desperation*
> *I rushed into a shop where they sold me some oil called Huile*
> *de Bronze of Molinard, after three days application of which,*
> *one's face takes on such a South-of-France-tan as you can't*
> *believe – entirely natural & doesn't come off as the skin is*
> *stained! What do you think of that? All one needs is a little*
> *darkish powder to dust over one's face, as one puts it on at night*
> *& washes off in the morning. Keep this to yourself, it is too good*
> *to give away [. . .]*
>
> *Do restrain Joan – it will all come back to me if she gets into*
> *trouble with my mother & it is not really worth it for those*
> *queens.*[12]

---

* The identity of Jeanette is unknown.

Joan and Alan were about to be separated again for two months since he was intending to stay abroad and write and so, despite Graham's cautionary note, he proposed. A couple of days before Christmas when Joan and her parents were to sail to Gibraltar for three weeks, the couple met for an evening out:

> We left the Café Royal in a taxi, and I suddenly asked her. She said 'yes'. We drove to Admiralty House: then I said 'St. Margaret's, Westminster' and the taxi took us there, while I could not mention the subject for fear she thought I was drunk when I asked her, or was joking: but in the evening at a party at Rosa Lewis's, I dared speak of it and she was enchanting again [. . .] Since then I've alternated between rapture and despair – despair at losing my own freedom, rapture at the thought of her. Is she stupid? Am I perverted? Are we poor? Graham, to whom I called, and who is now in England, is not too pleased.[13]

From Government House Joan wrote to Alan that she could not feel more miserable and depressed. She wished she loved him only a quarter as much as she did, as then the separation would not seem like years and years. Alan felt himself unable to stay away from her. He followed the Eyres Monsells a short time afterwards and they eventually met in Algeciras. His diary continues:

> Suddenly, while dressing for dinner, Joan appeared. 'Darling!' in at the door. I hurried down and asked her mother to a cocktail, terrified (but Joan had told her, I now knew and was not angry, but only apprehensive of what Sir B. might say). The cocktail was a success and we dined together, successfully too. Lady E.M. couldn't be more charming, and with a hardness, or rather directness, behind the charm which I like. She is shy, and

like all her children quite blind. I wished I could have cut my hair before she arrived.[14]

When Alan was with Joan he felt tongue-tied and 'lamentably failing in spontaneity [. . .] Ought I to take liberties with her person when she is alone in my room? But she is not the sort of girl I want to violate; and I think we both are reticent.'[15]

As was feared, Sir Bolton abjectly failed to be won over by the attractions of Joan's would-be suitor; unable to hide his lack of enthusiasm, the best he offered was an invitation to come to Dumbleton sometime. When the end of the holiday came and the Eyres Monsells returned to England, Alan stayed behind to travel and write in Spain and Portugal.

At the end of January 1933, Joan was a bridesmaid at St Margaret's, Westminster, for the wedding of Nancy Beaton, Cecil Beaton's sister. Beaton had spent hours posing his two youngest sisters, Nancy and Baba, as models for his photographs, and as a result they had become well known and fashionable in the world of 'Bright Young Things'. The wedding was a lavish and highly theatrical affair masterminded by Cecil. He did not want Nancy to be accompanied by 'lumpy girlfriends looking like bad imitations of musical comedy brides-maids in tulle skirts of pastel shades'.[16] Instead the bride was to look like a snow queen. The eight bridesmaids behind her were harnessed to one another with garlands of flowers in sleeveless, low-necked dresses, shivering in the cold. They were probably chosen because they were of similar height rather than because of any close friend-ship with the bride.* In the church, there were tall silver Venetian

---

* Other bridesmaids included: Baba Beaton; Lady Violet Pakenham, who later married the novelist Anthony Powell; Joan Buckmaster, the daughter of Gladys Cooper; and Margaret Whigham, subsequently Margaret, Duchess of Argyll.

posts and artificial flowers arranged by Constance Spry. The crowds gathered outside St Margaret's; for Cecil Beaton, acting as master of ceremonies in lavender-grey trousers and a white top hat, the wedding was the glittering success he intended. A month later, Joan was once again a bridesmaid at the wedding of a couple who were well known in hunting circles: Diana Coventry of Croome Court, Worcestershire, and John Mason. Joan, wearing 'buttercup flamingo', had also been a bridesmaid the previous year, and was to be a bridesmaid again in 1934: she obviously looked the part.

Joan wrote, rather confusedly, to Alan about their marriage plans and finances. Alan had also arranged to stage a play.

I loved to hear about your play. It will obviously be wonderful & how exciting the first night will be!

The thing is you must not write for money. You won't will you, as if you do, you obviously won't write such good things as if you didn't. Graham agrees with me about this. In fact this is the real reason he is not absolutely delighted. He says I ought to wait years and years before I marry you so that you don't have to think about getting money quickly & won't spend any time writing articles just for money. But that would be too awful, wouldn't it?

I don't see that we shall want any more money than you usually have. Sir B. ought to give me about £1000, don't you think, & I couldn't possibly want more than £250 for everything for myself, so all the rest would be enough for the house, food & servants & you wouldn't want more than you always have. (I hope you realise after this what a sensible, practical girl I really am) [. . .]

I stayed with Billa last weekend which was heaven, especially as no one else was there so we just sat in front of a fire & talked the whole time. We went to a dance of the Jones's which was really rather fun on Saturday. There was a dreadful hunting

scene in one of the rooms so Billa & I turned it round & wrote
the only three rude words we knew on the back in lipstick which
seemed very funny at the time. (Some nice man rubbed them
out after though, so we aren't disgraced.) [. . .]

I nearly forgot to tell you some very good news – Graham
says Lady E.M. likes you very much indeed which she really
couldn't help doing could she?[17]

They also discussed how to make Pryce-Jones more acceptable to
his prospective father-in-law. Unfortunately, he said he could not
shoot because he always closed the wrong eye in a panic when a
pheasant came over, and when he played golf he could not hold a
mashie properly, but he could at least try harder. But wouldn't it be
awful if he really did like it? In her next letter Joan wrote:

I'm afraid I was a little optimistic about the £1000 Sir B. ought
to give me, but it doesn't matter now as he will die quite soon as
last night we made a wax image of him and melted it in front of
the fire so I shouldn't be surprised if he is already in his death
throes [. . .] I quite agree with your economic theory and we
must certainly have a house at Granada as it is quite one of the
loveliest places I have ever seen [. . .] I rang up a shop the other
day and said that I would design some clothes for them and I've
got to show the things I've done which is rather unfortunate as I
haven't done any. However if I could do some I might make
some money which would be very useful.[18]

Betjeman wrote to Alan congratulating him and giving him advice.

I am so sorry I haven't written before. Of course I'm delighted.
You've scored all along the line. But there is one thing you must
do before you marry – you must explain that you were once

inverted. She won't mind at all. In fact she obviously knows as she is quite aware that old Graham and I and all our friends are inverted. I think it is mad not to be honest and clear up the embarrassment of a prickly conscience. Actually inversion is an additional charm. It worked very well with Philth [Betjeman's nickname for Penelope] although I have now decided I daren't marry her – money and emotion and fear getting in the way.

Oh Bog, I am pleased – though very sorry for Dotty. You must marry at once. 'Delay has dangers' as my favourite poet the Reverend George Crabbe says. Those eyes of hers like tennis balls and that undeniable depth and constancy. Of course it's what we all need and those who are supposed to make bad husbands – like you – always turn out the best. Bog, I am glad. I have a lot of important things to tell you when you return. There's no more need to write for money. I hope you've written a good play. You will become a great author. I will tell her she must marry you at once.[19]

During Penelope's long absence in India, John had met Billa Cress-well at a weekend party at Sezincote, a Regency mansion in the Gloucestershire countryside. A few days later Billa and John met in his London flat and lay on a sofa, where they kissed and cuddled. He then proposed to *her*, and she accepted despite his shortcomings which, as he pointed out, included the fact that he had no family background to speak of and little income. 'Finally there's no getting away from the fact that I love you, darling Billa,' Betjeman wrote. 'It's the most restful and consoling affair I have yet experienced, and it's quite enough really to know that you exist with those extraordinary clothes and that loud voice and that white and painted face. Moreover we're one up on everyone else because we've suffered [. . .] Meanwhile I will tell Philth's friends that I don't want to marry her – can't afford it. Dishonesty is the best policy – and the kindest

at present. I love you, I love you, I love you.'[20] Joan, one of the few
to know about this latest development, wrote immediately to Billa:
'Darling, darling, darling Billa, Betj told me last night and I am so
thrilled about it I don't know what to do. It's nearly as exciting as
Bogs and I. It is HEAVEN and I think really he is much nicer than
Graham or anyone (except Alan). Darling what a heavenly quartet
we shall be.'[21] However, shortly afterwards this new affair ended
abruptly. Penelope sent a telegram from India telling John to do
nothing until he had heard from her. Betjeman backed down and
in July – after more emotional turmoil – John and Penelope married
in a registry office in Edmonton, although they were too frightened
to tell the Chetwodes beforehand. Billa reflected afterwards unflat-
teringly that John 'was a sort of joke we all knew really. His hair was
like last year's nest [. . .] It was just the sort of thing he did. He liked
girls and he liked the idea of being in love.'[22]

Graham, meanwhile, had a new boyfriend – 'madly attractive as tall
as me with great shoulders & the smallest hips'[23] – and went to stay
with Somerset Maugham and his lover, Gerald Haxton, at the Villa
Mauresque on Cap Ferrat. They 'couldn't have been more charming hosts. I played lots of tennis & lay in the sun & found the
loveliest place in Nice when we went in for our fucking.'[24] Immediately afterwards, Joan and Graham went skiing in Austria. Joan was
a less enthusiastic skier than her brother, although she thought the
mountains were 'divine'. Her father, 'that odious Sir B', had given
her £20 for Easter, which was 'really rather "sportin" of him'.[25] She
had been reading Samuel Butler's *The Way of All Flesh*, a 'heavenly'
novel about the damage caused to children by tyrannical and over-
bearing parents. It was a book, she felt, that all parents should be
forced to read. She and her brother had both also read Alan's latest
book, a short biography of Beethoven which was dedicated to
Graham. 'I think it is the first readable book that I have encountered

that deals with music & the life of a composer,' Graham wrote to his friend. Unfortunately, the press was less enthusiastic. The review in the *Observer* was entitled 'A Strange View of Beethoven'. Not only had Pryce-Jones made the composer out to be a snob and a cad, he was also apparently 'stupid' which was why he wrote 'that kind of' music. The review was also sceptical of Alan's claim that 'an amateur is more likely to write real criticism than the qualified critics'. He was likely to remain an amateur if he confined himself to libelling the dead, the reviewer added.

Eventually, if Alan was to come to Dumbleton, Joan had to face her father and talk to him seriously about her marital prospects. If she had any doubts about marrying Alan they were outweighed by the benefits: marriage would get her away from her father of whom she was terrified. Sir Bolton played the role of a typical unreformed Victorian paterfamilias to perfection.

Darling Alan,

I thought I had better say nothing more to the family till you came back; however last night Lady E. M. said Sir B. would like to see me as she had told him. So, quite hysterical with fear, I tottered to his room to talk to him, & darling you can't imagine how nice he was. Lady E. M. must have said the most charming things about you. He talked mostly about money, & gave me a lecture on how badly & stupidly I'd been brought up, never having to know the value of money etc, etc. But if he only knew how economical I am the last half of every year when I've finished my allowance, he wouldn't say such things.

He asked, too, what sports you were fond of! So I said you had only given up hunting for the present as you were so much in London, & you adored golf. All of which is very nearly true, isn't it? He was very pleased, & said, 'Oh, he likes that sort of thing, does he?'

*So it looks as if everything is really going to be HEAVEN if
after two months of reflection you can still have the thought of
St. Margaret's (or the registry office as the case may be).*

Darling, I love you so very much, so do write again quickly.

Joan xxx[26]

In April 1933, Pryce-Jones at last came down to Dumbleton. The
first evening went well enough, and the following day when Sir
Bolton suggested a round of golf, another well-meaning guest tried
to extricate Alan from embarrassment by exclaiming, 'But you can't
expect Pryce-Jones to play with borrowed clubs.' Tennis was rejected
with similar finality. They settled on a walk around the lake in the
grounds instead.

Sir Bolton started the conversation with his young guest: 'I
gather that you want to marry my daughter.'

Alan said that he did.

'Well, now, there are a few things to discuss.'

Alan agreed.

'Where is your place?' his host asked.

Alan replied that, sadly, he had no place. His father was an
eighth child, and it was very unlikely that his unappealing childhood home in Wales would ever be his.

'And what job have you?'

Alan told him.

The dialogue continued until, at last, Sir Bolton said, 'And so,
Pryce-Jones, having nothing, without prospects, without a home,
you expect to marry my daughter, who has always had the best of
everything here, in Belgrave Square, on the yacht which a kindly
Government allows me. No, no, Pryce-Jones, come back in a few
years' time when you have something behind you.'[27]

The romance reached the gossip columns. The headline story
on the front page of the *Daily Express* for 2 May related to a crisis

in the government over a reduction in British tariffs to aid exports of coal to Germany. The headline of the story beside it read 'Daughter of First Lord Engaged, but her parents refuse their consent'. A photograph of Joan sat in the middle column of the page.

> The 'Daily Express' understands that Miss Joan Eyres Monsell, second daughter of Sir Bolton Eyres Monsell, First Lord of the Admiralty, and Lady Eyres Monsell, has become engaged to Mr. Alan Pryce-Jones, an assistant editor on the 'London Mercury', a monthly journal dealing with literature and the arts.
>
> The young couple are very much in love, but so far Miss Eyres Monsell's mother and father have refused to sanction the engagement. Both have strong literary inclinations. Mr. Alan Pryce-Jones is aged only twenty-four and besides reviewing books writes a good deal on architecture. His fiancée, barely twenty-one years old, is very tall, smart and good-looking. She has set a fashion by wearing Grecian curls at the back of her head. Miss Eyres Monsell is devoted to her brother Graham, who is a wonderful musician and lives in Paris. She has always moved a great deal in literary and artistic circles.
>
> Lady Eyres Monsell is immensely rich. The fortune she inherited cannot be less than £50,000 a year. She was formerly a Miss Eyres, and lady of the manor at Dumbleton Hall near Evesham.[28]

Sir Bolton's decision was final, and the following day a denial of the engagement appeared in the papers.

> 'There is no truth in it,' Mr. Pryce-Jones stated. 'It is true that I have known Miss Joan for a number of years, but there is no question of our being engaged.'
>
> Miss Eyres Monsell was equally surprised at the report. 'It's

awfully interesting but quite untrue,' she said. 'Mr Pryce-Jones has been a friend of the family for a long time and we are both interested in literature and art but that doesn't mean we must be engaged.'[29]

There was nothing they could do. Neither Joan nor Alan had any money behind them nor a steady income of their own, and neither family approved of the other, although the objections of the Pryce-Jones family rested more on vaguely hostile recollections of a time when his mother had been a debutante and resentment that her son had not been welcomed with open arms. Joan and Alan continued to enjoy one another's company among their close friends, such as Billa, who was also turning out to be not quite the sort of daughter her mother might have hoped for. Billa used to drive around London in a tiny car with the words 'Alan is a pansy' scratched into the paintwork. She, too, much preferred the company of artists and writers to that of young men of an officer class.

Betjeman came down to Dumbleton and Joan took a photograph of him posing by a window taken from the parish church, which had been placed beside the lake as a feature. John's head is flung back with his hand on his brow in mock anguish. Betjeman's first prose work, *Ghastly Good Taste,* had just been published. He captioned the picture, 'The author – an example of good taste if ever there was one.' He also composed a short poem about the marriage proposal. It was written in the extravagant, dramatic style of the nineteenth-century poet Sydney Dobell, the sort of thing Betjeman loved, the more obscure the better.*

---

* Sydney Dobell (1824–74) and fellow poets were members of the Spasmodic school, which typically used extravagant and intense language and situations, full of passion and anguish.

Dumbleton, Dumbleton, the ruin by the lake,
Where Boggins and Sir Bolton fought a duel for thy sake;
Dumbleton, Dumbleton, the Gothic arch that leads
Thro' the silver vestibule to where Sir Bolton feeds.
The groaning of silver plate,
The sickly social shame;
Oh heirs of Dumbleton! The Monsell in thy name!

A second poem for Joan, in which Dumbleton Hall is transformed back into the original Jacobean house – 'an ancient stonebuilt mansion' – was written 'As if by Longfellow':

Those old pinnacles and turrets as in good Queen Bess's reign
Still jut out before above the creeper, still the level lawns remain,
And within, upon the staircase, tapestries still catch the wind.
And there are tusks that Marco Polo may, perhaps, have
    brought from Ind,
Quaint old lanterns light the carpets, quaint old carvings
    deck the stair,
Sumptuous fabrics line the sofa such as Shakespeare used to wear;
And the heiress of the Cocks still retains the names of Eyres,
With Sir Bolton standing by her still receives one on the stairs;
Best of all his lovely daughter welcomes every author-guest –
Newer Shakespeares, other Beaumonts with their
    Fletchers come to rest;
Come to steal, perhaps, some kisses just as Shakespeare did and
Drake –
    Thus is kept thine ancient glory, Gothic Dumbleton, awake.

The manuscripts of the two poems were presented as a gift to Joan. John also composed a fable for Penelope entitled *SS Centipeda and Giomonsella, Martyrs* which he decorated with his own drawings.

The two martyrs are Joan and Penelope, both wearing haloes. It is a farcical story in which Penelope is both the daughter of a Spartan general and related to Julius Caesar. Graham appears as 'St Graham Hermaphrodite'.

Betjeman had perhaps exaggerated Alan's combativeness – by August he had fallen out of love. He confided all in a close friend, Patrick Balfour. Although heir to the Kinross title, Balfour had little money of his own, but he seemed to know everyone – among his closest friends at Oxford were Evelyn Waugh and Cyril Connolly, and he claimed that Connolly was the first person he ever went to bed with. His talent for knowing people made him the ideal person to write the 'Mr Gossip' column in the *Daily Sketch*. Patrick no doubt invited Alan's confidence, and his letters are full of pained examinations of his own, unsuccessful, love affairs, as well as those of others. Alan had just been to the Salzburg festival where he encountered a friend of Graham called Bobby Marshall. He had recorded more tortured reflections in his diary: 'I knew I was sunburnt and looking my best; but he is a "hearty", who has always led a perfectly normal life, and I am engaged . . . I don't want to go to bed with him (or do I?) nor he with me yet we can't bear to be apart.'[30]

Patrick wrote to Jim Lees-Milne:

Alan came and stayed with me in Essex before I left. He is not going to marry Joan – but do not spread it, as he hasn't told her yet. I think he is thoroughly wise. His three weeks in Salzburg must have done the trick, enabling to see the thing in proportion: & I encouraged him wanting to break it off. He talks of going miles away abroad somewhere for a year. I wonder if she will be very upset. He thinks not, and says she isn't really in love

with him so much as with the idea of getting away from home
& with the glamour of his life.[31]

A couple of weeks later he told Lees-Milne that he gathered 'from Alan's letters that he has not yet had the courage to break it off with Joan'.[32]

At the end of November 1933, Lady Eyres Monsell sailed for India and Australia with Joan and some Kettlewell cousins for four months, in order to part her from Alan Pryce-Jones and to persuade her to forget him. Their departure was published in *The Times* Court Circular.[33] A few weeks later – and with much greater anonymity – a young Paddy Leigh Fermor took a small Dutch steamer from Tower Bridge to the Hook of Holland.

4

Earning One's Living

E ven in her absence, Joan was a story:

> The other piece of news is that Miss Joan Eyres Monsell . . . is enjoying herself quite a lot, but in a different way to what she does in this country. She rides every morning (the ponies belonging to the Maharajah of Jaipur); she drives in a large and fast car, also belonging to the Maharajah, and she watches polo (Will she do this in England this summer? Probably not); she shoots; she's becoming a thorough sportswoman.[1]

Maharajah Man Singh II, who had inherited his title when he was eleven, was young, good-looking and extremely rich. Despite being married he also enjoyed the company of beautiful women. However much Joan liked watching him – and the maharajah was one of the finest polo-players of his time – she still had other things on her mind when she returned from India.

Joan and her mother arrived back in England on 24 March 1934. A month later, Cyril Connolly and his wife, Jean, hosted a dinner party at their new flat above a shop in the King's Road. Cyril liked to boast that his guests were chosen as carefully as instruments in an orchestra.[2] Along with Joan, who was at Cyril's right hand, the ten people seated around his table that evening included Evelyn Waugh and Peter Quennell. Afterwards, some of the party went on to the Florida nightclub. Cyril recorded his reactions to Joan in his journal:

> Found her very attractive. Talked about Alan, whom she says won't marry her without a grand wedding. We all got very tight at the Florida. Altogether a very pleasant balmy evening, a young party with two really pretty women. Terrible hangover next day, though amiable, tipsy and Eyres-Monsell-conscious in the morning.[3]

Cyril was at the start of what was to be a highly successful career as a writer and reviewer. He was a famously ugly man and looked like a pug dog – fat and prematurely bald with a little nose and a pasty complexion – but at the same time he could be wonderfully witty, intelligent company. Many beautiful women were attracted by Cyril's great charm. When he talked, he had the ability to make a woman feel that she was his intellectual equal. Joan and he became close friends, and for much of his life Cyril was at least half in love with her. She once photographed him lying bare-chested on the ground in a pair of shorts, with a croquet mallet at his side. She always kept the photograph in her bedroom, although as the years passed much of the picture was eaten by tiny insects.

At the end of 1933, when Alan had left for Austria, he still had not found the courage to tell Joan that he did not want to marry her. Joan wrote from Admiralty House to Alan's mother, Vere:

> *I very nearly came to see Alan off on Friday but didn't in the end – Of all the depressing and unsatisfactory things seeing people off is the worst. I'm sure I shall really enjoy India [. . .] Anyway I should rather be there than in London if Alan is in Vienna.*[4]

On her return from her travels four months later, Joan no doubt expected to resume their relationship. Unfortunately, in the interim Alan had fallen in love with another girl. Thérèse 'Poppy' Fould-Springer came from a French-Jewish family who owned extensive property in Austria and Hungary and at Royaumont, near Chantilly. In February 1934, Vere received a letter from Alan:

> *Thérèse Fould is by now really almost my greatest friend. She's almost a Madame de Sévigné; brilliantly witty and quite delicious too. The awful thing is that I would quite as soon spend the rest of my life with her (no that's not really true) as with Joan; and what makes it worse is that she's even richer prospectively. I seem only to take to the daughters of million-aires. They left today for Kitzbühel and I'm inconsolable – so much that after being up very late, I went out to Meidling [the Fould-Springer family home] this morning to have breakfast with them. But I suppose one ought not to marry a Jewess anyhow; especially if one is marrying someone else.*[5]

In April, by which time Alan had seen Joan again, he wrote in his journal.

> The whole family were there [Royaumont] and so unnecessarily nice that I'm sure, no I'm not, that they actually want me to marry Thérèse. But I must be wrong. Or has she said something? The awful thing is that I want to marry her.
> Then Joan – oh, it's absolute hell.[6]

Poppy was short, dark and plump – physically she could not have been less like Joan. She was barely twenty years of age, and even less well educated and less worldly-wise than her rival. She was deter-mined, however, and before long Alan decided that he would marry her after all and this time he had the support of her parents. His own parents, he wrote, knew nothing about Jews and were certainly not anti-Semitic, but they included Jews in the 'category of foreigners who were usually a trouble to know'.[7] A few months later, Patrick Balfour told Lees-Milne that 'Joan seems to have recovered and has some other chaps.'[8]

John Betjeman wrote to Alan from Uffington in October.

My darling Bog,

I was staggered by the announcement in The Times, particularly because I remember a man called Fould-Springer who had rooms under me at Magdalen and whom I very much disliked [. . .] Still you are not engaged to him, are you?

Oh Bog, Bog, how I miss you and how I envy your SUCCESS. Don't marry without a long period of probation. Think of Cracky, Sarx [George Schurhoff] (who has got a job as Superintendent of the Cancer Hospital in Vienna), Li and all those of our friends who immediately drift away, however much one likes them. Oh God – the difference of being married from being a bachelor. It is like living on another planet.

My God, Bog, have a care – I do hope I shall see you. I am not what I was at all. I find it even quite odd to speak to people I haven't seen for some time. It may even be a strain speaking to you. The fear of death is worse than ever, particularly when one works in a word factory. Avoid all work. I hope your marriage will enable you to do that. They are putting the electric light wires right across our view.

Love, JB[9]

In November, Joan was in Vienna but Alan refused to see her. She sent him a brief note, 'I'm so sorry you find it impossible to see me. I thought that we should remain friends, which is all I want.' Just before Christmas they did meet. Cyril held a party (in his diary he called it 'a very good landmark of 1934') attended by, among others, Joan, Patrick, Alan (without Poppy), Evelyn Waugh, Bunny Garnett, Henry Yorke and his wife 'Dig' (her real name was Adelaide), and the economist Roy Harrod. A few days later, Alan married Poppy Fould-Springer at Chantilly, with Patrick Balfour as best man. However hurt Joan might have felt at being jilted, it was because of Alan, who was such a social butterfly, that Joan was now invited to all the best parties and came to know everyone who was anyone in artistic and literary society.

In the summer of 1934, Joan and Penelope Betjeman went on a tour of Ireland on horseback, with a pre-war one-inch Ordnance Survey map as their only aid. At Clonmel they picked up two ponies and a rally cart which, although not smart, was comfortable and had room for their luggage, a spare saddle and a big sack of oats. They took it in turns to ride and drive. The larger pony fitted the cart better, so they rode the other, but she shied at any car and they had great trouble getting her to pass them, even when they were parked. Ireland seemed not to have changed much since the eighteenth century. 'There is still Georgian architecture everywhere, and you ride and drive along non-tarmac lanes for days without seeing a car or telegraph pole,' Joan wrote in the unpublished account she made of their travels. Everywhere there were still burnt-out ruins from the recent Troubles: the big classical barracks near Clonmel; large houses near Fermoy; and, on one side of the Shannon, the Hermitage – a Georgian house belonging to Lord Massey:

> It was destroyed in the Troubles by the Irish, who heard a foundationless rumour that English soldiers were to be quartered there. We borrowed brakeless bicycles and rode to see it, and found ragged robin growing in the lovely round hall, and ivy

growing over the pilasters and the remains of a plaster frieze of grapes and cornucopias.

On the other side of the river, at St Senan's Well, they met a woman who talked about fairies:

She did not think there could be any now, she said, no one ever saw them. Maybe there were some in the old days. They used to live in the hills or those ruined forts, like the one in the wood we had just passed. One man she knew had seen a leprechaun, and of course, there were banshees.

The people Joan and Penelope met they found hospitable, friendly and eccentric: 'An old woman in black came hurrying along the stony road from a remote farm. She was going to a funeral she told us delightedly. Hadn't we heard that Jimmy O'Brian was dead?' Everywhere they went they experienced something new. Joan's particular interest was in the buildings they encountered: dilapidated Georgian mansions in green fields with drives overgrown with grass, and 'colour-washed cottages and farmhouses, pale blue, yellow, pink and cyclamen, looking clean and neat'. She seems to have been particularly enchanted by Ballynatray house and village, near Lismore:

It has a wild garden of roses and tall mallows, and a ruined abbey, haunted and romantic. Inside the abbey a statue of St. Molanafide, a 5th century saint, has rosaries and flowers laid before it by the villagers, and a stone in the wall will grant you wishes if you kiss it and sleep for three nights with three ivy leaves off it under the pillow. For dinner we had cold venison shot in the park. Afterwards, in the dusk, herons flapped slowly along the pale water. The Irish call them Judy of the Bog (or sometimes Norrie of the Bog). All night we heard the call of sandpipers and the whistling of curlews.

Writing nearly seventy years later, Deborah Devonshire said of the house:

> In the 1930s Ballynatray took paying guests and Penelope Bet-jeman and Joan Eyres Monsell slept there on a riding tour. One of the party discovered an unwelcome object far down in the bed: the mustard plaster worn by someone who died of pneumonia. I cannot help wondering if John Betj. invented it. It would have been typical of the house – and of John. The last time I went to Ballynatray, three pigs and a couple of hounds were asleep in the sun, guarding the door.[10]

In her recollections of the trip to Ireland Joan frequently mentioned that she was taking photographs although unfortunately these Irish pictures have been lost. 'We wanted to take a photograph of it [a Queen Anne deanery] and as no-one seems to mind in Ireland we walked up to the front door and rang the bell.' The account, which must have been written at the end of the journey, remains only in typescript. She may have hoped that it would be published – and the very fact that the typescript was put between red covers and preserved suggests that she took some satisfaction from it. Although, as her letters demonstrate, Joan could write very well, she had more confidence in herself as a photographer. John Betjeman's attitude as deputy editor of the *Architectural Review* was that the 'Archie Rev' was nepotistic: he used the magazine to commission work from his friends. In the second half of 1933 alone there were articles by W. H. Auden – 'What is Wrong with Architecture?' – two more by Patrick Balfour, 'London, Morecambe and Elsewhere' by 'Cracky' Clonmore, a poem, 'Pylons', by Stephen Spender, and Betjeman himself wrote a piece on railways.

There was also an item on Nazi architecture. It was Betjeman who suggested that Joan should photograph buildings, and make them a speciality, since they were both so interested in architecture. Betjeman's friends were also Joan's friends. They were all creative people and doubtless gave her encouragement, and so photography became something more than just a hobby. From the mid 1930s onwards she described herself in official documents as a 'journalist'.

Cameras were easily portable. She could even take them abroad with her when she travelled, and Joan travelled a great deal. Traditional 'female' subjects did not interest her – Joan did not photograph nature, flowers or fashion. In all her hundreds of pictures there is nothing to do with 'being a woman' per se, neither are there pictures relating to social concern or politics in an era when there was no lack of significant political events. Aside from places, buildings and monuments, Joan photographed people – especially her friends – and these are some of her most evocative pictures. John Betjeman wrote to Billa, comparing Joan's pictures of her plump figure lying in the grass to those found in a glamour magazine: 'Whenever I feel sexless I only have to turn up those photographs Joan took of you, to feel that I have read *London Life* cover to cover.'[11] Joan took two photographs of the poet and aesthete Brian Howard; in one Howard lies languidly along the length of a sofa, and in the other he is draped across Joan's lap, enacting a kind of dissolute and irreligious pietà. But among all her photographs, there are no pictures of her family, not even of the babies or children. It is as if they were beyond the pale. Graham detested being photographed even more than Joan, and there are even fewer pictures of Graham than there are of her. 'All photographers are "bullshitters",'[12] he said, although presumably he excluded his sister from this assertion.

Success as a photographer at least gave Joan a certain amount of independence, and brought her a small income other than that controlled by her father. She was undoubtedly fortunate, however;

unlike other contemporary woman photographers – Helen Muspratt, Barbara Ker-Seymer, Edith Tudor Hart, Dorothy Wilding, Madame Yevonde – the Eyres Monsell money meant that photography need never be Joan's primary income. She was, in effect, a semi-professional. Folded among the pages of her sister Diana's album there are instructions for developing film – 'Wash for 1½ hours [. . .] Light may be turned on again when film has passed through developer 10 times' – but although there was certainly space for a darkroom at Dumbleton, Joan did not develop her photographs herself. Her archive contains very many cardboard boxes, manila envelopes and cartons of prints and negatives, but apparently they were always developed by other hands.

At least as a photographer Joan could have some say in the matter of making her own images rather than being solely the subject of others' view of her. Just how welcome Joan found this publicity it is difficult to say – she was essentially a private person – but two of her closest friends, Patrick Balfour at the *Sketch* and Tom Driberg at the *Daily Express*, were gossip columnists, so she can have had no illusions and must have just gone along with it. As Alan Pryce-Jones said, 'experience had already taught her to be wary.' Why the gossip columnists were attracted by Joan is made clear in a story in the *Bystander* in July 1933 of a party held at Admiralty House at which both she and her sister Diana were present: 'Diana Eyres Monsell is unusually tall; she has a sincere, honest, character, and makes friends slowly. Her sister Joan is smart and up-to-date . . . It was interesting to see the contrast in the sisters and their friends.'[13] In other words, Diana, who was chiefly interested in dogs and horses, was worthy but dull while Joan was more fun and made better copy. A couple of months later in yet another piece in the *Bystander*, Joan was described as 'very amusing and well-known among the high-brow set. Her engagement was announced some little time ago but promptly denied, but she is a strong-minded young lady and it is certain she will always strike out on her own.'[14] In December the same magazine published 'Young and Original, A Gallery of Portraits', which included a quarter-page photograph of Joan, who, it said, was 'one of the more intelligent and original of London's ex-debutantes'.

It is remarkable the extent to which one can find out the life Joan led and who she mixed with throughout much of the thirties by consulting the magazine and newspaper archives from those years. One can even trace the colours of the evening dresses she wore from the writers in the society columns: red, turquoise blue, 'a lovely green lace dress', a dress of black and white printed crêpe-de-chine, 'cyclamen purple', a white dress and a bracelet of orchids around her wrist. Along with the *Bystander*, Joan was also a particular favourite of a magazine published by the *Illustrated London News* called the *Sketch*. This weekly had lots of high-quality photographs to illustrate its articles and trivial gossip about high society. In October 1932, its columnist Mariegold reported that Osbert Sitwell gave Joan lunch at the Ritz. A month later at the Embassy Club it was informing its readers that Joan Eyres Monsell's 'good looks are in the best tradition of royal beauty, for she was wearing a positively Imperial purple dress'. Shortly after her return from India in 1934, Joan attended Wagner's *Ring Cycle* by herself but she went to the ballet *Euclid* with a young man about town, Hamish Erskine. In June 1934, the *Sketch* devoted a whole page to Cecil Beaton's bathroom at his house in Wiltshire. One of the bathroom walls was decorated with the outlines of the hands of his friends. The friends included Augustus John, Tilly Losch, Rex Whistler, Lady Colefax and Siegfried Sassoon, and just below the window, to the left of the towel rail, were Joan's fingerprints. The social engagements sometimes crossed into the more private; in the same week that Sir Bolton Monsell told Alan Pryce-Jones that there was no question of marriage to his daughter, the *Sketch* published a page full of photographs under the title 'Young Mayfair in Worcestershire'. The pictures were of a recent house party given by Coote Lygon and her sister Mary, known as 'Mamie', at Madresfield Court. Their guests that weekend included Joan, 'the brilliant young author' Alan Pryce-Jones, John and Diana Mason and Mark Ogilvie-Grant who was 'well-known as a clever artist'. All except Joan appeared in a photograph captioned, 'In this snapshot a group of the young Intelligentsia may be seen engaged in the simple pleasure of making daisy-chains.' Another 'charming picture' was of Joan by herself, posed demurely under a cherry tree; perhaps she acquiesced because she was so at ease with her surroundings.

Although refused permission to marry, Joan and Alan had continued to spend much of their time together. The friends they saw most of were the two youngest Lygon sisters either at Madresfield, near Malvern, or at Halkin House, the London family home on the corner of Belgrave Square. In the absence of their parents, Lord and Lady Beauchamp, the Lygon children lived as they wished; they and their friends enjoyed all that the two houses, their servants, cars and horses could provide them with. They had oysters and Chablis for lunch, and drank the finest champagne whenever they wanted. Two years earlier, Earl Beauchamp's indiscreet homosexuality had led to his downfall, and the Lygon family fell apart. Much as they loved their indulgent father, they knew about Lord Beauchamp's 'failing' and even used to warn their visiting male friends to lock their bedroom door at night. In 1931, the earl's brother-in-law, the Duke of Westminster, who both hated and envied him, had denounced him to the king. Shortly afterwards, on a June afternoon, a delegation of three fellow Knights of the Garter was shown into the drawing room at Madresfield, to persuade Beauchamp to resign his official posts. They warned him to leave the country by midnight in order to avoid arrest. Lady Beauchamp obtained a divorce shortly afterwards, detailing in the petition that throughout their married life 'the Respondent habitually committed acts of gross indecency with certain of the male servants, masturbating them with his mouth and hands'.[15] Lord Beauchamp's brother-in-law sent him a note which read, 'Dear Bugger-in-law, you got what you deserved. Yours, Westminster.' Beauchamp spent the rest of his life travelling abroad as a fugitive from justice, restless and homesick.

The story was retold, albeit with necessary changes, in Evelyn Waugh's *Brideshead Revisited*. Lord Beauchamp is transformed into Lord Marchmain, the beautiful Mamie was Julia and Coote, Cordelia. But the great unhappiness which befell this generation of the Lygons outlasted that of their fictional counterparts. In August 1936, Lord Beauchamp's second son, Hugh Lygon – with whom Waugh was said to have been in love at Oxford – died of a fractured skull after a car crash in Bavaria. After the scandal the Lygon children were deserted by many of their friends, who no longer wished to know them. Joan, however, was constant by nature and non-judgemental in her friendship. Coote always remained one of her greatest friends and it might even be said that by agreeing to be photographed at Madresfield – for the Beauchamp scandal was well known in society if not by the world at large – Joan was making a public statement in the weekly magazine.

Just as Joan was finding a degree of independence and fulfilment in photography, it was perhaps to be expected that Graham's hopes of becoming a concert pianist should come to nothing. His father, Bolton, had no sympathy. Having failed to make a career of the army or to take a degree at Oxford, or even to become a successful explorer like his cousin, Gino Watkins (it was Major Jackson who wrote up and published the account of his adventures), Graham had now proved himself a disappointment at something he had chosen to do for himself. Aged thirty, uninterested in hunting, shooting, politics or work of any 'manly' kind, and now seemingly unable to succeed even at an 'artistic' profession – the word in itself a euphemism for homosexual – Graham had a nervous breakdown. In an undated letter from this time, he wrote to Alan Pryce-Jones from Italy.

> *Alan dear,*
>
> *Here I am in a frightful pensione, full of old English spinsters and retired naval officers being psychoanalysed by a certain Dr. Williams, who, it appears, is very expert.*
>
> *All this as a result of a nervous crisis at the [?Sharfeseas] when their charming and very able Dutch doctor from Monte Carlo begged me to come here and see him.*
>
> *In the intervals of the hideous boredom of being all alone I am put to the indescribable embarrassment of telling someone who is outwardly an elderly, dull, proper, middle class English-man, how I dislike my father, what sort of boys I like and if, as a child, I would toss off with my right hand or my left. The more intimate details of my sexual enjoyment haven't been touched on yet but I live in fear.*
>
> *What I shall do if I'm not roaring dotty in a fortnight, I don't know, but if I make any plans I will tell you.*
>
> *Do write to me*
> *Love*
> *Graham*[16]

He subsequently went for treatment at the Mayo Clinic in Boston, Massachusetts.

Graham's struggles, while acute, were by no means extraordinary. Just a few years younger than the 'Lost Generation' who had sacrificed so much in the First World War, many young men and women Graham's age could never, through no fault of their own, live up to the expectations of their parents. Just as daughters were still obliged to become debutantes and marry, so it was taken for granted that sons would manage their estates or go into respectable professions. There were many upper-class parents who alienated their children, both by interfering in their lives or through their own preconceptions of what their children should become. Refusal to conform to these preconceptions was taken as proof of immaturity, and a demonstration of wayward behaviour. Such inter-generational disconnection was made worse by a bully like Bolton. If the intensity of Joan's relationship with Graham can be explained by the absence of a loving father in her childhood, when he was browbeaten by their father, she became even more protective of him. Joan and Graham *contra mundum*.

Unfortunately for her parents, Joan's identification with 'artistic' types extended far beyond her brother, and most of her male friends – including Mark Ogilvie-Grant, Maurice Bowra, Patrick Balfour, Tom Driberg, Robert Byron, Brian Howard, Eddie Gathorne-Hardy and John Banting – were either homosexual (Joan herself wrote 'queer') or at least sexually ambiguous. The 'artistic' bohemian people she felt drawn to just happened to be more interesting, and simply more fun. Legally, however, they were also indulging in criminal behaviour.

Brian Howard, his sometime boyfriend John Banting and Eddie Gathorne-Hardy were the most outrageous. The flat Brian and Eddie shared at 39 Maddox Street was so decrepit that there was fungus growing on the stairs. According to John Betjeman, the atmosphere was sometimes enlivened by Banting throwing knives 'when in the mood'. All three were regulars of the gossip columns. At Eton, Brian Howard had seemed the most sophisticated and flamboyant of pupils, his poetry already praised by Edith Sitwell. Then, at Oxford, he cut an extraordinary figure – 'tall, dark, pale-faced with enormous eyes and very long eyelashes, fantastically distinguished in appearance',[17] and with two black spaniels trotting beside him. He seemed destined for a brilliant career, but it never happened. He became a critic for the *New Statesman* and wrote occasional articles and poetry for other magazines, but his reputation, after years of drink and drugs, was one of underachievement and of wasted talent. But all that lay in the future. 'I would prefer to think of him in the dewy dawn sunlight, champagne in hand, all set for glory,'[18] said Alan Pryce-Jones, of a distant, youthful memory.

Eddie Gathorne-Hardy was the second son of the Earl of Cranbrook, and was Brian's 'companion in fantasy'. He wore horn-rimmed spectacles and was high-browed, both literally and figuratively. He had a bent for scholarly research, an enthusiasm for recondite Cornish culture and was also an accomplished botanist. His character was a mixture of formality and excess, as well as impossibly demanding. There is a well-known story of a conversation between Eddie and Maslin, the repressed homosexual family butler:

'Do you know what I'm going to do today, Maslin?'

'No, sir.'

'I'm going to go up to London, Maslin, and I'm going to pick up a very nice good-looking guardsman, take him back to my flat and I'm going to have him, Maslin.'

'You're a very lucky young gentleman, Mr Eddie.'[19]

He was a gift for writers; Miles Malpractice in Evelyn Waugh's *Vile Bodies* is largely based on Eddie.

Robert Byron was another member of the Eton and Oxford circles in which Joan found herself and helped influence both her aesthetics and her imagination during this period. In 1927, he, Mark Ogilvie-Grant and their friend David Talbot Rice had travelled with rucksacks on their backs up Mount Athos in Greece.* Byron, who was among the writers invited by Betjeman to contribute to the

---

* PLF always maintained that *The Station*, Byron's book about these travels, was the book that inspired him to carry on from Constantinople to Greece. When he set out on his great walk across Europe he had Ogilvie-Grant's rucksack on his back.

Architectural Review, had been an exuberant and rather overpowering presence at both Eton and Oxford. His influence on John's taste and writing was considerable. Brian Howard said of Byron that in his company one felt 'like an empty electric battery which has suddenly and mysteriously become recharged'.[20] Passionately interested in all things Greek and Byzantine, he loved travel and published early. Byron's friend, Christopher Sykes, wrote that for Robert:

> foreign travel was part of an immense design of life. He was a gay young man, apparently living for pleasure. He rarely spoke seriously about these things in my hearing. When his second book, The Station, came out in 1928, I read it with surprise at the gravity and scholarship it displayed.[21]

In September 1935, Byron attended the Third International Congress of Persian Art and Archaeology at the Hermitage Museum in Leningrad. The group he travelled with included Christopher Sykes, William Allen – who was an authority on the Caucasus – and Joan who, according to the *Yorkshire Post*, 'has been studying Persian art all last summer in the intervals of the Jubilee season'. Despite many other temptations and Russian generosity, delegates gathered every morning in a small dark theatre to listen to lectures which many of them must have found obscure. Byron, who was correspondent for *The Times* during the Congress, wrote in his summing up:

> Yet duty prevailed, even over those who had failed to realize, on successive previous evenings, that after ten courses of hot and cold hors d'oeuvres, with appropriate vodka, a Russian banquet was still to begin. Two medals and two books on Persian art were the hosts' reward to each heroically Iranian-minded guest. And by the end each guest realized that he or she had in fact

contributed something (if only a smile and a subscription) to a real intellectual event.[22]

Byron was, in truth, completely without illusions – the tradition of archaeological learning had been all but extinguished during the Revolution. He continued: '[It] survived thanks to the few brave men who refused to be intimidated by public odium and destruction of their fellows.' Recognizing their service by allowing contact with foreign minds was the least that could have been done. Having been to Russia a few years earlier, Byron was better placed than most to assess the continuing effects of the Soviet experiment. He wrote to his mother:

> *The people look uglier than ever – one couldn't believe ugliness on such a scale was possible unless one had seen it. There is the same total ignorance and disregard of standards in other countries – for example, now there is an Underground in Moscow (for which the plans were prepared before the War) no one can believe that anywhere else has had such a thing in years. All the modernist buildings have grown shoddy and horrible in three years' weather. The persecution continues – since the murder of Stalin's friend Kirov here, between 20,000 and 80,000 people have been 'liquidated' i.e. sent away, heaven knows where, after being given a few days notice to sell all they possessed.[23]*

Aside from the Congress there was a great accompanying exhibition with treasures from remote museums all over the Soviet Union. There were also the glories of Leningrad's architecture to enjoy – and Joan had taken her camera with her. How much she found of interest in the academic papers it is difficult to say – to any but an expert, lectures on 'The Systematic Classification of Persian Pottery between the 10th–14th Centuries A.D.', 'The Function of the Bactrian Kingdom as a Clearing House of Ideas' and 'The Sassanian Development of Vault, Dome and Buttress and the Revolution Caused by these Developments in European Architecture' must have seemed very abstruse, to say the least. Joan perhaps felt the effects of her negligible formal education, but she was on a mission to educate herself.

Byron's most famous book was *The Road to Oxiana*, his account of a ten-month journey he made with Christopher Sykes from August 1933 to June 1934. Many years later, Bruce Chatwin was to regard *The Road to Oxiana* as 'a classic text, indispensable' and he must have discussed Byron – one of his heroes – with Joan, but it seems that it was one of Byron's previous books that had an influence on her. *First Russia, Then Tibet* was published in 1933.

Tom Driberg, who wrote the 'William Hickey' social column in the *Daily Express*, was another of Joan's close friends and regularly found a place for her on his page. In November 1935, after Sir Bolton had stood down as MP for Evesham and been raised to the peerage as Viscount Monsell, 'William Hickey' reported:

> Tories in the Government are profoundly relieved by the news that Sir BOLTON EYRES MONSELL is to remain First Lord of the Admiralty. On his elevation to the peerage he will probably take the unimaginative title of Lord Monsell. He was originally Monsell: gained Eyres by marriage. His daughter, Joan – unusually tall, with attractively narrow eyes, very fair skin – has one pursuit which is exceptional in government or any other circles here. She is busily learning Tibetan.[24]

5

Love – and Marriage

While her sister Diana prepared for a traditional upper-class life, political and social upheavals were never too far away and had an impact on Joan's own circle. They were of course of daily concern to Sir Bolton. In April 1935, Diana married Major Alan 'Tim' Casey, late of the Royal Dragoons, at St Margaret's, Westminster. Casey had been a contemporary of Graham at Sandhurst, but Diana met her husband while staying at Kedleston Hall in Derbyshire; Casey was the new local master of foxhounds. Joan and her sister Patricia were the two adult bridesmaids and carried bouquets of red flowers; there were four little girls and a page who wore a uniform of the Dragoons of 1830. It was a large society wedding, attended by the Japanese, German and French ambassadors and the Chinese minister. Sweden, Italy and Finland were represented by their naval attachés. Sybil gave the newly married couple four Jersey cows from the Dumbleton herd as a wedding present, and after a honeymoon in Vienna the Caseys became farmers at Market Overton in Rutland – Cottesmore hunting country. Unfortunately, along with the marriage came Miss Bailey, Tim's cook and housekeeper from the house he had lived in as a bachelor. Miss Bailey refused to allow Diana to enter her own kitchen; a situation which lasted while living in two houses until, at last, Miss Bailey's death thirty years later.

Back in early 1933, Billa Cresswell and John Betjeman had attended a Labour meeting in Cheltenham. Afterwards, as Billa told Alan, there were questions: 'would the Labour government abolish fox-hunting, and if not why not?' and 'how many acres of land that could be cultivated were given over to deer forests?' Then they sang the Red Flag. Goodness, she was moved![1] The Labour Party had been humiliated in the General Election of 1931, losing four-fifths of its seats. In the same election, Oswald Mosley failed to win a seat as the leader of the New Party. Having started his political career as a Conservative MP, Mosley had subsequently joined the Labour Party before resigning over its unemployment policies. The New Party, which he had launched, originally attracted a great deal of moderate and cross-party support – Alan Pryce-Jones was briefly a member – but afterwards Mosley moved further and further to the right. A visit to Mussolini in Italy impressed Mosley deeply, and having wound up the New Party he founded the British Union of Fascists (BUF). Bolton Eyres Monsell's constituency, Evesham, was rural, and depended on market-gardening. Like much of Worcestershire it was badly hit by the agricultural depression of the 1930s. Many of the villages had been emptied of their young men by the First World War and for the younger generation there was considerable unemployment – the nearest industry was in Gloucester. For a constituency like this, fascism, which offered protectionism and isolationism, had considerable appeal, and Mosley himself considered standing in Bolton's seat in 1935, or at the very least putting up a BUF candidate. The constituency was seen as vulnerable, especially as Sir Bolton's twenty-five years in the seat were at an end. In March 1935, the *Gloucestershire Echo* reported that Mosley, one of the most dazzling orators of the twentieth century, spoke for an hour to nearly a thousand people at the Public Hall, Evesham. Six months later in Pershore, the headquarters of the BUF in the Evesham constituency, he gave a speech attacking the Labour Party as communists for backing intervention in the Italian–Abyssinian war. In the event, however, there was no BUF candidate in the Evesham election in November 1935, nor anywhere else. The newly created Lord Monsell's replacement as the Conservative candidate, Rupert de la Bère, was returned with an increased majority of over twelve and a half thousand. Mosley had missed his opportunity. Billa wrote cheerfully to Alan in Austria on the eve of polling day. She was an ardent Tory. Indeed, there was no party reactionary enough for her, though she was quick to inform him that she was not a fascist – far from it. She was just 'feudal'. Instead of the Tory squire she said she had hoped for, two years later Billa married Roy Harrod, an Oxford economist and a supporter of the Liberal Party.

Diana's wedding took place shortly before the signing, in June 1935, of the Anglo-German Naval Agreement – the most controversial event of her father's political career. The terms of the agreement allowed Germany to build up her strength in submarines, but her overall tonnage was limited to only 35 per cent of that of Britain. Konstantin Neurath, the German foreign minister, did not believe that agreement was possible, so he had sent his rival Joachim von Ribbentrop to negotiate, and then be seen to fail. To everyone's surprise, Sir Samuel Hoare, the new British foreign secretary, agreed to the terms but it was the First Lord of the Admiralty, Bolton Eyres Monsell, who signed the agreement on Britain's behalf. Ribbentrop proclaimed that this was the happiest day of his life, and Hitler was suitably impressed. Winston Churchill attacked the agreement both at the time and in his memoirs as a defining example of the futility of appeasement. In April 1936, the German ambassador, Leopold von Hoesch, who had attended Diana's wedding, died suddenly of a heart attack. Hoesch, a career diplomat, was popular and well liked by British politicians, admired for his ability to promote the smooth running of Anglo-German relations. However, he had made known to Neurath his unhappiness at Ribbentrop's growing relationship with Hitler, and had denounced Hitler's occupation of the Rhineland in March 1936 as a deliberate provocation to France and, ultimately, Britain. By now, Hoesch had become a thorn in Hitler's flesh, and his death could scarcely have been more convenient. Ribbentrop was appointed German ambassador to the Court of St James in his place.

There were many members of the upper classes who had been attracted by fascism – Sir Oswald Mosley's social connections were, after all, impeccable – so when Ribbentrop arrived they were all too glad to be taken in by his apparent charm. In Worcestershire, Avon Bank and Wood Norton Hall were particularly receptive houses, and Ribbentrop was invited to shoot at Wood Norton. In Gloucestershire, Lord and Lady Redesdale were ardent fascists: Diana Mitford, their daughter, married Mosley, and her sister Unity befriended Hitler. Whatever Bolton's own private opinions, he was a member of the government and so, as a sign of goodwill, he too invited Ribbentrop to Dumbleton Hall for the shooting. To show his gratitude, Ribbentrop presented the Monsells with a pair of dark blue silk curtains embroidered with a swastika; they were hung so that one could see them as one came out of the lift. Monsell finally stood down as First Sea Lord on 5 June 1936 but, at Ribbentrop's invitation, Lord and Lady Monsell (as they now were) attended the Olympic Games in Berlin in August that year. The press reported that while in Gemany, Bolton also had a meeting with Hitler at Stanley Baldwin's request:

Mr Baldwin has always had a great admiration for Lord Monsell, who retired from active politics a few months ago, although still, by the standards of Westminster, a young man. He is a modest, unaggressive type of statesman, and has long been credited with the ambition to live the life of a country gentleman, though his visit to Herr Hitler suggests that the Prime Minister is anxious to keep his services available to the State from time to time.[2]

The Monsells had still not returned to Dumbleton by the beginning of September, and so, in the absence of her mother, Joan opened the Evesham Hospital Carnival. The weather was reported to be perfect.[3]

Joan's weekends at that time were usually spent at Dumbleton or with the Lygons at Madresfield. You had to be very jolly and young to be invited to a Dumbleton party. One weekend Gerald Berners, who lived at Faringdon House, collected the ballet dancer Frederick Ashton from Didcot station and drove to Dumbleton for what turned out to be a wild weekend, where everyone got drunk and a lot of clothes got flung about. Billa, while swinging from the ceiling and performing a striptease, broke a vast bronze candelabra.[4] 'I was starkers, my dear, absolutely starkers!'[5]

The Hall still maintained a very high standard of living. The butler, Thomas Spencer, whose wife was the head cook, was in overall charge of fifteen resident servants. These included two foot-men, a housekeeper, cooks and four kitchen maids. Spencer kept the staff in order, and arranged with the housekeeper and cook to organize meals and accommodation for family and guests. He was also in charge of the wine cellar and the silver, which was kept securely locked in a massive safe. The Hall had extensive cellarage for wine and for food, including the game – they were especially full after the shooting parties. Shooting was Bolton's favourite pursuit, and he had taken great trouble to shape the Dumbleton woods into one of the best and most difficult shoots in the country. The house-hold staff all lived in, apart from the butler and odd-job man, although the male staff were separated by different staircases which led to individual bedrooms. At Belgrave Square, accommodation

1. Joan was born in February 1912 at her family's house
in Belgravia and christened Joan Elizabeth Eyres Monsell.

2. Charles Kettlewell in Kamchatka in 1882:
'he had little in the way of camp lore.'

3. Dumbleton Hall, 'a substantial, stone-built mansion containing accommodation for a Family of Distinction', was purchased in 1875 and later extended.

4. The lion skin in the Dumbleton drawing room was one of the many trophies from Ewart Grogan's African expedition.

5. Sir Bolton and Lady Eyres Monsell on the yacht *Heartsease* in 1934;
they employed a full-time crew of fourteen.

6. Joan with her sister and cousins at Sandbanks in Dorset, *c.* 1917.
Left to right: Diana Eyres Monsell, Gino Watkins, Peter Daniell, Pam Watkins,
Joan, John Christian, Tony Watkins, Mary Christian.

7. Joan in 1926. Social life in the country revolved around fox-hunting and pony shows.

8. Joan as a debutante in 1930; she claimed that all she had learnt at school was how to curtsey.

9. Graham Eyres Monsell, c. 1930: 'they sold me some oil called *Huile de Bronze of Molinard*, after three days application of which, one's face takes on such a South-of-France tan as you can't believe'.

10. Joan skiing in Austria in 1933:
the mountains were 'divine'.

11. John Betjeman at
Dumbleton in 1933. Betjeman had
published *Ghastly Good Taste*
and captioned the picture,
taken by Joan, 'The author –
an example of good taste if
ever there was one.'

12. Brian Howard, photographed
by Joan: 'tall, pale, dark-faced with
enormous eyes and very long eyelashes'.

13. Eddie Gathorne-Hardy in 1932. He and Brian Howard
used to share a flat so decrepit that fungus grew on the walls.

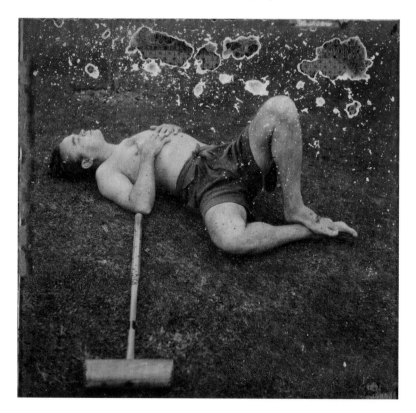

14. Joan kept this photograph of Cyril Connolly in her
bedroom in Greece, where it was eaten away by insects.

15. Joan by John Banting, a fashionable Art Deco painter.
A handsome and glamorous figure, he used to throw knives
'when in the mood', but was a close friend.

16. In 1933 Joan was engaged to Alan Pryce-Jones but he fell out of love.
He married in Austria the following year.

17. John Betjeman wrote to Billa Cresswell, 'Whenever I feel sexless
I only have to turn up those photographs Joan took of you.'

was much more cramped and the staff all ate, worked and slept in the basement. Servants travelled between Dumbleton and London by bus or by train and if they travelled to Paddington they went on by taxi to Belgravia. Fruit, vegetables, eggs, milk and meat were also sent up daily by the early train from Evesham to London, to Cowdray for the polo, or to the Monsells' yacht, the *Heartsease*, which they owned for a couple of years in the 1930s, employing a permanent crew of fourteen. Bolton kept a Rolls-Royce and a Lagonda, as well as a little two-seater car which he would drive at speed up and down the drive with the ladies, making them squeal with excitement. The Hall, village and family in many ways supported a small welfare state, providing employment and looking after its people. Milk came from the dairy and eggs from the hens, and whatever else was needed was supplied. Like every country house, Dumbleton Hall relied for its smooth running on a plentiful supply of cheap labour, but in the hard years of the late 1920s and the 1930s Depression, there were plenty who would gladly have exchanged this cheap labour for the unemployment they faced. The view from the country house basement was still a good deal more attractive than that from the dole queue.[6]

Joan's small green pocket diary for 1936 is the only one of hers that survives from these years. At the beginning of the diary there is a list: 'Great Symbol; Psychic Heat; Illusory Body; Dreams; Clear Light; Intermediate state; Transference'. Her Tibetan classes continued every Tuesday evening. Some days in the diary are also marked by Tibetan letters or hieroglyphs, which she was seemingly using as a private code. Joan was not conventionally religious, but at this period in her life she was fascinated by all things Tibetan, and, since the two elements are so closely bound up together, that included both culture and religion. More to the point perhaps, Joan was also always self-questioning – in her letters she was always blaming herself for her indecision. On the final page there is some doggerel verse:

see arriving on the scene
Joan, the happy scholar of home
one shoe laced, and one undone
where to begin? Ah, there's the fun
one gate leading from the Park
one book praised by Freya Stark
one to marry, black as ink
maharajah – Maeterlinck*
gives no advice, but Graham says
do you hesitate with your [story?]
patchwork means a sense of quiet.
must the light be on or off?
must he be a tough or toff?
how many sheets? Can you pull the plug?
on the bed? Or neath the rug?
at the keyhole? Crowds? Alone? 'I don't know' cries Schizo Joan.

The Maharajah of Jaipur was frequently mentioned in the London society columns of the 1930s. In July 1935 the *Bystander* published a picture of Joan and the maharajah together at a charity party – cabaret, supper and dancing – in aid of the Artists General Benevolent Fund. Joan possessed an Indian jewel: precious stones inlaid in gold. Many years later when Joan sold her jewellery to build a house, this was one piece she held back. But the full story of her admirer, the 'one to marry, black as ink/maharajah', she did not reveal.

The arrangements Joan jotted down in the diary show that 1936

---

* Maurice Maeterlinck (1862–1949): Belgian symbolist poet and playwright.

started at the Chelsea Arts Club Ball on New Year's Eve. On 29 January, she was lunching at the Ritz; the next day she went to a concert with Billa. On 1 February at 7.30, Joan was at the Café Royal to meet Cyril Connolly. The Café Royal, at the Regent Street quadrant, was enjoying a revival of popularity. The old Café, which in its glory days had been the resort of Oscar Wilde, Lord Alfred Douglas and Max Beerbohm, had been destroyed, and the mirrors and golden caryatids only survived in the grill-room. In its place there was an ugly modern restaurant encircled by the spacious Café Gallery, where one could dine and drink until the early hours of the morning and could always find friends. As Osbert Lancaster remembered, 'the food was good and cheap, the house burgundy at five bob a bottle excellent.'[7] When he came to draw the Café, he included Connolly among its diners. For the coronation of George VI they produced the *Café Royal Cocktail Book*, compiled by the President of the Bartenders' Guild. Hundreds of cocktails were listed, from the A.1 ('invented by Albert') to the Zubrowka ('invented by S.T. Yakimovitch – If extra kick is required a dash of Absinthe may be added. Shake and strain off into the cocktail glass, putting a small piece of lemon peel on top'). Cocktails were consumed almost religiously. Patrick Balfour wrote an article for the *Listener* called 'Society'.

> Later I proceeded to a cocktail party, to which my neighbour at luncheon had invited me. This is perhaps the most popular form of entertainment among the upper tribes of the British Islanders. It is a refreshingly simple function, at which the guests drink coloured liquid from little glasses, crowd together, prattle without restraint about anything that comes into their heads, and the evening proceeds are carried away by a garrulous enthusiasm which is positively child-like in its intensity.[8]

JOAN

Cyril's is the name which occurs most often in Joan's diary. Lees-Milne described dining at Cyril and Jean Connolly's King's Road flat to Ann Gathorne-Hardy, to whom he was briefly engaged:

> The Connollys are marvellous people to know [. . .] They are quite rich, about £1200 a year I should think, and they like to spend it all on food, drink, travel and their friends. They are both extremely intelligent; he is brilliant, untidy, dirty and ugly. They give lots of dinners at which 8 or 10 sit down to the most gorgeous meals [. . .] They never go to cinema or plays after, instead one sits round the fire and drinks [. . .] Above all they know and invite all the people one likes best in England.[9]

The guests the night he was invited included the Peter Quennells, the Peter Rodds*, John Sutro, Christopher Sykes and his sister Angela, Countess of Antrim, Joan, Coote Lygon, and the publisher Kenneth Rae. Connolly loved to play the role of host; organizing successful parties gave him considerable pleasure – and there were many successful parties in the Connollys' untidy rooms. This bohemian disorder had one serious drawback however: none of their pets had been house-trained. Alan Pryce-Jones recalled 'a pair of lemurs, which frolicked up and down the curtains, in spite of, or because of, a chronic looseness of the bowel',[10] and Aldous Huxley, a fastidious neighbour during a time they lived abroad, claimed that he had once watched Jean Connolly, after she had distributed raw meat to their tame ferrets, wipe her blood-stained fingers down the front of the Chinese coat she was wearing.[11]

Connolly, who believed that he was destined to be a serious novelist, left many unfinished excerpts of draft novels among his papers, hundreds of pages with which he could do nothing. In 1935, his

---

* Peter Rodd and Nancy Mitford married in 1933.

single finished novel, *The Rock Pool*, was at last published by the Obelisk Press (in the copy Connolly gave Joan, he said it was from 'Auntie C'). The book, which is about decadent inhabitants of a resort in the south of France, had previously been turned down by British publishers as obscene on account of its lesbian content, but some contemporary critics received the book generously. *The Rock Pool* seems wooden and awkward, as if Connolly so loved being the centre of attention that he could not even share his self-absorption with his own creations. In the main, Connolly was a journalist, although – as he was always happy to admit – he would prefer to lie in bed or in his bath than write. While expressing a personal preference for the lingua franca of American novels he was, simultaneously, reviewing non-fiction for the *Sunday Times*, novels for the *New Statesman* and, together with the crime writer Francis Iles, crime fiction for the *Daily Telegraph*.[12] Joan apparently took Cyril's advice on what to read. In her diary she wrote down a list of recent books: *Butterfield 8* by John O'Hara; *Tender is the Night* by Scott Fitzgerald; *Frost in May* by Antonia White; two thrillers – *The Murder of My Aunt* by Richard Hull and *Malice Aforethought* by Francis Iles – and a horror story, *The Werewolf of Paris* by Guy Endore. Perhaps *The Southern Gates of Arabia*, an account by Freya Stark of what is now the Yemen, was one book wholly of Joan's choosing; it is unlikely that Cyril would ever have wanted to go to Arabia.

Joan's diary also records a visit to an exhibition of Paul Nash's work with John Betjeman, a 'Byzantine Party', and, on 21 February, her taking of the 6.13 boat train to Paris, where, on the 27th, she attended a Surrealist exhibition in the rue de Clichy. Later in the year, she went to see an exhibition of work by the Jewish-Hungarian artist and photographer László Moholy-Nagy, a former professor at the Bauhaus who had left Germany for England when the Nazis came to power. In addition, she made arrangements for lunches, cocktail parties, and the occasional visit to the ballet or opera (ever eager to learn, she took the score with her, so that she could follow the music). In September she went with the Betjemans to Rome, where they stayed in a house belonging to Gerald Berners. Betjeman wrote to Berners: 'Joan and Pegriloppy are very cultivated. Never out of the Galleries. We enter every open church. I am taking notes now like Peyellowppy, so as not to get muddled. Joan is very keen on churches.'[13]

Joan was now·a young woman of twenty-four, endlessly interested in all sorts of things and leading a full and varied social life. Furthermore she was both beautiful and intelligent – in itself a source of endless surprise to the press. However, the pocket diary for 1936 offers little insight into her emotional life and the entries peter out long before the last pages. And it offers no hint of what was for her the most important story of all: 1936 was significant, because it was the year Joan met and fell in love with John Rayner, the man she was to marry.

John Rayner was born in Dulwich in August 1908. His background was solidly middle class. His father, Jack, was a journalist; the literary editor of the *Weekly Dispatch* from 1915 and its news editor in the 1920s. Through his father's connections, John grew up in a literary household. In 1919, Jack bought the goodwill and stock of the Eldar Gallery in Great Marlborough Street, which promoted contemporary artists, particularly Walter Sickert. As a boy, his son attended a preparatory school in Seaford near Newhaven – the future art historian and spy Anthony Blunt was a fellow pupil, while John had a lasting memory of rejecting the sexual advances of the headmaster. From his prep school, John won an exhibition to Cheltenham College. Although his mother continued to deal in art to help with the family finances, when Jack Rayner died unexpectedly in 1925, John, aged seventeen, had to leave the school. The editor of the *Weekly Dispatch* gave him a job, starting him 'on line' – paying him by lines printed. This arrangement swiftly changed to a regular salary when he saw John's ability, and the young man was soon writing gossip columns under the name of 'John Grosvenor'. In September 1931 he took a job as assistant to the features editor of the *Daily Herald* at a salary of twelve guineas a week, and two years later he became features editor himself. In January 1934, when he was still only twenty-six, John was taken on by the *Daily Express*, which offered him a commencing salary of twenty-five guineas a week. He became in turn associate features editor, literary and features editor, and, in 1938, day assistant editor, by which time his salary had risen to thirty-five guineas a week.

Under the editorship of Arthur Christiansen, John – who was known within the office and by many of his friends as JR – had dramatically altered the design of the paper, giving it more interesting formats, bigger and bolder typography, and more colourful headlines. Traditionalists might not have approved but everyone copied him, and by the middle of the 1930s the *Express* was the biggest selling newspaper in the country. Christiansen also surrounded himself with some of the most forceful, energetic men of his generation, so that his conferences were conducted in a spirit of short-sleeved exuberance which set the tone for the next day's paper. A former editor of *The Times*, Sir Edward Pickering, reminisced about his years on the *Express*:

Alan Moorehead and O'Dowd Gallaher were monopolising the foreign bylines; Tom Delmer was beginning to establish that long list of countries that he was expelled from; Tom Driberg was having a glorious row with Frank Buchman of MRA [Moral Rearmament]; Jimmy Agate was a frequenter of the office at midnight correcting his book reviews with meticulous care; John Rayner was producing feature pages as elegant as his own shirts; Lucy Milner was looking more elegant than any Woman's Page illustration.[14]

Rayner was tall, broad-shouldered, and in his passport he described himself as having grey eyes. Not only was he good-looking, he also knew how to look good. Tom Driberg – one of Joan's many flamboyant, and gay, male friends – had got to know him when he was still working for the *Daily Herald*. Meeting at a party, Driberg said that he had nowhere to live, so John invited him to stay in his flat in Devonport Mews in Bayswater. It became a long-lasting friendship. Driberg had attended Oxford with John Betjeman and Cyril Connolly, and like many of that crowd his university career came to an abrupt end. When he arrived in the examination room still hungover from a night's drinking and instantly fell asleep on the table in front of him, the college authorities told him to pack his bags. After working as a waiter in an all-night cafe and as an occasional prostitute, in 1928 – with help from Edith Sitwell – Tom found a place at the *Express*, writing the social column. He made it his own. Rather than fill his paragraphs solely with trivial social chit-chat, he enlivened them with commentaries on social and political trends and artistic fashions – and Joan, of course, was one of his favourite subjects. His writing was open-minded, witty and interesting: like Driberg himself, it was never dull.

It was Tom who introduced Joan to John Rayner. In February 1936 an article appeared in the *Express* under the subtitle 'Vision of Beauty Changes with the Years – Five Experts Look at Mrs. Brown Potter (Toast of the Nineties) and Reveal Today's Ideals'. The article was inspired by the recent death of Cora Brown Potter, an American society lady and contemporary 'beauty' who had become a stage actress. Five *Express* writers were asked to write a brief paragraph on current equivalents. Between them they chose the actresses Marlene Dietrich and Luise Rainer, and a Miss Pamela Treffry

('character, beauty of line, repose – such an antidote to dental dis-
plays and assertive ingenuousness'); Tom, as 'William Hickey',
proposed the blues singer Ethel Waters ('bone-structure like a Benin
carving'); and John Rayner, the features editor, chose the Hon. Joan
Eyres Monsell – 'Very blonde, high cheek-boned, looks best in
country or riding clothes. When she was in Budapest crowds used
to wait outside the hotel for her to come out so that they could get
a glimpse of the "English Venus". She is a daughter of Lord Monsell, First Lord of the Admiralty.'[15] Whether or not the Budapest story
was true – and it probably owes much to journalistic invention – in
a very public fashion John was showing his interest.

In 1933, John Betjeman had been in desperate need of increasing
his income in order to marry Penelope Chetwode. Fortunately, his
friend Jack Beddington – the director of publicity at Shell – was
keen to encourage drivers to use more petrol and, at the same time,
associate the company with a caring stance on the environment and
English heritage. Together, the two men persuaded the controlling
director of the *Architectural Review*, Jack Regan, that a series of
county guides would be both good publicity and a profitable adventure. Betjeman produced a dummy guide to his own favourite
county, Cornwall, and saw that his salary would be raised to £400 to
cover the extra work involved. Betjeman had a very real love of the
appearance of books, their print, layout and varieties of type, and
although he resigned from the *Architectural Review* in 1935, he continued to work for Beddington as general editor of the *Shell Guides*,
distributing the writing of them among his friends. For Hampshire,
Betjeman asked John Rayner. Jack Beddington wrote to JR, specify-
ing that he would be paid a fee of fifty guineas with an addition of
up to ten guineas for travelling expenses: 'You will use Maurice
Beck as your photographer and you will get the work done this
summer [1936].' When the guide was published in 1937, the following year, under the quirky title *Towards a Dictionary of the County*

of Southampton, commonly known as Hampshire or Hants, it turned out be one of the most successful in the series. Beck's photographs, however, are rather dull, and he did not share the car with JR. Instead, John took Joan with him in order no doubt to survey Joan as well as the county – she certainly took no photos. By the end of the trip they had fallen in love. The problem being, however, that John also had a wife called Molly and they had a son named Nicholas.

In the spring of 1937, Tom Driberg, Peter Quennell and Joan all sailed for New York on the SS *Berengaria*. (This was reported in the *Tatler* as 'Tall, golden-haired Joan Eyres-Monsell . . . has gone to join her brother in the USA.'[16]) Quennell was unsatisfactorily married for the second time and had turned his eyes to Joan, but she was receiving cables from Rayner in London. On Tuesday 5 March, Tom reported in his 'William Hickey' column, 'Last day of trip. Bright sunshine, calm seas. We reach Quarantine about 6.30 this evening, dock at 8. I am lucky, say homecoming Americans, to be approaching New York for the first time, after dark when the lights make it even more impressive than by day.' The homecoming Americans, he continued, included buyers from big New York fashion houses who had been to see the Paris collections:

> Quietly dressed middle-aged women they find the trip a rest after seeing 3 or 4 shows of 200 to 250 dresses each day for a week, picking from every 200 perhaps 10 suitable for sale in the States. On board is America's first consignment of new Paris models: 'How dreadful if the ship sank with all those dresses,' said a young woman.
>
> Most original fashion note last night was provided not by France or America, but by Great Britain's JOAN EYRES MONSELL, who came down to dinner wearing a purple dress,

a scarlet and gold Eton jacket, a single extraordinary earring. It consisted of a bunch of 42 small gilt safety pins. No mere fashion plate, Miss Monsell has spent as much as she could screwing up her pretty but myopic eyes over a Tibetan dictionary. No mere highbrow either, she has been winning satisfactorily at trente-et-un.[17]

Perhaps being in love had given Joan confidence. Any woman who dressed with such flair knew exactly what she was doing and by now she must have become so used to being in the papers that she had decided that she would enjoy it. Joan spent a week with Graham. His treatment at the Mayo Clinic over the last couple of years had gone exceptionally well. At the time, Elton Mayo, an Australian, was professor of industrial relations at Harvard Business School. After a month of daily talks and reading psychology, Mayo asked Graham to take on the treatment of an outpatient at Boston Psychiatric Clinic, and he had shown such sensitivity to his patients that Mayo had given him further responsibility. As a result, Graham started to lose his own shyness and gain confidence: Mayo commented that he now preferred work to nightclubs. Subsequently, Graham was appointed as research assistant in industrial research at the Graduate School of Business Administration, and joined a team looking into the sociology of industrial workers – he seemed finally to be at ease with the world. Seeing Joan, however, gave him the opportunity to let his hair down. As he wrote to Alan Pryce-Jones in April, after Joan had returned to England, 'Joan's hectic visit to the New World ended in such a gay and drunken week in New York as I have seldom lived through.' Perhaps Joan was also letting off some steam before resuming her affair with a married man.

Molly Rayner had first met her husband John in 1933 and, after finding that she was pregnant, they married in October that year. She was a woman who liked to drop names and she had social aspirations: there are posed photographs of Molly with her baby son in both the *Tatler* and the *Bystander* in 1935. She followed the magazines whereas the magazines followed Joan. In the summer of 1936 the couple spent a month travelling round Greece. 'Greece v. cheap, beer v. good, lovely melons, women don't wear belts, too hot and so walk very well,' John wrote to his mother. But by then he had interests elsewhere. It was as if Molly didn't quite fit. To begin with, Molly Rayner had no idea what was so wrong with her marriage to John but she eventually hired a private detective to follow her husband. The detective reported back that she had nothing to worry about: John was drinking so heavily in the Fleet Street pubs with his fellow journalists that he was likely to die soon from alcohol poisoning, so her problems would be over. Aside from physical attraction, John had in common with Joan a love of places and nature, music, art, reading, wine and good food, not to mention – and this is by no means trivial – an affection for cats. He was also inclined to tease. These traits, as well as other pursuits and interests, informed the way he thought and lived and the people with whom he chose to share his life.[18]

In mid 1937, soon after Joan's return from America, John left his wife and moved in with Tom Driberg. In October, when Molly heard that John and Joan were in the south of France on holiday, she telephoned Tom to find out more and asked if her husband had been seeing Joan lately. Tom, out of loyalty, lied to her, saying that, on the contrary, he had been taking Joan out to dinner, and had usually arrived back to find John at home all by himself. He also claimed that he did not know they were in France together. The raggedness of the break continued – Molly was expecting another child. Their daughter, Amanda, was born in April 1938. John always claimed afterwards – probably out of guilt – that he had somehow been tricked by his wife into getting her pregnant, to prevent him leaving home. In later years, apart from paying monthly maintenance and sending Christmas and birthday presents, he had little contact with his first two children.

For some time while he was still married, Joan and JR were spending weekends together at Tickerage Mill near Uckfield in Sussex. Dick Wyndham, 'Dirty Dick', the owner of the mill, was an artist and a photographer who had won the Military Cross in the First World War. He was a very tall man, thin and gangling, and he dressed appallingly in filthy flannel trousers – his fly buttons invariably undone – and an old ragged mackintosh, but he possessed immense charm. In his emotional life, one attractive woman followed another. It was said that, on his regular trips to the south of France, when he drew up at a wayside hotel, the proprietor, who was an old acquaintance, would invariably greet him with the same remark, '*Que madame a changé!*' as he led his clients to their room.[19]

Wyndham had inherited Clouds in Wiltshire, a house built for his family by Philip Webb in the 1880s and decorated by William Morris, but he had found its upkeep impossible and sold it in 1936. In its place, Wyndham bought Tickerage, a far smaller mill house flanked by a mill pond with a shallow lake lying at the bottom of a valley beneath a steep slope covered with apple trees. If Dick was not abroad, he invited gatherings of friends. Although these were essentially masculine affairs, girlfriends were welcome, and a long procession of women found themselves invited to the mill, Joan among them. At one such weekend Joan photographed the host and guests. Along with JR and Joan, the guests included Patrick Kinross (Patrick Balfour's father having died, he had inherited the title), Constant Lambert, Angela Culme-Seymour (who was married to Kinross), Tom Driberg, Cyril Connolly, Stephen Spender and his boyfriend Tony Hyndman, and Mamaine Paget, who later married Arthur Koestler.

Connolly loved Tickerage. In his 1945 book *The Unquiet Grave*, he listed it as having the magical qualities which helped him keep angst at bay:

> The mill where I sometimes stay provides another cure for Angst; the red lane down through the Spanish chestnut wood, the apple trees on the lawn, the bees in the roof, the goose on the pond, the black sun-lit marsh marigolds, the wood-fires crackling in the low bedrooms, the creak of the cellar-door, and the recurrent monotonies of the silver-whispering weir, what could be more womb-like or reassuring? Yet always the anxious owner is flying from it as from the scene of a crime.[20]

Wyndham was a generous host, and he provided good food and good wine. He was also a good listener who enjoyed good conversation. Tom Driberg said these weekend parties were the best he ever attended. Many years later, Mamaine Paget's twin sister Celia recalled in a letter to Joan:

> *It's good to remember the old days at Tickerage: the intellectual treasure hunts (you won one of them), the bluebell wood, walks across country on summer nights under the full moon with nightjars whirring, the marvellous food and wine, playing croquet – John Piper says when he went there once we were playing it uphill. Dick certainly was a very special person, and I miss him still.[21]*

Once the decree absolute came through in March 1939 dissolving JR's marriage to Molly, he was free to marry Joan. Their modest wedding took place in July at Caxton Hall Register Office in Westminster. They were both dressed in blue and Joan wore a spray of orchids. John Betjeman was one of the witnesses, the other was a Mr E. G. Wood – a young man they had met on the stairs together with the young woman he himself was marrying. John's colleagues did not find out until they saw the story in the evening papers. This struck them as impressively casual and aristocratic, the effect he had doubtless intended. The wedding was widely reported. While John Betjeman was just a 'friend', Mr E. G. Wood got the headline: 'Cabby as Witness at Wedding'. The *Daily Mirror* even carried his photograph, sitting at the wheel. After all, both JR and Joan described themselves as 'journalists' in the marriage register, and knew how to make a good story for the press.

Joan's parents can only have been relieved that she was at least now married and no longer living openly with a married man. They must long have abandoned hope that she would live any sort of respectable life. And JR had a reasonable salary so he was not marrying Joan for her money. Cyril Connolly, however, whose marriage to Jean had collapsed amidst adultery, recrimination and general mayhem, said Joan's wedding was the unhappiest day of his life.

6

Wartime London

Joan and JR started their married life in his small flat in Blue Ball Yard, an eighteenth-century yard with stables off St James's Street in Piccadilly. JR wrote to his mother that it felt like starting all over again, and that life was very enjoyable. But, within weeks, Joan was almost a widow. In August they went to stay in Hammamet in Tunisia, where Graham had been lent a house. They hired a car for four or five days and drove down to the oases and the city of Kairouan. John was bitten by a dog and they were frightened that it might have been rabid, but the Institut Pasteur confirmed that it was not *enragé*. However, a week or so after their return to London, John fell ill. Joan looked up typhoid in a medical dictionary and he seemed to have all the symptoms, but the *Daily Express* staff doctor turned out to be incompetent and had no idea what John was suffering from. When his temperature rose above 104 degrees, a tropical disease specialist was called in, but he diagnosed malaria and gave him the wrong medicine. Finally, at Joan's instigation, Lord Dawson of Penn, the physician to the Royal Household and former President of the Royal College of Physicians, came to see her husband. He only needed to stand at the door of John's hospital bedroom to give a correct diagnosis of typhoid fever. John was moved into a private nursing home in Portland Place, where he lay ill and delirious for days. Amidst all this, on Sunday 3 September, Neville Chamberlain broadcast to the nation announcing that the country was at war.

Joan wrote to Penelope Betjeman from Blue Ball Yard.

> *Darling Penelope,*
>
> *John has been desperately ill with typhoid, in fact on Tuesday everyone was sure he was going to die but suddenly he fell asleep & got over the crisis. Since then he has recovered a bit and his temperature is down a lot. It used to go to nearly 106. He was delirious for several days, the most nerve-wracking thing & most unfair that he should suffer mentally as well as physically. He still has three special nurses & tubes of oxygen outside his door & the most depressing thing is he is almost certain to have a relapse.*
>
> *I am sleeping at [B]elgrave [S]quare now, except when I slept at the nursing home, as it was so gloomy here alone. I feel very unreal & the war hardly exists. Let me know if you ever come to London.*
>
> *Best love Joan.*[1]

In the midst of all this the October edition of the *Architectural Review* included a seven-page report and photo shoot on Père Lachaise Cemetery in Paris, full of pictures of row upon row of funeral monuments, weeping angels and long avenues of cedar trees. The article ought to have been the highlight of Joan's career so far and a matter of great satisfaction. Instead it was all too horribly real. Her new husband had almost died and she could not know what horrors the declaration of war might presage. Slowly, John recovered but at Christmas he was still too weak to leave Portland Place. Joan went to stay at Tom Driberg's new house, Bradwell Lodge in Essex. The lodge was a half Tudor, half Georgian house with a belvedere – a room built by a former owner on top of the house with a view all around, so that he could watch out for smugglers. Her fellow guests were Tom's brother Jack, Constant Lambert and Patrick and Angela Kinross. In the mid 1930s, Patrick had changed from being a gossip columnist to travel writing, with books on journeys through Asia and central Africa. With the imminence of war and his father on the point of death, it had seemed a desirable time to prepare for some sort of permanence by marriage. But his choice of wife could not have been more disastrous. Angela Culme-Seymour was very beautiful. She had a complexion like camellia flowers, large dark eyes and long bewitching eyelashes, but Angela was not made for permanence: she had left her first husband, Johnny Churchill, while changing buses in Malaga in the south of Spain – it had seemed a good idea at the time.[2] JR, although unable to come himself, had sent Tom a house-warming present of a visitors' book, an inch and a half thick, printed with the name of the house and Tom's initials. Rationing had not yet begun, so there was plenty of food, but Tom could scarcely boil an egg, so he hired a cook from a London agency. The cook turned out to be 'a highly superior Scottish matron' who had previously held posts in ducal households and had never worked without the assistance of at least a kitchen maid. She did not hide her pained surprise at the inadequate and chaotic kitchen arrangements, but the cooking was splendid. Her forbidding presence rather chilled the Christmas spirit and Tom was relieved when she left.[3]

JR attributed the typhoid to the ice in a gin and tonic which he had drunk after a hot walk along the beach at Hammamet. There were no long-lasting effects from his illness, although he believed that the typhoid triggered his deafness in later years. Joan had saved his life, and he remained perpetually grateful to her for her generosity in summoning Lord Dawson, but the considerable bill had to be paid off in £50 instalments and Joan had very little money of her own. At the beginning of January, while still in the convalescent home, JR wrote to John Betjeman. He had noticed that Betjeman, who now made regular radio broadcasts, was giving a talk that day on the Home Service about the poet Sir Henry Newbolt.

> *I hear you are in a state about the war. I have been in here for*
> *nearly 4 months & hope to be out in under a week. But will*
> *have to convalesce. Have you any books to recommend, old or*
> *new . . . ? I wish I cd. leave the [Daily Express] & become a*
> *bird watcher, preferably in Surinam. Love to* ∏ *[Penelope], tell*
> *her we are married in the eyes of the State, & if she quarrels*
> *with that she's a King's Enemy. JR.*[4]

Finally, JR was able to leave hospital, and after spending time in their London flat, Joan and he went down to Brighton, Cornwall and Dorset in order to convalesce. Meanwhile, Betjeman was making attempts to join the armed services, but in January he was turned down on medical grounds by the RAF; he later claimed he had been rejected because the interview exposed his fear of spiders. He wrote to Joan to ask if her father could help. Joan herself was trying to find work as a photographer. She replied from Cornwall:

> *Darling John,*
>   *I am trying to find out about the navy but I don't think Sir*
> *B. will be much help. He is at Yarmouth sending trawlers to*
> *their death, I suppose. What about Piers Synnott [under-secre-*
> *tary at the Admiralty]? He ought to know about the right*
> *department but I think it is very difficult to get in unless you*
> *start in the usual way.*
>   *It was very enjoyable staying at Brighton & we saw Bosie**

---

* Oscar Wilde's former lover Bosie (Lord Alfred Douglas) was a friend of John Betjeman.

who talked a lot about you & hoped your new book of poems
wouldn't be all free verse & nasty modern stuff.

Do you know any oriental buildings anywhere? I can only
think of the Pavilion, Sezincote, Pagoda at Kew at the moment
but thought they might do for the Archie Rev. if I can find a lot
more. Or has it been done a million times?

Best love to you & Penelope
from Joan (& John)[5]

Unaware of his own obvious unsuitability for such a role, Betjeman
next tried to join the Royal Marines. This too proved fruitless.
Instead he took a post offered to him by Kenneth Clark with the
film division at the Ministry of Information, and then in the following year, 1941, he went to work as press attaché at the British
embassy in Dublin.

In the spring of 1940, JR was still far from well. He caught flu.
He was no better than at Brighton, he told his mother. His feet were
aching, he could not walk, and his ears were singing. This was still
the period of the 'Phoney War', while everyone was waiting for
something to happen and when there had been no significant land
operations in western Europe. It was still possible to visit the south
of France with a permit, and so, in search of more sunshine and
warmth than they could find in England, John and Joan went to
Auribeau-sur-Siagne in the Alpes Maritimes for five weeks. Auribeau
was a pretty little village close to Cannes, surrounded by hills forested with mimosa trees, with the River Siagne running in the valley
below. On arrival at their *auberge*, JR had another bout of fever with
sweats and shivering, but he was assured by a local doctor that this
was not the typhoid returning. Joan and he were happy there, enjoying the good, plain food the *auberge* offered and playing chess while
he slowly mended. And it was in Auribeau that Joan discovered that
she was pregnant. She sent Driberg a postcard:

Darling Tom,

If you write to J.R. will you send it to me as I have already had a letter from my family, not that it is likely to shock our American host as he has spent the afternoon telling us of his hetero sex life including how he made money in a Paris hotel sleeping on Sat. nights with English women over the week-end to see how it's done in France. Also if J.R.'s lawyer wants to communicate tell him to send to you to forward. H. Noailles is permanent address of J.R. who has grown beard & looks like Van Gogh self portrait. V. attractive, I find. We eat partridges & drink Château neuf Vieux Telegraphe 1929 v.v. good. Joan xxxxx

N.B. – followed by liqueur called Frigolet, efficacious for making boy babies (so they say locally). In fact, may all our troubles be little ones.[6]

John had now been absent from work for over seven months. He wrote to his editor, Arthur Christiansen, to explain why his conva-lescence had been so prolonged and announced his imminent return. Tom Driberg urged JR not to worry. Christiansen had broken his leg stepping out of a taxi in the blackout and would be away for two or three months. Another colleague was off work with a nervous collapse and Tom had sprained his ankle, also while get-ting out of a taxi in the blackout.

When Joan and John were still in France, she had a miscarriage. After everything that had happened, the realization that she was pregnant was a piece of good news at last. It must now have seemed cruelly depressing. that this good fortune had ended too suddenly – another disappointment. It was so early in the pregnancy that she did not feel the need to call a doctor, while John's reaction was simply to go for a long walk. When he came back they had a row. Joan had grown up amidst a large family, not just her brother and two sisters, but uncles, aunts and many cousins, and she saw a lot of them. She was twenty-eight, she had a husband and for the first time in her life she had a home of her own. She wanted a family too. But, she could at least reflect, there was still time for children – and she looked back on this holiday with pleasure.[7] She could not know how deep her desire for children would later be.

On their return to London, the couple moved from St James's to a flat at Verulam Gardens on the Gray's Inn Road, which was convenient for Fleet Street now that JR was back at work. They liked their flat very much. 'We look out on to a green lawn and old green trees, jackdaws and pigeons and there is a little more room than in Blue Ball Yard,' JR wrote. He invited his mother to come and view the flat but warned her that there were fifty-nine stairs to the top. The artist John Banting was asked to paint the piano. He also wanted to paint a ceiling, preferably over a bed, on the principle that one saw more lying in bed than at any other time. Banting was a fashionable decorative artist who had recently, in February, exhibited at the International Surrealist Exhibition in Paris. His clients had included Diana Mitford, when she was married to her first husband Bryan Guinness, and Eddy Sackville-West, for his private rooms in the Gatehouse Tower at Knole in Kent. He was a rougher kind of bohemian – the way he shaved his head made him look like a rather glamorous criminal – although Nancy Mitford thought he was wonderful.[8] In 1933 Banting had painted a portrait of Joan – the only portrait ever commissioned of her. The picture was both exaggerated in size and simplified, almost a *reductio ad absurdum*. Arched eyebrows, bright blue eyes, pink cheeks, red lips set in an oval face with wavy blonde hair and supported by a long neck: clean, precise, brightly coloured, modern, very Art Deco. Joan and JR also bought another of his works. In a characteristically self-deprecating fashion, Banting offered to exchange it for another if they did not like it: 'It is possibly not a very good mixer amongst all and every varied sort of person and also it is one that one might easily get tired of after a time.'⁹ And he quoted Picasso as saying that 'the way to kill a picture is to hang it on a nail'. Joan had her own fully developed artistic taste, very far from the family portraits, ships at sea, and green landscapes among which she had been raised.

A. J. A. Symons – AJ, the author of *The Quest for Corvo* – was also a friend. Symons was a dandy who modelled his flamboyant style upon Disraeli. He read books on etiquette, wore a monocle and a lavender-grey suit, and he spent hours practising calligraphy.¹⁰ Like JR, he was also a considerable bibliophile. Because of the blackout various friends who came to dine, including AJ, spent the night on their sofa. In a letter dated July 1940, he thanked Joan for 'the best dish and some of the pleasantest hours I have enjoyed since peace left us. I suspected you of being a blue stocking; I had no idea you were a cordon bleu.' AJ had evidently taken a great liking to her, and wrote that he had never known any woman so agreeably, unobtrusively, charmingly rule any roost. Joan was an excellent cook, and there were two things at which she excelled: soufflés, and the ability to produce partridges on JR's birthday on 31 August, a day before the shooting season began.

Once war had started in earnest, weekends out of London became especially welcome. When AJ invited Joan and JR to stay at his home in rural Essex in August 1940, he instructed them to bring only their thinnest clothes, a croquet set and lightest spirits. Their fellow guest was Constant Lambert, whom JR liked greatly for his intelligence, rapidity of mind and sense of fun. Together they sat drinking some of the last bottles of treasured clarets and Sauternes in the blackout. They also went to Bradwell Lodge, where Tom's visitors' book records seven weekend visits when the Rayners were either on their own or in the company of A. J. Symons, Constant Lambert and Cyril Connolly, or with Sefton ('Tom') Delmer of the *Express* and his wife, the artist Isabel Nicholas. The atmosphere was not always as easy as they might have hoped. In her unpublished memoir, Isabel recorded that there was always a coolness between Tom Driberg and herself, while 'no two Toms could have disliked each other more' than Driberg and Delmer. But, she said, both Tom Driberg and JR had great affection for Joan and understood her perfectly. They called these times 'Famous Last Weekends', as if they were living in the constant fear of some apocalyptic event. Eventually, there actually was a 'last weekend'. In 1940, shortly after the Battle of Britain, Bradwell Lodge was requisitioned by the Air Ministry for use as the Officers' Mess of Bradwell Bay.*

Sefton 'Tom' Delmer was an *Express* foreign correspondent. He had been a contemporary of Osbert Lancaster at Lincoln College, Oxford, but he would never have been counted among the 'aesthetes' – in fact he had been most definitely a 'hearty'. Born in Germany and German-speaking, he had seen the rise of Nazi Germany first-hand. He had even had friendly relations with Ernst Röhm, the leader of the Brownshirts, who he described as a 'jovial little soldier of fortune'.[11] This had, in turn, given Delmer access to Adolf Hitler; in 1932 he had walked through the burning embers of the Reichstag at Hitler's side. After a year in France, Delmer spent two years in Spain reporting on the Civil War and was then in Poland when the Second World War broke out. Delmer was a large, Falstaffian figure – highly intelligent and shrewd. He claimed that he had first determined to marry Isabel after seeing a bust of her sculpted by Jacob Epstein in the Tate. After working with Epstein, Isabel had lived and studied in Paris among the left-bank avant-garde. André Derain and Pablo Picasso had both painted her, and Alberto Giacometti had also sculpted her. Isabel wrote in her unpublished autobiography:

---

* There is no bay at Bradwell.

Alberto worked all night, but at five every evening we drank at the Lipp. Picasso used to sit at the table opposite and one day, after staring at me particularly hard, he jumped up and said to Alberto: 'Now I know how to do it.' He dashed back to his studio to paint my portrait with little red eyes, wild hair and a vertical mouth – one of five he painted from memory.[12]

Isabel was still in Paris using Balthus's studio when the Germans invaded France. She left in the company of the Jewish-Romanian poet Tristan Tzara. When they parted, he headed south while Isabel stayed in Bordeaux, awaiting departure. The then third secretary of the British embassy, Donald Maclean, told her not to leave until a British ship arrived. The ship that picked her up, the *Madura*, was the last one to leave and it took four days to reach Falmouth. 'I remember taking a walk up a hill. When I reached that fine short grass I fell on my knees and kissed it,' she wrote. Isabel – who was exuberant and pretty and could drink and swear as well as any man – became very close friends with Joan, and it was through Isabel that Joan later became friends with both Giacometti and Tzara. Isabel wrote:

I was delighted to see Joan again We met for a drink one day at the Café Royale. We both ordered martinis with a dash of absinthe. This was not the sort of drink either of us ever drank – tho' I had grown fond of ordinary pernod. We had about three of these and not surprisingly took taxis home. However the effect was stunning. I fell into bed and had a kind of paralysis. I found I could not move my limbs. When Tom came home he sent for a doctor who shook his head and said this is the beginning of the end. Later Joan phoned to ask what had happened to me. We had had a shared experience. Too much order perhaps. Joan said we might have been arrested.[13]

The first major Luftwaffe attack on London came on the evening of Saturday 7 September 1940. Joan joined the Holborn Division of the British Red Cross, walking every night from Gray's Inn Road through the most densely bombed part of London to Holborn tube station, to work as a volunteer nurse. JR told his mother, Gertrude, that Joan was nursing, washing dishes and spending her nights in the tube stations. 'The Commandant of her division commended her for her good work and ventured to say she would do well in whatever sphere she found herself.'[14] They were now having two or three raids every day, 'but nothing like Sevenoaks where we were this weekend, parachutists slowly descending, bullets near, etc. Very exciting,' JR wrote. Gertrude's food parcels from Devon were greatly appreciated. For Christmas, she sent a duck – a 'soft, delicious, sizzling and succulent bird'. She also sent barrels of cider, jam, geese and chickens. There was a steady demand from John to knit him socks, for which he provided the wool coupons. Shopping for even such everyday items as umbrellas or pens became difficult, because they were so scarce.

Joan was asleep in bed with JR in Verulam Gardens in early April 1941 when three bombs fell only ten yards away. The next time the Gardens was hit it caused great damage. Fortunately, neither Joan nor JR was at home, but the flat became uninhabitable. A month later, JR wrote to the treasurer of Gray's Inn asking for a rebate on the rent of their flat: 'I am sure you will understand it is financially difficult as well as personally distressing for us to move from Gray's Inn though our own troubles hardly bear comparison with those of the rest of the Inn.' The Delmers, who lived in Lincoln's Inn Fields, were also bombed. At the time, they were holding a dinner party where their guests included Ian Fleming and Prince Bernhard of the Netherlands. Joan and JR lived temporarily at the Athenaeum in Piccadilly before taking a flat at Palace Gate, a block designed by the modernist architect Wells Coates. John wrote that he was sorry to leave 'the nicest flat in the world', at smouldering Gray's Inn, whereas Palace Gate – all glass, steel and concrete – had much less appeal. The flats were very small, but they had their own bomb shelter. The Rayners' flat was next to that of Peter Watson, who was by now an important collector and patron of the arts. It was here where John Craxton and Lucian Freud first encountered one another and formed their early creative partnership, and it was also where Joan first met the two young artists. Joan's friendship with John, or Johnny, Craxton was to last until the end of her life. When she first met him Craxton was a very tall, very thin young man who had just failed his army medical. He arrived looking skeletal – he had had pleurisy at school – and clutching a volume of William Blake's *Poetry and Prose* only to be dismissed by a sergeant who told him he would be as much use to the war effort as a three-legged horse.[15] With the encouragement of the Official War Artist Eric Kennington, together with Peter Watson and Joan, Craxton returned to painting. Joan also bought a picture by John Piper. JR wrote to Piper's wife Myfanwy that the sight of the picture made it worth getting up in the morning to see it in the flat.[16]

The bombs continued to fall, but London life went on. 'The destruction in the West End is incredible,' wrote Robert Colquhoun, another of Watson's artists. 'Whole tracts of streets flattened out into a mass of rubble and bent iron. There is a miniature pyramid in Hyde Park not far from us built up of masonry and wreckage taken from bombed buildings. These heaps are all over London.'[17] The raids provided work for Joan, however. Cyril Connolly published Joan's picture of Chelsea Old Church with its bombed rafters jutting upwards like the prow of a ship. The National Buildings Record also commissioned some of her excellent Blitz pictures. In July 1941, the *Architectural Review* published 'The End of Last Time, First Instalment of a Survey of Bomb Damage to Buildings of Architectural Importance': 'To provide obituary records of such buildings is a task THE ARCHITECTURAL REVIEW feels an obligation to undertake and one that can appropriately be started in issues raised by the war.' Whether any of these were by Joan it is impossible to say, but on one page there is a picture of Gray's Inn: two men and a woman in a fur coat stand and look at the smoking ruin; to one side, in front of the building, a little pile of chairs and boxes sits, waiting to be rescued. This was how it must have been for Joan.

The October 1942 edition of the *Architectural Review* included an article called 'Victorian Necropolis, the Cemeteries of London' by R. P. Ross Williamson. While most photographs were published anonymously, on the copy of the *Review* which she kept Joan wrote that these pictures – the cemeteries at Kensal Green, South Norwood and Abney Park, South Kensington – were hers. The final photograph showed fragments of a gravestone at Norwood, destroyed in the Blitz. It was where JR's father was buried.

The war also meant a new role for JR. He had left the *Daily Express* in November 1940 and started working for the Ministry of Economic Warfare (MEW) in Berkeley Square. He told Gertrude that he was working harder and for longer hours than at the *Express* and reading so many documents marked 'secret' that it was lucky that he was naturally uncommunicative. From his office window he could see the effects of the German bombing on the leafless garden below, where the sun showed up the bomb craters in the grass. The following year, JR was posted to the PWE – the Political Warfare Executive. The PWE, which operated from Woburn in Bedfordshire (the workers were billeted on the estate), was responsible for producing 'black and white' propaganda for use against Germany, Italy and the occupied countries. White propaganda was open and obvious, while black propaganda sought to give the impression that the PWE were actually operating inside Germany or elsewhere in Europe, and its impact depended on being able to identify completely with their German targets. In September 1940, Sefton

Delmer had also been recruited from the *Express* by the Special Operations Executive (SOE), which was based at Apsley Guise in Bedfordshire, to organize black propaganda broadcasts to Germany. There could have been no job better suited to his talents. He invented a Prussian character called 'Der Chef' who, as a right-wing German patriot opposed to the Nazis, apparently broadcast nightly within Germany. To attract audiences, he would include salacious material condemning the depravity of the Nazis – the broadcasts were often a mixture of pornography and patriotism. The German High Command condemned their 'quite unusually wicked hate propaganda'. In the summer of 1942, a particularly graphic broadcast about a supposed orgy involving a Kriegsmarine admiral was picked up in Moscow, and elicited a strong Foreign Office protest from Sir Stafford Cripps, the British ambassador to the Soviet Union. Delmer's own chief replied that he didn't consider the broadcast to have been depraved, and 'in this case moral indignation does not seem called for'.[18]

The PWE was also charged with the production of forged documents, leaflets and publications – all designed to disrupt German morale and their power to continue fighting. Isabel, as an artist, also found herself employed to produce pornography, such as a painstakingly realistic picture of a foreign worker with a bright blonde girl. This was distributed in Greece where, she discovered later, Paddy Leigh Fermor had seen it. She was also pleased with her production of a Göring menu card – Hermann Göring being considered a particularly decadent Nazi. The menu included an apparently standard typological frieze, which on inspection turned out to be a chain of men, women and boys in sexual experimentation.

Joan, meanwhile, sought distraction from her photography and volunteer work. The war was experienced by many as a period of intense living, and the disruptions it caused put many marriages under strain. Joan considered that her marriage was sufficiently modern to encompass her taking lovers, and she was not the only one to think that way. If her husband was away from home or working late and Joan wanted to go to a nightclub – many blackout hours were spent in wartime nightclubs – then she felt free to take the young John Craxton along with her:

> She was a dazzling beauty and I, an awkward 20-year old, was utterly stage-struck when she invited me to dance with her one evening at the very smart Boeuf sur le Toit night club.* The manager tried to remove me as I was wearing sandals, but was promptly reprimanded by Joan.[19]

Going to a nightclub was one thing, but sleeping with other men was another, and Joan slept with Cyril Connolly. This was particularly galling for JR, who had always been jealous of Connolly's success with women, and also resented his writing talent. As the editor of the magazine *Horizon*, Connolly was in a reserved occupation. At his Bedford Square office he was invariably attended by female acolytes he had both taught to sub-edit and instructed in the art of cooking. Peter Quennell remembered him slouched in a massive chair: 'it suited Cyril, who preferred a semi-reclining pose to sitting upright at a table; and having placed a board across the arms which carried papers, books and pens, he strengthened the stout defensive enclosure – at a distance only the crown of his head was visible – that protected him against intrusion.'[20]

Joan slept not only with Cyril; she also slept with Alan Pryce-Jones. Alan had returned to England from Austria in 1937 because Poppy was Jewish, and had then stood for parliament in Louth in Lincolnshire as a Liberal; the party was the only one that believed

---

* The 'Boeuf sur le Toit', a fashionable gay nightclub, was named after the famed nightclub in Paris.

in rearmament. He joined the officers' reserve and, as a German-speaker, served in the Intelligence Corps after war broke out. He also worked on the battle order of the German Army at Bletchley Park, and was in France at the time of Dunkirk. While Alan's family moved out of London to Kent for safety, he took advantage of their absence for casual encounters with both sexes, as he wrote in a poem:

Suddenly a diamond shone in the roots of his hair
And live love, the expensive and successful, burst like a next-door
Neighbour in the room, calling us names and shocking for
The reckless, the impossible, the huge catastrophe,
Bullying us with the size of the moment. But we
Lay fascinated, spilled and blown, shiftily.[21]

John found it impossible to cope with Joan's attitude, and became unhappy and aggrieved. There were rows which put too much of a strain upon their marriage. To escape the situation, Joan thought it best to go abroad, and so she took classes to train as a cipher clerk. In the meantime, and for the sake of convenience, Joan and JR continued to live together quite amicably under the same roof. Neither wanted their parents to suspect that their marriage was in difficulty. In September 1942, JR wrote to tell his mother that Joan and he were spending a week in Zennor in Cornwall, on the farm where they had stayed when he was convalescing from typhoid. On Christmas Eve, they dined with Cyril, Mamaine Paget and a girl called Barbara Skelton. A week later, John spent New Year's Eve at the Ritz with ministry people. The dinner was quite good but the waiters were clumsy and kept spilling soup down his neck.

Dumbleton itself was now a part of the war effort. John had already divided his considerable collection of books between the Hall and his mother's house in Devon. It was to be some years before he saw them again. At the outbreak of war many landowners were quick to offer up their mansions, there being a feeling that being able to choose one's tenant gave a degree of control.[22] In 1941, a lease was drafted to let the whole of the top floor and half of the ground and first floors of Dumbleton Hall to the BBC. A clause was included: 'To lease the premises for housing white British or other nationals only, for not more than 50 persons.' Instead, the Women's Land Army took over. The girls were all field workers, who every day were sent out wearing fawn Aertex shirts and corduroy breeches to thresh, hoe, and pull beets and potatoes on neighbouring farms. Often they found themselves working with Italian – or even German – POWs. The Italians were particularly keen on scented soap, which they asked for in exchange for the little wooden toys they made. Lord Monsell himself was absent for much of the time, but Lady Monsell continued to preside over Dumbleton Women's Institute and enjoyed the company of the Land Army girls. In January 1943, Joan and JR were allowed a few days' compassionate leave at the Hall – Joan would shortly be leaving for Algiers, her first posting as a cipher clerk. They never lived together again.

7

Encounter in Cairo

By 1942, JR's role in the PWE was to work as a rapporteur for a committee which met weekly to examine the propaganda rumours – known as 'sibs' – suggested by various government departments. He became known as the 'Sibster'. Sibs were rumours disseminated in the UK and abroad for the purpose of misleading the enemy on a wide range of subjects. Collecting material for weekly meetings and then getting those around the table to agree lines of action required much time and diplomacy on John's part. After a few months, he found that trying to reconcile the conflicting interests of all the departments concerned was unrewarding and he lost patience, the situation doubtless exacerbated by the strains of his home life with Joan. When he learned of a possible job in Algiers after the Allies landed in November 1942, he requested a posting. Although he did not achieve his escape, he was soon occupied with more congenial work. Isabel's marriage was also in trouble too, and she and John began an affair. JR was often at Apsley Guise, so he and Isabel came in frequent contact and were able to conduct a clandestine relationship. Sefton Delmer's account of the break-up of his marriage ignores the affair, however, and is almost as colourful as his propaganda.

In the evening I listened at intervals to the [radio] programme as it went out, suggesting improvements here and there, sub-edited and 'angled' fresh items of news as they broke on the Hellschrei-ber [a facsimile-based teleprinter] or our British or American agency tapes [. . .] Never did I get to bed before one a.m.

Let no-one, however, imagine that my sleep was uninter-rupted. For at three a.m. the door of my bedroom would softly open, a hand switched on the lamp on my bedside table, and a girl's voice spoke.

'Mr. Delmer,' it said sweetly through my dreams, 'Major Clarke's compliments.'

Standing beside my bed, solicitously offering me a large buff envelope containing a dispatch, I saw a blonde angel, blue uni-formed, breeched and high-booted. From under a crash helmet peeped corn-coloured curls. Her slender waist was tightly strapped in a leather corset. There she stood awaiting my com-mand, her crimson lips slightly parted – the dream vision of a James Bond fetishist. But this was no dream.[1]

According to Delmer, the dispatch-rider with the page proofs of *Nachrichten für die Truppe* did not leave until several hours later.

All this soon became too much for Isabel. First she insisted on separate rooms, so that she would not be disturbed by my dawn visitor. Then she got herself a job as an artist designer for one of the department's productions in London. She went off to live there and only visited us at R.A.G. [Apsley Guise] at remote intervals. That was the beginning of the end of my first marriage.

The account is every bit as fanciful as it sounds: at the time Delmer blamed JR for the break-up of his marriage, and felt considerable animosity towards him thereafter.

Once she was back in London, Isabel went to work at Bush House for a magazine called *Il Mondo Libero*, under the direction of the journalist Victor Cunard. The magazine, which was about life in England, was intended for distribution in Italy. Although her life was now much more relaxed after the exhausting hours of PWE, anxiety over the failure of her marriage – and the feeling that the affair was a betrayal of a close friendship – was making her ill. 'You look awful,' Delmer told her one day when she met him. 'I don't want to be married to an old woman. A magazine isn't worth it.' Joan, however, wrote to Isabel to say that if she was having an affair with John, she was quite ready to accept it. As far as she was concerned their friendship was unaffected – and yet Joan herself still wondered if her own marriage could be saved.

Graham had returned to Europe in uniform, not in a Guards regiment but in the Intelligence Corps of the US Army. In August 1942 he was stationed at Matlock in Derbyshire. After a visit to John Betjeman in Dublin he had gone back to Dumbleton, where he had spent a few lazy days with Joan and his mother. He wrote to Betjeman, telling him he was reading his second volume of poetry, *Continual Dew: A Little Bit of Bourgeois Verse*, 'which I hadn't seen for a long time: it brings some sanity into one's unreal life'.[2]

Soon, though, Graham left England once again, this time for North Africa, where Operation Torch had successfully driven out the Axis powers in late 1942. The region was to be the base for the Allied invasion of southern Europe in 1943. Its strategic importance had also led to Joan's posting there in January of that year. Graham's 'unreal life' continued, although he and the others entertained one another with their letters, and Graham remained the aesthete.

In April 1943 he wrote to Alan Pryce-Jones from Algeria.

JOAN

My dear Alan,

I can't remember if I have written to you or not since being out here. I know I wrote on the ship but that letter went to the bottom with everything else.

There's a good deal one could say if it were not for the censor & pretty funny some of it is. Life on the whole though is rather a bore here: work is copious and enjoyable, relaxation and fun non-existent. Patrick Kinross arrived for a few days from Cairo about a month ago with the most unsettling tales of gay life there, great apartments, parties & fun, with Eddie Gathorne-Hardy, Rommy [Romilly] Summers et al [. . .]

Joan was here for a short time, as you probably know, but left for Madrid which she says is full of grand tarts and spies. I wonder how she will enjoy Lady Hoare's knitting parties for the female personnel?

There is no-one of fundamental interest & one goes drearily to bed at about 8.30 on those nights when there is no work to bring one back to the office.

Write me a word about yourself – let me know if you know anyone new coming out.

Bless you, Graham[3]

After Algiers Joan was redeployed to the British embassy in Madrid, a city which was a hotbed of intelligence and counter-intelligence. She probably already knew the ambassador and his wife. In 1936, Sir Samuel Hoare, a cool, rather prim man had succeeded Joan's father as First Lord of the Admiralty; his ambitious wife, Lady Maud, was Coote Lygon's aunt. Spain under General Franco was ideologically aligned with the Axis powers, which had supplied both soldiers and material to the Nationalists in the Civil War. When Hoare arrived in Spain in 1940 Italian and German fascists were deeply entrenched in every walk of life. The embassy staff were overworked and overcrowded. Three years later, when Joan came to Madrid, the political tide had begun to turn. After the defeat of Stalingrad early that year and the fall of Mussolini in July, Franco had begun to realize that an easy German victory was much less likely.

Madrid gave Joan time to think and to reflect on her marriage. She was aware that John was still trying to go abroad – he was even trying to learn a little Italian. He no doubt had in mind the planned Allied landings in Italy, and the likelihood of his being posted there the following year. In October, she wrote to him from the city.

Darling – it is really appalling how quickly the time goes here & it is with horror I realize that I have been away nine months now – I am filled with the guilt at the easiness of my life here & at the thought of starting another winter coping with flats and rations by yourself. I do hope Is is staying with you. Anyway I really am about to make great decisions and changes (if situation allows) as much as Madrid grows on me it is a great waste of time being here & doing the work I do – There are two things I want to know first –

(a) how much chance is there of your leaving London in the future? (I know I keep asking you this but as I haven't heard what you are doing for so long I thought you might have more plans.) There is nothing I should hate more than to arrive in London to find you leaving for Rome.

(b) a much more difficult question & I promise you that this isn't the first & preparatory letter of a long series on the same subject – Do you really want to start our same old life again? I know this sounds as if I'm making you take all responsibility and decisions, but I've tried and can't and I think it is you who would benefit more by a change than me, as I shall have the same difficulties and disagreeable habits such as putting the

*blame on other people, whatever I do. It is hard to write like this
and not let absence influence me and I am sure I am always
nicer away, but I'm afraid when I come back everything will be
the same and I shall be as bad-tempered as ever. Another point
is I shall never like living in England. I am trying to put all the
difficulties & everything in its worst light & it is torture not
being able to see you to discuss everything altho' I'm sure we
should never arrive at a decision.*

*Do please write to me. You must be off your head with work.
I have been in bed with sinusitis but better now. I've taken to
bull-fights. English names going back on hotels & shops &
English photographs & ads in papers. Falange crowd on F.'s
birthday still shouting Franco-Hitler.*

I've hated writing this letter & now feel most miserable.

My Love JR[4]

Joan uses John's own 'JR' monogram as her signature; it was as if she
was demonstrating that she still felt tied to him, and even in love.
In her most intimate letters – to JR and later to Paddy – Joan made
two complaints about herself: her bad temper and her indecisive-
ness. This letter still reflects the thoughts about herself that she had
turned into doggerel in her 1936 pocket diary:

> *Can you pull the plug?*
> *on the bed? Or neath the rug?*
> *at the keyhole? Crowds? Alone?*
> *'I don't know' cries Schizo Joan.*

Many years later, looking back on the failure of her first marriage,
she wrote simply that, in one another's absence, 'we gradually drifted
apart.'[5]

Patrick Kinross found the outbreak of war unexpectedly liberating. He had joined the Royal Air Force Volunteer Reserve in 1940, when he was thirty-six. Writing to James Lees-Milne he seemed carefree. The pilots at RAF Bomber Command were:

> *not at all the hoary toughs I had expected, but sensitive,*
> *pink-faced striplings, very affable and impressed by one's*
> *superior intellect [. . .] Now I am back in the Air Ministry in*
> *the Middle Eastern Department, which is quite interesting. I*
> *don't know where I shall sail, but it may not be for another few*
> *weeks, I may go to Fighter Command for a week in the mean-*
> *time. So I am getting a fairly comprehensive picture of Air Force*
> *matters. Tonight I am going to see Lord Lloyd [of Dolobran]*
> *again, & I am hoping he will do something for me in Egypt.*

But, as with Joan and JR, Kinross's marriage to Angela Culme-Seymour had also failed. Angela was incorrigibly promiscuous. On the death of her father-in-law she had travelled up to Scotland for the funeral sharing a sleeper with a painter called 'David something'. Patrick had been hopelessly naive ever to think about marrying her. His letters continued:

> *Meanwhile, Jim, my private life is at an end. I have discovered a*
> *whole host of infidelities by Angela over the past year or more,*
> *and I don't really see that it is any good going on with it. It seems*
> *she is incorrigible & perhaps a little mad. I thought that I was*
> *going to be able to make some sort of a job of her, but I see that I*
> *have failed, & that perhaps I could never have succeeded. It is*
> *time for somebody else to take it on – if she can find it on . . ., I*
> *suddenly found – or at least thought I didn't love her any more. I*
> *don't know what will become of her. I shall divorce her if I can*
> *get the evidence, but may have to wait until after the war [. . .]*

Thank God I am going to Egypt & a new life & interests. What a life. What a war. But I regret nothing. It is all experience.[6]

When Patrick wrote again to Lees-Milne it was as Pilot Officer the Lord Kinross, c/o RAF HQ Middle East, Cairo. He told him he sometimes still felt waves of resentment against Angela but he was far more detached than he had been a few months beforehand. 'She was like a cat who basked there for a bit enjoying the cat's prerogative, serenity without responsibility, and then slipped out.'

Patrick also wrote about Robert Byron, who had drowned a couple of days before his thirty-sixth birthday when his ship was torpedoed by a U-boat off Cape Wrath in Scotland on its way to Egypt. 'I wonder if he would have achieved anything, with all his dynamic qualities, or if his lack of judgment & balance would always have frustrated him. One will miss him tremendously after the war. Of all one's friends, he was the strongest personality.' And he had seen Randolph Churchill, the prime minister's son. 'He was nice, much improved by military discipline. Obviously like Tom Mitford and so many others, he should always have been in the Army, and in any other generation would have gone into it as a matter of course.'[7] But only weeks before the war ended, Tom Mitford died too, of injuries sustained in Burma. He was thirty-six. 'It is almost unbearable,' Nancy Mitford wrote to her sister Jessica, 'if you knew how sweet & nice & gay he has been of late & on his last leave.'[8]

War had brought dissolution and changed everything. It had destroyed lives and it had destroyed marriages. For Joan, however, the war was to bring about a new world altogether.

In December 1943, JR flew to Algiers to work with a joint US–British Psychological Warfare Branch, planning operations for when the Allies would confront German forces in Italy. Algiers was bursting with American, British and French personnel, but John found lodgings with Graham. The city was at its least attractive: convoys of shabby trams, jeeps and army trucks, cars and people crowded the streets. Food shortages had given rise to resentment against the Allies and the mood amongst the French and Arabs was sullen.

In early January JR flew to Palermo in Sicily, in order to begin broadcasting to mainland Italy, and soon moved on to Caserta, Bari and Naples, from where, at the end of the month, he was flown over Anzio harbour. He recorded seeing smoke pall, a burning tanker, petrol cans, a cruiser and the wounded. The main Allied landing had taken place ten days earlier. Put in charge of the Political War-fare Branch (PWB) 15th Army Group, John became responsible for all combat propaganda activities in the army area: from the coordi-nation of news leaflets to front-line broadcasting by way of radio transmitters and loudspeakers. It took him six months to reach Rome. On 5 June, Liberation Day, JR and the British troops entered the city amid mass celebrations. Huge crowds took to the streets, cheering, waving and hurling bunches of flowers at the passing army vehicles, and the pope appeared on the balcony of St Peter's to address the thousands of Italians gathered in the square beneath him. JR and his colleagues set about producing the first newspaper for the civilian population, only to have to scrap it the next morning to include news of the Normandy landings. Twenty-four hours after their arrival, they had Rome's radio working; helping the Italian press return to pre-war, pre-fascist freedom became one of his major tasks. There was information to be disseminated and there were new ways of presenting it.

JR soon found a house to move into in the Via Gregoriana at the top of the Spanish Steps. He had a maid called Ana who kept pigeons for the table. If he came back late and unexpectedly with hungry guests she would hurry up to the roof to kill some of the birds, and provide a polenta in no time. In August, he was joined in his flat by Evelyn Waugh. Waugh recorded in his diaries that Mondi

Howard, who was also attached to the PWB, had arranged for him to stay with John, whom he hardly knew, and that the flat was charming. On 22 August 1944, Waugh recorded:

> A week of easy living, getting stronger and eating better. Rome short of water, light and transport. The few restaurants madly expensive. Ranieri open for luncheon only. Most of the hotels taken for various messes. My day, on the average, has been to wake at 7 to the bell of S. Andrea del Frate, tea with John Rayner in pyjamas, read the enemy broadcast news, dress slowly and go out, either by foot or in a borrowed car to see one of the churches [. . .] Usually dinner at Via Gregoriana, electric light every four days, on other days a single candle or a storm lantern. Often official guests of John.[9]

Although Rome had been liberated, the Germans had not been decisively defeated. Field Marshal Kesserling, the German commander, was under orders to contest every inch of Italy. His troops fell back as far north as Florence, held the city for three weeks and blew up the bridges over the River Arno. Working under continual German mortar and sniper fire, JR and his colleagues produced a daily newspaper on the south bank of the river, using a jeep engine as the power supply for their printing press. The paper was sent through the German lines to circulate to the Italians on the north bank. Fighting continued throughout the autumn and winter. Sometimes John found time to write to Isabel.

> *Have become v practised in the art of travelling light, sometimes sleeping under pines, sometimes in shell-shattered palaces, sometimes in the bedroom outside, which is a Baroque Borromini with an owl in it [. . .] As the jeep bounds on I think of the misty hanger; and you no doubt think of olive groves and*

cicadas & the intolerable burden of the midday sun. I believe
the brain is sd by those who have investigated it to be suspended
in the skull by the thinnest film of liquid. In such a bath the
whole body passes the day & most of the night.[10]

At the beginning of October, he wrote, 'No news of Joan's alleged
visit; vague talk in note of Sir B. getting her here or where you were
offered, that's all.' And then a month later, on 12 November:

As to Joan, I have no word from her at all, no mention of her
from any rare contact (e.g. Graham who stayed a few days). I
think she must be pretty up to date you know, in principle any
way, I shd have supposed, but one can't send knives by letter,
only nuances. In any case, don't you worry.[11]

JR also told her that he was 'v. cold, no hot water, haven't had a bath
for 6 months, am ageing, creased, balding, dictatorial'.

Sometimes, when he and his colleagues found themselves too
close to the front line for safety, JR confessed that he was terrified.
He found that the best way to cope when danger threatened was to
curl up in the back of the jeep and fall sleep. Shortly after writing
his last letter to Isabel, the jeep in which John was travelling
crashed, and his back was broken.

Control of Egypt was of strategic importance throughout the war.
Although the country was nominally independent under the rule
of King Farouk, British influence was still dominant, and Cairo
became a major hub of operations for Allied forces, despite the
population being largely sympathetic to Germany. The city itself
was a major base for Allied operations, and espionage and counter-
espionage on both sides, but remained relatively untouched by
fighting. The fiercest battles were, of course, around El Alamein, to

the west of Cairo, as the Germans fought in vain to reach the Suez Canal.

Cairo could not have been more different from life back home. There was no wartime austerity and rationing and all needs were provided for – a shop called 'Old England' advertised itself as selling 'best British briar pipes, lighters, cutlery, camp beds, tables, leather goods, travelling articles, flashlights, batteries, photo frames, cameras, films, albums'. Museums were closed and there were no tourists as such, but everyone seemed to thrive. The Turf Club still provided gambling and polo and people met for tennis and squash at the Gezira Sporting Club. For the officers and troops there were clubs, hotels and restaurants. Coffee and rich pastries were widely available. Even the hordes of beggars holding out their bowls for *baksheesh* prospered, while the morale of the troops was said to depend mainly on the price, quality and availability of the prostitutes.

Most British residents, as distinct from troops on leave, kept to the relative shelter of Gezira Island, separated from the mainland by a number of bridges on either side. It was here that Paddy Leigh Fermor, an officer with the Special Operations Executive, and Billy Moss, a young officer in the Coldstream Guards, had found a large rambling house which they shared with suitable friends. The house was called Tara, after the legendary palace of the kings of Ireland, and it was presided over by a Polish countess called Sophie Tarnowska. 'They were all in their twenties, with active times behind and ahead of them. The household quickly cohered in a private Bohemian world under Sophie's kind reign – someone teasingly said she was a sort of Wendy surrounded by Lost Boys of riper years – and afterwards the memory of Tara proved a lasting bond,' Leigh Fermor wrote later.[12] It had many bedrooms, a ballroom with a parquet floor, and a piano borrowed from the Egyptian Officers' Club, all of which made it ideal for parties.

At the outbreak of war in 1939, Paddy had returned to England from Romania, where he had been living with Princess Balasha Cantacuzene on her estate at Baleni. He had met Balasha, who was sixteen years older than him, near the end of his walk across Europe from the Hook of Holland to the city he always called Constantinople. Back in England, he initially joined the Irish Guards, but during training, which he loathed – 'my job is blacking the grates!'[13] – he fell ill. When he recovered, he joined the Intelligence Corps. Once again he thought the training 'idiotic', and he wrote to Lord Lloyd of Dolobran, who had recently been made a government minister by Churchill, trying to get back to Romania.[14] Instead, Paddy soon found himself attached as a liaison officer to the SOE, which had recently been formed to carry out reconnaissance and sabotage operations in Axis-occupied countries. The SOE – or Ministry of Ungentlemanly Warfare as it was sometimes known – was a better home for Paddy's natural talents. As a Greek-speaker, he spent much of the war in German-occupied Crete, where he helped organize local acts of resistance.

Another of the inhabitants of Tara was Xan Fielding, the man Paddy loved most of all. Born in Ootacamund in India, Xan, like Paddy, was a son of the Empire, but had been brought up in a large house in the south of France. He did not learn until he was an adult that his mother had died in India when he was born. As a child he had been brought up by his grandparents who told him that they were his parents, and that his aunts were his sisters. After periods at the universities of Bonn, Munich and Freiburg, Xan went to Cyprus, but he detested the British colonial administrators, who distrusted him in turn because he had bothered to learn Greek. He was sacked from his post at the *Cyprus Times*. The same British administrators made his attempts to run a bar a failure, so he went to Greece, where he found refuge on St Nicholas, a small island in the Bay of Chalkis; an anthropologist friend, Francis 'Fronny' Turville-Petre, had turned the island into a kind of gay commune. In the summer of 1940, following the Battle of Britain, Xan joined the Cyprus regiment and then, after the invasion of Crete, he volunteered for service with the SOE. The first question at his interview was 'Have you any personal objection to committing murder?' And he had none. Paddy and he met in the village of Yerakari, in a green, fertile valley of the Amari. Together with Paddy, Xan helped build up military intelligence on the island. Xan was short, dark and wiry in build; physically he could pass himself off as a Cretan much better than Paddy ever could. Eventually, he grew discontented with his work on Crete and applied to be transferred to the French operations of the SOE. After parachuting into France, he was picked up almost immediately with false papers and sentenced to be shot. The next day, however, he was taken out of his prison cell only to discover that the Resistance had bribed his captors, and he was released.

Although it was Paddy and Billy Moss who were to take the credit – and Paddy always had a tendency to myth-making – the first references to kidnapping a general are in the SOE archives. In September 1942 Xan Fielding had a plan for landing on Crete with the order to make an abduction. At the time this proved impossible but twelve months later Tom Dunbabin suggested that two be taken at one fell swoop.[15] On leave back in Cairo, Paddy and Billy Moss came up with new plans to kidnap the garrison commander on Crete, General Kreipe. On 26 April 1944, the general's car was stopped in front of his house, the Villa Ariadne. With the help of partisans, Paddy and Moss, who were dressed as corporals in the German Feldgendarmerie, coshed the driver and bundled the general into the back of the car. With Moss driving, they progressed through Heraklion for an hour and a half, bluffing their way past twenty checkpoints. They abandoned the car, leaving behind documents in English to prove that the kidnap had been carried out by British commandos, and to minimize reprisals on the local population. Kreipe was taken up into the mountains and concealed in the caves. A fortnight later the general was spirited away by motorboat to Egypt. The Kreipe kidnap made Paddy a celebrity. A combination of psychological strain, exhaustion and the general harshness of mountain life made him ill, however, and on 19 May 1944 he was admitted to hospital with polyarthritis. He spent about three months in hospital, during which time Sir Bernard Paget, the Commander in Chief of the Middle East Command, pinned the Distinguished Service Order on Paddy's battledress jacket, which he was wearing over his pyjamas.[16]

Paddy had a girlfriend at the time called Denise Menasce. Her family were upper-middle-class Sephardic Jewish bankers and businessmen, who had been made barons in the Austro-Hungarian Empire. Denise was dark, pretty and intelligent, as well as bilingual in English and French. She had become mixed up with the military set and their friends at Tara. Paddy went back to Crete in October, leaving her pregnant and vulnerable.

Would you be very bored with me if I wrote a miserable and depressed letter. Please don't be, Paddy darling, for I am feeling as low as low can be this evening and I just have to write to somebody – so you will just have to be my victim. I'd give anything to be in your arms and be cuddled, and made a fuss of, and be told I was quite nice and sweet. You've never really seen me in my black moods. They are as bad as yours only drink doesn't help. I tried that all evening, but in vain. You've only seen your little imp behaving like a wild thing, and jumping around you in a surge of joy to have you back for an extra 24 hrs. But tonight I am rather a different person – somebody you haven't yet met, and which I don't think you like. A little woman of 24 who feels stupid, empty, and very much alone [. . .]

Paddy darling, this is such a revealing letter, I am rather ashamed. I usually am terribly reserved talking or writing about my real self – so please forgive and forget this – somehow you have walked so completely into my life, that I find myself telling you my most intimate thoughts.

That baby is also rather worrying me. Even though I am not a slave or in the least bit melodramatic. I suddenly feel full of importance at having it. No man can really understand what conception means to a woman. It becomes life, creation, it gives a tremendous sense of strength and power. Instead of having been possessed and destroyed, you realize that you carry in you the power of life – And yet . . . tomorrow morning Mrs. Boswell is going to see a doctor, and look rather shamefaced, and get into the most sordid explanations as to where, why, and how – and how much!! What an anticlimax.

Paddy my poppit, don't please, please, think I am really minding about this. I am not like Sophie, and quite realize that this is normal and necessary. So please forgive my trying to embellish in my own eyes tonight, what is going to be rather hell tomorrow.

Am awfully sleepy so will stop now. Goodnight darling. Bless you and forgive this.[17]

For the next couple of months, Denise wrote to Paddy nearly every day or so about her feelings for him and what she was doing, making a kind of diary. Two days after her abortion she wrote, 'A hasty note to say that all is well, so that my letter makes no sense at all.' She hoped he did not get all her letters in a pile. 'Tonight we are all eating caviar at Suzette's and going dancing afterwards – it now makes me miserable to dance tangos with anyone else!!'

By the summer of 1944 the atmosphere in Spain had changed considerably since Joan's arrival. After D-Day and the liberation of France the Franco regime had finally accepted that Germany was losing and that they should back the United States and Great Britain. They had blocked the export to Germany of tungsten, which was indispensable to the manufacture of aircraft and weapons, and the Spanish government now operated under terms of strict neutrality. In October 1944, after leaving Spain, Joan arrived in Cairo – a dusty, dirty, overcrowded city she came to love. The British embassy was a large colonial house with a columned veranda on two storeys and wrought-iron railings adorned with Queen Victoria's imperial insignia. Inside, its high rooms were hung with silk damask and furnished with antique chairs and Persian rugs belonging to Sir Miles Lampson, the ambassador.[18] The cipher room at the embassy was on the ground floor, with steel bars across the windows. The room was usually filled with over twenty people, and lipstick-marked cups of half-drunk tea were scattered amongst used carbons, dispatch books, partly chewed slabs of chocolate and countless cigarette butts.[19]

Joan was sharing a house with two old friends, Eddie Gathorne-Hardy, who was still lecturing for the British Council, and Patrick Kinross, who was now the RAF press officer. The house, which Joan called 'a white box with windows'[20] and Paddy said was 'a crumbling Mamaluke palace',[21] was joined to the ninth-century mosque of Ibn Tûlûn in the old part of the city. Joan had certainly heard about Paddy – everyone had – and before long she had met Denise, befriended her and even consoled her in her troubles. Denise wrote to Paddy: 'I am now going to write to Joan and pour out my sorrows to her.'[22] A few days later she wrote again to the elusive major:

> *This afternoon I sat on Sophie's bed and longed for you to come in a 'coup du vent', and yell for a brandy and ginger ale – look at yourself – that look I know so well in the glass – and dash off for some rendez-vous – reeking of Sophie's eau-de-Cologne – Darling, when will you come back – do please soon.*

JOAN

Ps Am giving a party for my birthday at Tara, on Dec. 1st.
Could I have the pleasure of Major Leigh Fermor's company.
R.S.V.P.[23]

Paddy had also already heard about Joan. After his illness he had gone to the Lebanon in order to convalesce and then he had spent a few days in Crete, where he received a letter from Billy Moss. It was dated 5 December 1944: 'A good thing has turned up in the shape of Joan Rainer [sic], and we have seen quite a bit of her recently. She's got a good brain and she talks a lot about bull-fights and Spanish poets. I think you would like her.[24]

When Joan at last met Paddy Leigh Fermor at a party, shortly after Christmas 1944, both were immediately attracted to one another. Joan, who would not have admitted to being attracted by his glamour or his fame, found him irresistible. For Paddy, who saw himself as a Byronic figure, loving to dress up and engage in acts of derring-do, Joan was yet another challenge. They could not keep their hands off one another – not that Paddy was immediately going to abandon all her competitors. It was not long before he received a typed letter from Denise Menasce (normally her letters were handwritten).

> *Paddy, you little double-crosser, trying to kill two birds with one*
> *stone! I should have thought your technique was more polished*
> *. . . It ought to be by now. That maybe explains the Greek love*
> *call (just heard it) 'I desire Major Leigh Fermor'. For 'Qui trop*
> *embrasse mal etreint.' My sweet little independent dachshund, I*
> *think some charitable soul ought to buy you a lead . . . Though*
> *who will ever hold it is a difficult problem. Maybe you can*
> *organize it so as to have a cinq à sept, sept à neuf, neuf à*
> *minuit, and a sleepy cession de minuit au petit jour. Though I*

feel you might get your time table wrong which would lead to
the most awful chaos. Also there might be a slight complication
about names. As calling Ines Joan, and Joan Denise, might lead
to trouble. My advice is: take a little notebook into your bath-
room, and learn up what you are going to say; and to WHOM.
   Poor Paddy
   Ton Hispano Mauresque
   Consolation P.S. I know the conclusions you draw from rude
attacks. You may be right.[25]

Ines Walter, an habitué of Tara as well as a confidante of Denise,
was described by Stanley Moss as 'enormously *décolletée*, happy in
the role of a Hungarian peasant'.[26] She was also engaged to Bernard
Burroughs, a diplomat.

By February 1945, when Paddy had returned to England for
extended leave, Denise had accepted that Joan was a rival. However,
he had sent her a pair of earrings ('an enormous success . . . I practically sleep in them'):

> *Yesterday Joan and Eddie came to lunch, & Xan and Inez [sic].*
> *I thought it was a good lunch, and it certainly was a very gay*
> *one, as nobody thought of leaving before 4.15. I retract all I ever*
> *said about Joan, she is a very charming girl, I regret to say I will*
> *always be slightly jealous of any serious rival, however charming*
> *she may be. I do really like her a lot, and have made plans to*
> *see more of her.*[27]

Joan made only intermittent entries in her new pocket diary. On 6
January 1945, her first entry for the year, she wrote, 'Grumbling &
disappointed of small things = treats arranged for oneself to compen-
sate for unhappiness.' However much she was attracted by Paddy,
this was still wartime, and all relationships seemed up in the air.

There was little certainty of any future for them; Paddy was hoping to go to the Far East – as Xan was to do – where the war was far from finished. And Joan had yet to extricate herself from her own unsatisfactory marriage to a man for whom she still had lingering affection. On the pages of her diary she jotted down notes on 'differences between Jung and Freud' and details of a trip to Beirut in February. She frequently arranged to lunch and dine with Patrick Kinross. She also mentioned Denise and, on one occasion, the Aga Khan. The names of Robin Fedden and his wife Renée and Amy Smart appeared often, and they became friends with whom she remained on close terms for many years after the war. Robin Fedden was both a Quaker ambulance driver and a magazine editor. Amy Smart was a painter – her paintings inspired by Sufism – born into a Syrian–Lebanese Christian family. Amy's mind, Kinross said, was at once masculine, oriental and feminine,[28] and she and her husband Walter surrounded themselves with artists and writers.

At the end of April, Denise wrote again to Paddy.

I had a long letter from Joan – she says she's written to you post haste. Her plans are still very vague, as both Aly [?]* and her in laws are going to Kenya, and she'll decide afterwards. She disapproved of your idea of going to the Far E. because, she says, of your health. Also rather depressed me by saying that the only commodity left in England was sex with a big S so I suppose my darling you won't be finding life too difficult.[29]

Joan went on leave, travelling by train from Beirut to Damascus, and from there she went to Baghdad, where she attended a party before taking another train to Kirkuk. In Kirkuk, she visited the museum. She was now in Iraqi Kurdistan. Over the following week

---

* Aly is unidentified.

she took photographs and made notes in her diary, which she used for writing a long account of her journey into the mountains of Rowanduz, with the apparent intention of publication.

The railway ends in Kirkuk, a Kurdish town in N.E. Iraq, and there among the Iraqis in uniform or Arab Dress, one sees groups of Kurds dressed in their baggy trousers, long coloured sashes and fringed turbans. The young dandies often with a pink rose in their mouths [. . .]

The food was Turkish and delicious, rice and meat dishes, eggs, chickens, once a large fish shot in the river with a revolver, flat pancake-like bread, combs of wild honey, and to drink – mastaw, fresh curds mixed with water and snow and between meals innumerable cups of coffee or tea from a samovar.

The next five days were spent travelling in the road-less mountains with our host, his three brothers and a bodyguard of Kurds which grew as we went along, riding or running in front of us, always charming and gay, singing or dancing when we rested and rolling about with laughter at the slightest cause. We rode all day over very mountainous country, fording (once swimming) rivers or crossing ravines by perilous bridges that seemed to be made only of twigs and mud; twice we rose in pitch dark (the oriental lack of punctuality made us start hours late every morning), along the edge of precipices, torrents roaring somewhere below and enormous ferocious sheepdogs rushing howling at us from the few habitations we passed. At the end of the day we came to some relation's house, vast meals were produced from nowhere and the Kurds slept on the floor in their cloaks, their rifles beside them.

The country was always superb; meadows of long green grass and flowers, irises, hyacinths, tiger lilies, rivers of every sort, walnut and cherry trees growing round the villages huddled in deep valleys, oak forests full of wild boar, rocky gorges and steep bare mountains and always, as a background, the huge snow capped mountains on the Turkish frontier. And the Kurds were always singing of fighting or love, or discussing their independence.

By the time Joan returned from Kurdistan a week later, the war in Europe was at an end.

Paddy was still away. After two months in England, during which time he was awarded an OBE at Buckingham Palace, he was deployed briefly in Germany and Denmark. His VE Day was spent in London, however, far away from Joan. No letters between the two remain from that time but clearly they were still in touch. Xan was now in the Far East. Paddy applied to join him but was rejected – perhaps because of his health; there was no lack of unemployed ex-servicemen looking for work and Paddy, demobbed, was one of them. Joan took him home that summer to meet her family but they must have wondered about his prospects. Joan herself of course was still a married woman, if in name only.

John had returned home to England for convalescent leave and treatment on his back shortly after the accident in November 1944. At Christmastime he was well enough to go to Paris with Isabel, and he skated along the banks of the Seine in his plaster cast. On New Year's Day 1945, he flew back to Italy. Isabel took a job in Paris working for the BBC and Radiodiffusion française, and visited her friends from pre-war Paris: Balthus, Picasso and Braque. She was now divorced from Sefton Delmer, and she wrote to John suggesting marriage. They could live abroad but retain a 'niche' in England. 'There is a great deal to be said for legality [. . .] I was thinking how odd it will be when we are officially encouraged to be together rather than, as at present, frustrated whenever possible.'[30] John, however, had been offered a post in Ceylon with the Supreme Allied

Commander South East Asia which, despite Isabel's anxieties about his fitness, he was determined to take. In July, he sent a telegram suggesting she come to London for a few days. By then, however, Isabel felt that the relationship was over. She seemed to believe that he lacked the will to continue with it. In her memoir she wrote:

> Time to go and a time for tears. Saying goodbye to John was extremely painful: I suffered more than he did. The future was a large hole, once inside what would I find as the ship slowly drew away from the quay. I looked down between a large eel curving its way beside us: amazing creature born in the Sargasso Sea now here.[31]

John would have flown to Egypt, so the image is a metaphor. Isabel stayed on in Paris, waiting for Giacometti. One evening eight years beforehand, when she had last modelled for him, he had seen her from afar standing in boulevard Saint-Michel – a distant figure surrounded by space. For the whole of the war, even in her absence, in his mind she had remained his muse. She had received a letter from him written in Geneva and dated 14 May 1945. It was their first correspondence in five years, and she quickly replied. He immediately noticed how Isabel's handwriting had been altered by John's lessons in Elizabethan calligraphy.

On his way to Ceylon, John stopped off in Cairo, perhaps to see whether there was hope of rescuing his marriage to Joan. However, as she had already told him when she was in Madrid, she was not ready to return to England. She had made plans of her own: in September she was going to Athens to work as a secretary to their old friend Osbert Lancaster, who was now the press attaché at the British embassy. No doubt, if she had not already made it clear, she must have told him about the place Paddy had in her life. And so Joan and JR agreed to divorce. He carried on to Ceylon to join Lord

Mountbatten's staff in their headquarters, which were in huts ranged across the botanical gardens in Kandy. He barely had time to settle into his job as head of psychological warfare before the Japanese forces in South East Asia surrendered on 12 September. Mountbatten then transferred to Singapore taking many of his staff, including John, with him.

8

Athenian Adventures

As the Germans started their retreat from Greece in October 1944, rival leftist and pro-monarchist parties within the country began their descent into civil war. Before long, much of Greece came under the sway of the Communist National Liberation Front (EAM) and its military wing, the National Popular Liberation Front (ELAS); together they threatened the weak, newly installed provisional government with their long-term intention of transforming Greece into a Soviet-style state. The first shots in the Battle of Athens were fired on 3 December 1944, during a huge demonstration in Syntagma Square outside the Greek Houses of Parliament, where demonstrators waved flags and chanted EAM slogans. More than twenty people were killed, and many more wounded. Although at the time there was a small British military presence to maintain order and oversee much-needed relief supplies, nothing could have stopped the communists from taking over the territory they controlled, even though Stalin seemed happy to respect Churchill's romantic care for Greece, so long as he had free rein in eastern Europe and the Balkans. There was much hostility towards the British presence in Greece in both the British and American press. Unfortunately, the British ambassador, Rex Leeper, had made matters worse through his tactlessness and by berating the correspondents for the way they had reported the events.

As a consequence, the Foreign Office decided to send out an official press attaché, and the man they chose was Osbert Lancaster. There could have been no better choice. Osbert had spent the war at the Ministry of Information – a department he described as 'a Home of Rest for Intellectuals in war time'[1] – monitoring German news bulletins and briefing journalists for the Foreign Office. He had also continued to work as a cartoonist. His pocket cartoons featuring Maudie Littlehampton, which John Rayner had encouraged him to draw for the *Daily Express*, as well as other propaganda drawings had captured the mood of the nation.

Primrose Leeper, the ambassador's wife, feared the worst on being told that Osbert was coming to Athens. She had heard the name, but expected someone highbrow and precious. In fact, he fitted in wonderfully even if, with his bulging eyes, handlebar moustache and loud, checked tweed jackets of the sort worn by bookies, he cut an extraordinary and incongruous figure at the embassy. Although Osbert's job was actually to muzzle the press, his briefings, his frankness, his idiosyncratic manner and sense of humour so baffled and charmed the correspondents that they went out of their way to attend. Despite the Americans often finding his British accent incomprehensible, after Osbert's arrival press relations improved markedly. His experience gave him a rare ability to talk on equal terms with the embassy, the Foreign Office and the military as well as with the press, for, at heart, he was one of their number.

On Boxing Day 1944, after four weeks of chaos, Churchill flew into Athens and arrived at the embassy still wearing his air force overalls. He stayed three days. A conference of warring parties, including ELAS, was hastily summoned and a truce agreed.

As a gesture to show their growing confidence in the Greek government, the Athens branch of the British Council was reopened. The British Council had been set up in 1934 – as the British Committee for Relations with Other Countries – in order to promote the

English language and an interest in British culture across the world, as well as a sympathetic appreciation of British foreign policy. Athens was one of its early branches, and it was also the last to close during the war, having been evacuated only in 1941, when local staff destroyed its office records to protect themselves from persecution. In the spring of 1945, Maurice Cardiff, an ex-SOE officer who had spent the last months of the war working with the communist resistance in the Aegean Islands, was summoned to the British military headquarters. Here he found Colonel Kenneth Johnston, whom he had known in Cairo, busy stuffing files into a briefcase. To his considerable surprise, Cardiff found himself being asked to take over the running of the Council, an organization of which he had scarcely heard and which had nothing to do with the army.

Johnston had been recalled to London, and was due to leave by plane within the hour. As he talked he went on filling his briefcase, and when he finally snapped it shut, he led Cardiff down the corridor, still talking, to the lift. In the entrance hall, he at last stopped and asked Cardiff if he would accept. Smiling encouragement and with an assurance that everything would be all right, Johnston ran down the steps and dived into the car which was waiting to take him to the airport.[2]

Another of Colonel Johnston's last-minute instructions to Maurice Cardiff had been to find accommodation in the centre of Athens suitable for use as an Institute of Higher English Studies, and after considerable searching he found an appropriate building. He drew £14,000 sterling in gold sovereigns from the bank and took it to the lawyer's office in a small suitcase, completing the deal over cups of Turkish coffee as they counted the gold and arranged it in little piles on the lawyer's desk.[3] As Cardiff settled in to his daily work at the British Council office, he found himself bombarded by letters from London advising him of the imminent arrival of additions to the staff, either to assist him in Athens or to set up out-posts in Salonica, Patras or elsewhere,

The new institute's director was Rex Warner, a powerfully built man of, in Cecil Day-Lewis's words, 'Homeric boisterousness'. A classicist and a writer of acclaimed modernist novels, he added a certain prestige and gravitas to the institute and the Council that funded it. The staff found him genial and popular and apparently 'rock-like'. Back in London, Paddy Leigh Fermor was looking for a job which would take him to Greece in order to be with Joan, who was already in Athens. When Colonel Johnston set about recruiting a deputy director to work with Warner, Paddy immediately applied and was accepted; he might have lacked a university education or office experience but he had other assets – not least his knowledge of Greek and the fact that he was a hero of the Greek Resistance. In many ways, Paddy was the exact opposite of Warner. There was nothing rock-like about him, rather what Cardiff perceived as 'a restless vitality', and 'a readiness to take on anything mentally or physically, which left no doubt of his being able to prove, if needed, a sterling champion'.

In early November, Joan wrote to Patrick Kinross, telling him how much she already felt at home in Athens.

Darling Patrick,

Thank you so much for your letter and I adored reading Penelope [Betjeman]'s which I herewith return. What an extraordinary person she is and how I long to see her again. She certainly seems to have solved the almost impossible problem of how to be happy but I'm not sure how you and I together would have appreciated domestic life in a vicarage.

I am furious that I missed Tom [Driberg]. Has he still got that delicious moustache on top of his head?

I can't complain as I'm having a gay time here and I do

think Greece comes up to all my expectations. There is also a
delicious pagan atmosphere of NO GUILT, *which I appreciate*
very much, having suffered too much of it on account of my
up-bringing.

I am seriously setting about getting a flat now, as the
Grande Bretagne has turned into a terrible totalitarian military
barracks, and Military Controllers burst into my room whenever
I am in bed for a day saying; 'This is a military billet and not a
private hotel and you will get up for dinner or go straight to
hospital.' Needless to say, with a little judicious bribery, meals
are brought to me all day long but I am beginning to suffer
from persecution mania. You must come and stay in the spring,
when I hope to have a yacht too. (This is the most bloody
typewriter I have just been lent and you must not judge my
secretarial powers by this.)

Osbert sends you his love. He is very nice to work for but I
hardly know him socially, on account of my lowly position I
suppose. However I can't say I am sorry as I don't find Embassy
or Brit. Council sets particularly amusing. Paddy arrived last
week which adds to the general exhaustion of taverna life, and
Francis Noel Baker* is here again, but he is surrounded by
Ambassadors, ministers and sinister agents the whole time.

I haven't forgotten your retsina, but it is impossible to send it
by bag and I am waiting for an accommodating friend to bring
you some. Up to now it has been difficult to send as all the new
wine is starting and one drinks it still fomenting and it is no
good for travelling. I hope your ibis is well. I feel very nostalgic

---

* Francis Noel Baker (1920–2009) joined the army in 1940 and was commissioned
into the Intelligence Corps. In 1945 he was elected Labour MP for Brentford and
Chiswick but was always strongly anti-communist. His family owned an estate on the
island of Euboea.

about your delicious Sunday lunches in the garden. All descrip-
tions of England sound too gloomy, except from a Betjeman
point of view. Poor Graham had a cold, guilt, indigestion and
melancholia the whole time he was there. I feel like staying on
here if I could get some land somewhere, as I am getting very
tired of work. I can't think of a more beautiful place to live. Tell
Eddie [Gathorne-Hardy] this too and give him my best love and
say I am writing again.

    Forgive this rambling boring letter. I keep being interrupted
and I have just spent a nerve-wracking half hour at the B.
Consulate swearing on a stack of bibles about my divorce.

    Give my love to Amy [Smart] and best love to you
    Joan.[4]

Most of the last pages of Joan's pocket diary for 1945 have been torn
out. However the entry for 30 December remains and simply reads
'PADDY' and '72452' – presumably a telephone number. He had
been back to Cairo – perhaps for a final party – and the doors of
Tara were closed for the last time. In Greece, there was new company to be found and the British Council and institute were soon at
the heart of ex-pat cultural life. This expanding social circle also
embraced the artist Nikos Hadjikyriakos-Ghika, the poet and critic
George Seferis, George Katsimbalis, a poet and editor of the *Hel-*
lenic Review, and Osbert Lancaster. However unlike Joan, who had
reasons to stay on now that her work was finished, Osbert soon
returned to England. After Warner, Joan and Paddy, there also
arrived Graham's Eton contemporary Mark Ogilvie-Grant, who was
recovering from four years as a German POW.

    'Pretty Joan has turned up, everybody very pleased to see her,'[5]
wrote Nancy Mitford, who had worked at Heywood Hill's bookshop
throughout the war – not that she and Joan were ever close. For
Paddy it was time to break old ties. At Easter he went to Paris to say

goodbye to Denise Menasce for the last time. Afterwards she sent him a postcard of la place de la Concorde, writing, 'only a line to tell you how delighted I was to see you even if I didn't show it. It is wonderful to think that whatever happens it will always be the same between us . . . As ever, impishly, Denise.'

In Athens, the staff of the Council and institute continued to grow, Steven Runciman was made head of the British Council in Greece, while Maurice Cardiff was demoted to the role of acting assistant. Cardiff was more than happy to accept this inferior position. He was beginning to feel overwhelmed by the volume and nature of his responsibilities, such as superintending the innumerable packing cases sent out from London. The vast consignment of harsh British government service lavatory paper prompted aggrieved comments, especially from Greek colleagues and visitors. Runciman had begun the war as a press attaché for the Ministry of Information at the British legation in Sofia, until the staff had to evacuate hurriedly when the Germans invaded Bulgaria. Afterwards he served in Cairo and Jerusalem, and in 1942, at the Turkish government's request, he was appointed professor of art and history at the University of Istanbul. Paddy had first met Runciman in Sofia in August 1934, when on his way to Constantinople – 'suave and suede-shod and urbanely clad'. Although they eventually became friends, in 1946 relations between Paddy and Runciman were strained. And Cardiff admitted that Runciman terrified him. Friendly and charming though he was when they were introduced, he felt prompted to attach a mental label to his new boss – 'handle with care'.

Maurice Bowra, in his role as chairman of the British Council Humanities Advisory Committee, came out to lecture and was introduced to the staff of the institute. Given his strong feelings for Joan, he would have looked on Paddy as some sort of rival, and could not have been the most unprejudiced of observers. That said, in the subsequent report he wrote on the British Council in Athens, his reaction to Paddy unquestionably carries more than an element of truth:

> A misfit is Mr P. Lee-Fermore [sic] who has many excellent gifts but is unfit for office work. With his experience in Crete he has many unusual acquaintances, which is a great asset, and he might be better employed on a roving commission of making contacts, for which he is admirably fitted.[6]

Bowra's view was almost certainly shared by Steven Runciman. But the Greek political situation had shifted again. The communist guerrillas retreated from Athens to the north of the country and the British Army information officers thought that the British Council could set up some outposts to help counter their influence. When one of these outposts was opened in Salonica, Runciman decided that Cardiff and Paddy should go out and see how it was progressing. They could also make a tour through some of the more important towns, to assess what more might be done to further the Council's and the British government's aims. Joan accompanied them. Paddy's fractious relationship with Runciman and his unsuitability for office life now enabled them to escape Athens and see more of Greece. At the Ritz Hotel in Salonica – chosen because it sounded the grandest – the barman not only offered drinks but brought out for their inspection cocaine and hashish. Cocaine had no appeal, but the latter had romantic associations. Joan mildly disapproved, but Paddy and Cardiff bought a minute block of what the barman assured them was the best on the market. They stretched out on twin beds and puffed away conscientiously while Joan sat watching and complained that they ought to have eaten first. Joan, Cardiff observed, was much more withdrawn than Paddy, although her intelligence matched his. She was a wonderful person to travel with – but rather given to 'moaning'. She need not have worried. Inhale as deeply as they could, the joints had no effect other than to make Paddy and Cardiff giggle; they found the situation comical, anyway. The trio stayed several days in the city before setting off again over mountainous roads in an old army vehicle – a kind of half-open barouche with seating for twelve – and all the while Paddy regaled them with his tales. The stories would often climax just as Cardiff, who was the driver, heaved the barouche around a perilous hairpin bend or scraped the rock face on one side to avoid a chasm on the other. Sometimes envy would make him question if the tales were really true. But, of course, they always were.

Cardiff, for his part, had formed two early perceptions which helped smooth his own relationship with Runciman. At the time, Runciman was already at work on the history of the Crusades that would cement his reputation. If Cardiff needed to consult him he would open the door a little in order to give Runciman just enough time to cover his Crusades work – which he was doing in office time – with an office file. The second observation was more important. In response to any proposal, Runciman would invariably say 'yes', but the manner in which he said 'yes' varied. If his 'yes' was short, even curt, he meant it; if the word was long and drawn out on the other hand, this signified 'no'. Paddy did not grasp this fine distinction and he thought – or he allowed himself to think – that over the course of the summer of 1946 he had been given permission to go off on a six-week tour of the Greek islands or a trip around the Peloponnese.[7]

Xan Fielding was still in Saigon when he discovered that Paddy had found a means of getting back to Greece:

Paddy, me old dear, you're the worst of all monsters. Why this long impenetrable silence? I've written you several times but have had nothing from you since the delightful scribble from Garibaldi's.

Anne has mentioned you in several letters but never told me where you were or what you were doing. Yesterday I picked up an old copy of the Evening Standard and now at last I have some idea as to your whereabouts and occupation – Deputy Director of the British Institute at Athens! I envy you. I picture you in romantic white clothes sucking down retsina in Kolonaki – oh the gorgeous Helenistic [sic] fornication – pepper trees, sweet almonds and double beds. Give all my love and 2 or 3 of my tears to all our friends there – Christ I wish I were with you.

Life out here apart from 2 months in the Himalayas has not been much fun. Colombo was tedious, Calcutta foul, Rangoon worse – And Saigon itself troublesome but worse. Fortunately I managed to get away on my own for six weeks into Cambodia – the sunniest, most smiling country I've met east of Suez. As usual, I found myself backing an attractive, amusing minority against the unattractive established authorities; was involved in various intrigues, both erotic and political, with the royal household, and after a very thorough immersion in drink, sex and opium and after a personal rocket from the G.O.C., I'm once again back in Hq – but not for long. I hope to be in Bali or thereabouts by Christmas.

I've seen nothing of David [Smiley], the Bill & Co for ages. I gather most of them are on their way home & I begin to feel lonesome again – lazy, old and discarded and unwilling to settle down. All I want now is a sunny wine-producing climate and no responsibility. Maybe I'll achieve this in time.

Xan[8]

Xan was a proud but difficult man, never comfortable in his own skin. He feared humiliation most of all. At the end of the war there was no lack of highly talented ex-officers in search of employment, and many commissioned war veterans ended up as secretaries of

suburban golf clubs or running chicken farms. Xan was typical of
those who placed personal advertisements in the agony columns of
The Times:

> Tough but sensitive ex-classical scholar, ex-secret agent, ex-
> guerrilla leader, 31, recently reduced to penury through incom-
> patibility with the post-war world: Mediterranean lover, gambler,
> and general dabbler: fluent French and Greek speaker, some
> German, inevitable: would do anything unreasonable and unex-
> pected if sufficiently rewarding and legitimate.[9]

Paddy would have told everybody about it, but Xan did not. So far
as one can tell, the personal advertisement brought no success – it
was just another small private shame.[10]

Xan's time in the Far East was ended. He was back in Europe
and had made his way to Greece where he accompanied Paddy and
Joan on their travels and visited Lawrence Durrell on the island of
Rhodes. Durrell was living with his lover Eve Cohen whom he
intended to marry. Their house, which consisted merely of a studio,
a bedroom, a kitchen and a bathroom, stood in the eucalyptus-filled
garden of the Mosque of Murad Reis, together with a pair of Turkish
mausolea and a number of white marble tombstones. They talked
about books into the early hours, whilst Eve sat silent and submis-
sive at Durrell's feet until, exasperated, the mosque's mufti would
rattle his shutters to get them to stop. In the morning they all went
down to bathe in the sea at the Mandraki waterfront, a few minutes'
walk from the house. One day they took a trip to the ancient ruins
of the city of Cameirus, where Joan (whom Durrell called 'the Corn
Goddess') took photographs of Xan, Paddy and Lawrence Durrell
re-enacting ancient rituals, including a mock circumcision of Paddy.
'Our exploration reached an extraordinary climax when Xan leaped
a couple of yards from the coping of a high ruined wall on top of

an Ionic column twelve feet high which rocked frighteningly on its stylobate for several seconds. At last, as we watched with held breath, it became static with its new arrival poised on the capitol – for some reason, but most appropriately, with nothing on – with a flying stylite,' wrote Paddy.[11] Xan, he thought, looked just like Eros.

Joan took her camera wherever they travelled, snapping shops, bars, beaches, temples. That year, on Ithaca, she took a photograph of the head of a classical statue lying flat on the ground, where it may have fallen centuries past. Its features are still clear and discernible, although slightly weathered by time, and it is part covered by sand. Probably the picture was taken near to a beach, or actually on one. Beside it in the album where Joan kept her photographs, she placed a photograph of Paddy recreating the pose. This too is a close-up, so much so that one can see the very pores of the face and naked shoulders of a man whom Maurice Cardiff called 'Byronically handsome'. Paddy's eyes are closed, but everything about the photograph tells the observer how deeply attracted Joan was by him and the intensity of her need for him.

There are also two photographs of Joan which must date from around this time. During the war fashions had changed. From the Kurdistan pictures of May 1945 onwards she was wearing her hair long, as was the fashion of the late 1940s. In the first of the two Joan is lying in bed on her front, her head and shoulders are bare, as is her back, which emerges from under the sheet. Her elbows press into the pillow and she holds her head in her hands. Head, shoulders and arms make a simple triangle, her face and her expression are averted – she appears to look downwards – as if she was more truly herself when she did not look into the camera. In the second picture she is standing with what appears to be a sheet draped around her and falling onto the floor; it is gathered so tightly at the waist that she seems extraordinarily slender, like some kind of statue. She is only inches away from the mirror of a wardrobe door, with her arms raised in front of her face. The light comes from a window on the left, making the picture into a long, simple rectangle of alternating shapes of light and dark. Once again Joan's face cannot be seen. We do not know who the photographer was, but its style is quite unlike her own. These are intimate pictures done for the eyes of a lover. They are sensual, somewhat aloof and deeply private. This is Joan.

At the end of their stay with Lawrence and Eve, Paddy and Joan left separately for the island of Patmos. Just before they reached home, Joan wrote to Durrell:

> *I had a fantastic journey to Patmos. 4 days, 2 staying at Simi at the almost deserted monastery then Cos & Leros. The Abbot & I spent a lot of time lying in the hold on bales of fertilizers to keep dry. Patmos was lovely, everyone very kind. The monks pulled their beards a lot but that was all. Paddy arrived 2 days later when I had given up hope of ever seeing him again & was just leaving myself. He has been writing a lot & is about to send you some poems. I hope you got the book from the hotel. Come back to Athens; we shall be there in about 10 days. Love from us both to you & E. Joan.*[12]

In December, back in Athens after much travelling, Paddy discovered that Runciman was displeased with his use of British Council time and money, and his contract would not be renewed. Paddy was angry and unhappy to be forced out of a job he loved – the only peacetime post he had ever held, or would hold, in his life. After so many years away from England, both Joan, who was also without work, and he would have to return home for good. He too wrote to Durrell.

> *I found Joan a week after leaving you, entwined like a sleeping*

beauty in the beards of Patmos, and stayed there several days
rainy and thunderous like those described in your story. I
thought very seriously of settling down there this winter. It is one
of the most extraordinary places I've ever seen. We left for Samos
by caïque, but a storm blew up, and we were forced to put in at
a tiny island called Arki. As Joan and I stepped ashore, our bags
were grasped in silence by a fisherman, who led us up a winding
path through laurels to a large white house, quite alone among
vineyards, but with all chimneys smoking. An old gentleman
with white whiskers welcomed us gravely on the threshold, as
though he had been expecting us, and led us into a great
flagged kitchen, where in the shake of a lamb's tail, we were
seated with ouzos and mézé. A huge handsome old wife was
clanking pots over the fire aided by an army of daughters of
astounding beauty, the son of the house cleaning his fowling-
piece with a bunch of partridges beside him. Dogs and cats were
everywhere. Any amount of shepherds and fishermen were sitting
about talking or eating, and we were soon given a delicious
meal – avgolémono soup, fish, jugged hare and a splendid wine.
All this with scarcely an enquiry as to where we came from. In
fact we were addressed by our names with a gentle, incurious
courtesy. It was very strange, and a bit eerie, like the arrival of
Odysseus at the palace of Nausicaa's father, or the way-laying
and entertainment of travellers by magnificoes in Hungary. It
turned out that ships are washed up there so often that their
entertainment had become a matter of course. 'One day last
year,' Mr Kalantakis said (he's a Cretan), 'the sea brought us
seventy-two guests.' We stayed there four days, living in lovely
rooms and eating and drinking like heroes, and when the wind
changed said goodbye to our charming and munificent host with
real intentions to return another summer. One of our fellow
naufragés was a Karaghioziman, unfortunately without his gear,

but gave quite a good conjuring display to a kitchen crammed
with neighbours and dependents, ending up with the most
frightening bit of magic I've ever seen. He made us clench our
hands tightly together, saying he would turn them to wood;
shouted 'ONE! TWO! THREE! ALLEZ-SANS-
EMARCHE!' And well over half of the company remained
with their hands glued palm to palm, tugging and straining till
the sweat poured down them, at last they fell apart when he
touched their knuckles with his forefinger. He did it again and
again on my insistence and once linked a daisy chain of
half-frightened, half-giggling peasants helplessly together arm in
arm. It had all the excitement, and all the unpleasantness of
'Mario the Magician'. It had to be stopped in the end because
the children were screaming . . .

I'm leaving in about a fortnight, feeling angry, fed up, and
older than the rocks on which I sit. Fucking shits. But I am
writing quite a lot, and enjoying it enormously. I have, not very
originally, written a long thing about the islands which I am
sending you for criticism. Please do so, could you Larry, if it is
not too much of a bore for you. Write here if it will get [to] me
before the new year, if later to the Travellers' Club, Pall Mall,
London S.W.1., Xan's and my address. Have had two letters and
some more poetry, very good, from him . . .

I am writing this from the stove-side in Joan's room. We both
think very nostalgically of you and Eve among your turbaned
monoliths, and send love and kisses and every kind wish for
Christmas. Write quickly, love Paddy.[13]

On their return to Athens Joan also received a letter from Tom
Driberg asking her about coming to Greece, but she discouraged
him. She told him too that she had been unable to help find the

whereabouts of a friend of his. Her reply was sent on a postcard depicting Hieronymus Bosch's *Garden of Earthly Delights*:

> *It would be nice if you were to have whole suckling pigs &*
> *barrels of strong red wine – all that is very pleasant of course*
> *but you can imagine the disadvantages of living in this embassy*
> *& in a totalitarian state. I can't find your friend – perhaps he is*
> *one of the 300,000 still in prison since the Civil war or was one*
> *of the hundreds still shot daily. If you didn't see this picture*
> *when you were here it is worth looking at closely. Love, Joan*[14]

Unhappy as they were about being forced to leave Greece, it was a good time to go. The civil war had started again and would continue for several years. The communists were gouging out the eyes of the icons in the churches – it was symbolic of what was happening in the country beyond.

9

From Curzon Street
to the Caribbean

At the beginning of 1947, Joan and Paddy came back to an England in the midst of a harsh winter. It was bitterly cold. By the end of January, roads and railways were blocked by drifts of snow, power stations began to close for lack of coal and the electricity supply was restricted to nineteen hours a day. Bread, which had always been available during the war, was rationed for the first time because of a disastrous harvest the year before. For adults, there was a weekly allowance of a shilling's worth of meat and one egg. Should the meat turn out to be tough, the 'Advice for the Housewife' column in the *Listener* recommended adding a tablespoonful of vinegar to the water before boiling. There were endless variations on how to use dried egg to make savoury sandwiches. The machines for dispensing sweets on station platforms had all rusted up from disuse. It was almost impossible to find suitable accommodation, and it was more than two years before Paddy and Joan were offered anywhere satisfactory. In the meantime, together with Xan, they took what Joan called 'a hideous, furnished, tart's flat' at 11a Curzon Street, directly over Heywood Hill's bookshop.[1]

'Have you seen Joan? How is she?'[2] John Rayner wrote to Tom Driberg at the very end of March 1947. Two days later the divorce nisi was granted on the grounds of his adultery with Isabel Delmer. The suit was not contested, but the solicitor had been negligent, hence the delay. Rayner was now living in Australia, 'a land of milk, butter, honey, steaks, oysters, peaches, tweeds, woollens, books, sun, sea, kindness, geniality, the well-fed & well organised communist brake on industry'.[3] He had been anxious for the divorce to come through as soon as possible, for he was both arranging marriage to a new wife and booking her into hospital for their first baby. John had met Miranda Lampson in Singapore, where her uncle, Lord Killearn, was high commissioner. Killearn had been British ambassador to Egypt in his previous posting, and Joan already knew Miranda, who was slightly older than her. Joan's divorce from JR was just one of over 47,000 that year – it was a peak year for post-war divorces.[4] She wanted it to happen, but when it actually came through she was unsettled by it. For Miranda, it was a great relief, and on 7 May she and John were married in Sydney. Their first son was born legitimately a week later. 'Now grunting beside me is Mr. John Peregrine Rayner, a very nice little boy,' John wrote to his mother, who regretted that his parting from Joan had caused 'talk'.

Now that they were no longer soldiers in uniform, Paddy and Xan were keen to get started as writers, and they pulled all the strings they could. Xan, who lacked the anchor of Joan, was wondering what to do with his life, and wrote to Maurice Bowra. Bowra replied, regretting that he was unable to help.

I was extremely sorry to hear of the failure of your plans, especially after everything here had been fixed. I saw Birley* the other day and told him about it, and he was clearly most eager to help and will talk to the Ministry of Education people about you. But I have no great hopes of these bureaucrats. Anyhow do

---

* Professor Eric Birley (1906–95), historian and archaeologist.

nothing in a hurry about going to Peru or Annam in case
something turns up.

Joan and Paddy came here on a royal visit, Paddy wearing a
most eccentric cloak – a priest's or a goatherd's I can't remember
which, and carrying a bottle of whisky. They were both in very
fine form and fitted well into our academic atmosphere but then
Joan was always very high-brow, and I am sure Paddy won
scripture prizes before he was sacked for fucking the matron or
whatever it was that led to his downfall. Glad you have met
Pauline – one of the most eccentric girls I know, and I know a
good many. Indeed sanity seems hardly to exist in the other sex.[5]

Paddy had bought his cloak from a shepherd in the Pindus mountains of Greece the previous year and it was typical of him to wear
it. Bowra could never resist the temptation to be waspish. Joan and
Paddy frequently kept different friends, and as far as Bowra was
concerned, Paddy had intruded on his intimacy with his beloved
Joan. Despite having much in common – a love of all things Greek,
talking, war, medals and royalty – relations between Paddy and
Bowra never really warmed. Across the road from Bowra's Wadham
College, however, Richard Dawkins, the eccentric professor of Byzantine studies and modern Greek, an honorary fellow of Exeter
College and a man with an 'inexhaustible liking for the young',[6]
hero-worshipped Paddy and sent him innumerable badly typed fan
letters.

In the September 1946 edition of *Horizon*, Cyril Connolly had
published 'The Cost of Letters',[7] the results of a questionnaire he
had carried out among twenty-one contemporary writers. Questions
included how much a writer needed to live on and, if he could not
earn this sum by writing, what did he think was the most suitable
second occupation for him? Inevitably, the answers varied greatly
and frequently contradicted one another. Most estimates for living

expenses were up to about £1,000 (£37,000 in 2016), with Elizabeth Bowen's suggestion of £3,500 the most ambitious by far. Connolly gave his reasons: 'If he is to enjoy leisure and privacy, marry, buy books, travel and entertain his friends, a writer needs upwards of five pounds a day net.' Graham's ever-indigent friend, the artist Robin Ironside, was less hopeful: 'As an aspiring critic, mainly of painting, I require, for the satisfaction of my aspirations and having due regard to the present cost of living, a net income of £15 a week, an amount I have never possessed and am never likely to possess. Because I am too poor, I have never been to Greece or to America.' On contemplating a second career, John Betjeman wrote, 'I can only speak for myself. I would like to be a station-master on a small country branch line (single track).' Connolly's own response was frank: 'A rich wife.'

Paddy had no money of his own and when Joan and he first met he had published little. Joan may have believed in Paddy's talent as a writer but others in her family were fearful that his motives were as much financial as romantic. Joan drew an income from the estate which was supplemented by photographic assignments. The Dumbleton estate had survived the depredations of war in reasonable health but she was not wealthy. Formerly Joan had had a husband with a well-paid position, but she was now providing financial assistance for a lover with considerable charm and good looks but few clear prospects. Although Paddy succeeded in selling magazine and newspaper articles and reviews, which helped get his name into print, the rewards were small, and in the early years of their relationship Joan was forever giving him cheques for £5 or £10 (£185–£370). To her family, their lives together seemed eccentric and rackety ('my mother keeps asking me why I haven't got any clothes and making suggestions about how to get them,'[8] she wrote). When Joan went home to Dumbleton, she had to go to the estate office to collect the fare for her journey back to London, and this only changed when she came into an inheritance on the death of her brother Graham in 1993. As well as being a skilful avoider of responsibility, Paddy was always clueless about money. There were arguments and Joan's patience was clearly tried, yet eventually she decided to be as liberal as she could be. In 1950 she wrote to Paddy from Dumbleton:

> *I propose to pay into your bank account £30 a month from June*
> *for the rest of the year & an extra £50 to start you off & then*
> *you need not have all this bother & hell of asking me. It sounds*
> *terribly little darling but I do think you ought to try & make*
> *some money for yourself – I can't think why really but it would*
> *be much better for you from every point of view. Also it's about*
> *half of what I really must try to live on. Please don't think I'm*
> *doing this so that we can see less of each other but only so that*
> *we needn't be so much bothered by it all.*[9]

Paddy and Joan would have to live on £720 a year, plus whatever else they might earn from writing and photography – money was going to be tight.

All this made the idea of returning overseas seem more desirable. 'Pudding Island', as Lawrence Durrell called England with contempt, was grey, dreary and bomb-damaged. He wrote to Xan: 'I had no idea you were back in England [. . .] I didn't expect you'd reconcile easy to slow London. It's an old man's country – the island for contemplatives and quietists. I've no doubt you'll find your way out to the Mediterranean again.'[10]

The notion of 'abroad' represented liberation from all manner of British class conventions and inhibitions, as well as more definable things like warmth, sunlight, good food and good wine. It was also considerably cheaper.

The Betjemans invited Joan and Paddy to stay at their new home in Farnborough near Wantage. The Old Rectory was a large Georgian house with twelve acres of garden. John had insisted on buying the house because he was 'potty' about it. Situated amidst downland, ancient tracks and rolling cornfields, Farnborough had a population of just over a hundred and was the highest village in Berkshire. The water had to be fetched from a communal village pump and at night they used paraffin lamps. In the winter months the whole family huddled in the huge inner hall, which had once been a village schoolroom. But despite the lack of amenities and telephone there was 'corking' scenery across Watership Down, and there was also a library for Betjeman's considerable collection of antiquarian books. Immediately after their visit, Joan and Paddy went to the Camargue for the Easter of 1947. Joan wrote to Penelope from her hotel in Les Baux, thanking her: 'I did love staying with you so much & thank you a million times. I envy you your house & family so much, & you & John are just the wrong people to see before travelling – I feel like the Flying Dutchman.' The Camargue turned out to be a disappointment – 'pointless unless one rode about all day on a delicious white horse.' The gypsies all lived in motor caravans with Aga cookers and maple furniture. The local wine was not good but it was a more lucrative source of income than bull breeding. Bulls were still bred for sport, but those that were left were for eating:

> They were a special Camargue breed but Spanish bulls have been mixed with them a lot, until a fascinating old queer, The Marquis de Baroncelli de Javon, practically took over the whole Camargue. (Alas, he died aged about 75 a few years ago of a broken heart as the Germans had destroyed all his farm and house.) He stopped the mixed breeding & started again from the few remaining pure stock, and the same with the pure Camargue horses which were being interbred with Arabs . . . He must have had a wonderful life, dressed up in the cowboy clothes the

*guardians all wear, surrounded by the handsomest, worshipped
by everyone in the Camargue but now he is dead. I suppose the
'progress' which he fought all his life will completely swamp
what still remains of the real Camargue. It is lovely being in the
south again & this place is perfect. Delicious food & masses of
it for modest pension prices but nearly everywhere else is very
expensive & bad. I far prefer a horse to a bicycle.*[11]

In the summer of 1947, the publisher Lindsay Drummond Ltd
engaged Costa Achillopoulos, a Greek photographer, to produce a
book of pictures of the Caribbean. Costa, who had been brought up
in Paris and England, was completely cosmopolitan. Tanned, with
hair which had turned white overnight when he was twenty and
green eyes, he seemed to have been everywhere and know everyone.
In an age before mass travel he managed to sell his pictures without
difficulty to magazines and newspapers, and together with his Rol-
leiflex camera, he was forever on the move. He was also amusing,
self-deprecating and immensely good company. Paddy, who was a
friend, was invited by Costa to go with him – he even offered Paddy
his advance in order to make the voyage possible. Joan decided to
accompany them, and in his preface to *The Traveller's Tree: A Journey through the Caribbean Islands*, the account he subsequently
wrote of their travels, Paddy acknowledged Joan as the Egeria – or
spiritual guide – of the journey, and Costa as 'not only its photographer and painter, but our motive force that launched it, its only
begetter'.[12]

Paddy, Joan and Costa set sail at the beginning of October on
the *Colombie*, a French ship which had recently been refitted after
wartime use, and for the next six months they wandered by boat and
by plane through French, Dutch, British and American islands of
the West Indies – Guadaloupe, Martinique, Dominica, Barbados,
Trinidad, Grenada, St Lucia, Antigua, St Kitts, St Eustatius, Saba,

St Martin, St Thomas, Haiti and Cuba – to the point of exhaustion. Joan had her camera everywhere they went. When the photographs had been developed, she cut up the contact sheets and pasted the individual pictures into albums which Paddy used as *aides-mémoires* when he was working on *The Traveller's Tree*. There are few references to Joan in his book, but Paddy includes a description as Costa and she wandered around the great cemetery in Guadaloupe. Joan had an enthusiasm for tombs and cemeteries which Paddy completely failed to share – especially when he was obliged to follow them in the baking heat.

> Not even a dog was to be seen. But behind a tall crucifix stood a cemetery of such dimensions – Père Lachaise and Campo Santo gone mad – that, opening their cameras, Joan and Costa slid from their seats with sharp gasps of delight. For hours I trudged behind them round this blazing necropolis, down avenues of stucco vaults and tombs, Parthenons, temples of Vesta, and Chartres cathedrals, past urns and weeping angels, mournful marble Lucreces hung with brown wreaths and even shaded sometimes by evergreens white with dust, till they had seen and photographed their fill. These acres inhabited by the dead, these miniature halls and palaces and opera houses, were, it occurred to me, the real town, and the houses falling to ruins outside the railings were in the nature of a negligible suburb.[13]

By the time Joan had finished her third film with her last photograph – 'an ochreous Aztec pyramid built round the faded photograph of a very old Negro in postman's uniform' – they left this city of mausoleums like 'three pillars of fire'. 'The dust that settled on our steaming faces turned us into zombies. It penetrated every orifice of the head and temporarily robbed us of all our faculties.'

Their feelings towards each of the Caribbean islands varied from one to the next, but the British island of Dominica with its pretty little capital of Roseau – 'an Antillean Cranford' – was one of the best. Little Union Jacks fluttered from the gables of the houses and 'the brass plate of Barclays Bank gleamed in the morning air'. They visited the Free Library where 'two young Negroes sat in the reading room, deep in the *Bystander* and *Horse and Hound*', and Paddy wandered into the High Court, which was in full session. The Puisne Judge of the Windward Islands sat in his scarlet robe and wig under the Royal Arms, two ancient drums and a panoply of banners. An old peasant woman was being tried for murdering her husband with a hoe, and as Paddy entered the court an official was holding the weapon out for the inspection of the jury. It was like a scene from *Alice's Adventures in Wonderland* drawn by Tenniel.

The happiest part of their long odyssey through the islands was undoubtedly a prolonged stay at Pointe Baptiste, a house at the northern end of Dominica. They arrived one evening when it was growing dark and, turning downhill into a wooded hollow, they saw the windows of the house gleam through the tree trunks. After walking across the grass, they came to a large airy room and found drinks standing on a table amidst vast sofas and chairs and great quantities of books – 'exactly the sort of library one sighs for anywhere'. They stayed at Pointe Baptiste with their hostess, Mrs Napier,* who was a member of the Dominican House of Representatives, many more days than was necessary, painting and reading and writing. When at last they left, they began to move back south for a journey into Carib country to visit a community of some of the original inhabitants of the islands, who had lived there before the Europeans arrived. The guide and head of the retinue was René, a lean and gentle young man who had studied divinity, and he was followed by three enor-

---

* Elma Napier (1892–1973) was a Scottish-born novelist. She moved to Dominica in 1932 and became known as a writer, hostess, politician and conservationist.

mous porters who carried the luggage on their heads as they wound their way through the foothills of the volcanic mountain of Morne Diablotin.

> From my position in the rear it was an impressive sight: René led the way, then came the porters, as slender and graceful as caryatids under their globular loads. Joan's horse ambled after them, bearing a figure that looked as purposeful in its dark glasses and great straw hat as a mid-Victorian lady heading for the mission-field in Uganda. She was followed by Costa riding dreamily through the shadows in his sky-blue shirt and shorts, or alternatively, at pleasanter moments clambering up the gluti-nous pathway on foot. The path grew level at last, and through a gap in the trees we could gaze from our lofty headland into a deep gorge downy with tree-tops. The sea reached inland between the steep sides of the canyon to meet the emerging sea.[14]

At length they came to a Carib settlement: a meeting with the last survivors of an almost extinct race of conquerors, which was as impressive in its way as if the encounter had been with Etruscans or Hittites. A young Carib threw down a dozen coconuts from a palm tree before sliding down the trunk with his cutlass in his hand. The king of the Caribs opened the nuts and offered his guests the milk. He regretted that Mrs Napier had not accompanied them because, as her chief constituent, he wanted to have a serious chat about island affairs. When at last Paddy, Joan and Costa got back to Roseau they found that the old woman arraigned for murder had been acquitted that very afternoon – to general satisfaction – condemned instead to a year's imprisonment, and they were just in time to hear the fine summing-up of the Puisne Judge of the Windward Islands.

'We have been to practically every West Indian Island, British,

French, Dutch and American & my mind is, alas, not broadened, but battered out flat with travel,' Joan wrote to John Rayner as she neared the end of the journey. 'They are all very beautiful & all different, but a bit woolly and green to travel about in. All very well to stay beachcombing in one spot drinking rum and eating avocados under coconut palms by a phosphorescent sea. Haiti, of course, was far the most interesting. All the Voodoo Gods have great charm but I especially liked the chiefs of the Kingdom of the Dead – Le Baron Samedi, Le Général Criminel and le Capitaine Zombie.'[15] Haiti – unfortunately for Paddy – also had a picturesque cemetery, as well as an undertaker's with an assortment of headstones, crosses and coffins. Its signboard advertised the identity of the owner; at the top he had painted a little white tortoise, and at the bottom a death's head. The burials were provided by a Monsieur E. La Tortue, *L'Ami des Morts*. All of this was once again enthusiastically photographed by Joan.

From the Caribbean islands, Paddy and Joan went to British Honduras and carried on through Central America. Because of Guatemala's claim on British Honduras it was legally impossible for a British citizen to travel directly to Guatemala, but they succeeded in finding a guide through the jungle:

> *Paddy & I, (Costa wisely went the ordinary way) walked for four days through the 'bush' to Guatemala, encouraged by a charming Indian guide called Exaltacion Pook, but it was too tough to be pleasant – mud up to the knees, crawling a lot of the time through the undergrowth, pricked and stung by every leaf, climbing on or under, or, worst, along, huge fallen trees. There is no path since the hurricane a few years ago – but we saw baboons, huge butterflies & orchids, & slept in hammocks in villages where they had never seen what, alas, they called 'red people' before – or in palm leaf shelters in the middle of the forest.*[16]

From Guatemala they went south to El Salvador and on to Teguci-galpa, the capital of Honduras, which was celebrating Holy Week. Except for a few pages on Cuba, all the Central American republics were omitted from *The Traveller's Tree*. The differences in their culture and social history, Paddy felt, were so considerable that they would unbalance the book. Besides, he hoped that an account of his subsequent journey might yield a sequel. That book was never written, however, and the draft notes he made towards it remain unpublished in a couple of old exercise books. At the end of their journey they were tired. Joan wrote that she was longing to get back to London 'as really the people here, as opposed to the countries, have too little to offer'.

Paddy and Joan arrived at Tilbury on 20 May 1948. In *The Times* that morning they saw the headline 'British Correspondent Killed'. It was Dick Wyndham. According to a story filed from Amman, he had died the previous day on the northern outskirts of Jerusalem while on an assignment for the *Sunday Times*. He had been photo-graphing Arab troops as they moved into action when he was struck by a burst of machine-gun fire. Joan was deeply shaken and dis-tressed. Wyndham, that 'uncouth old schoolboy [. . .] a Sargent drawing of the 1914 subaltern come to life',[17] as Cyril Connolly called him, was dead. For Ian Fleming, he was 'one of the great Bohemian figures of his age [. . .] a fine, careless figure, larger and more varied than the life around him'.[18]

Wyndham's death marked the ending of Tickerage Mill, which Joan and that charmed circle of friends had known as a pre-war Arcadia. In another letter from Joan to Rayner she wrote about Dick: 'It makes me furious to think of it, what a hopeless, stupid waste it all is. I'm afraid we shall miss him all our lives.' Tickerage was being sold (a subsequent owner was Vivien Leigh), and Wyndham's pic-tures went to Sotheby's later in the year.

John was also dwelling on things lost. His wife Miranda was tall, blonde and slim and her physical resemblance to Joan was not unnoticed. John's letters to Joan have mostly been destroyed, but he had obviously not recovered from the trauma of the break-up of their marriage. Joan wrote to him: 'I got one letter from you this morning & another, very gloomy, some time ago, which I've been meaning to answer for ages. Thank you so much for them [. . .] You oughtn't to feel gloomy, at any rate you ought to have little guilt & remorse – that should be more my side of it – but what's the good? I shall obviously go on making a mess of things but I intend to try and enjoy myself while I do so.'[19] At the end of the following year they met briefly in London and talked over old wounds and regrets. Once again John told her about his unhappiness and afterwards Joan wrote to him:

> *Darling John,*
>
> *How unsatisfactory it was seeing you for such a horribly short time & how inadequate I feel about everything. I could kill myself for not having had a flat that week where we could anyhow have talked as long as we wanted. But I suppose these meetings in a void are always like that – too nerve-wracking & difficult whatever happens – & I doubt if we had talked for weeks whether we should have worked things out to our satisfaction – of course I had 'flu too and that didn't help. I do think you are wrong to feel that you could have changed things by some means or by behaving differently or by being different in some way – I know it was entirely my fault & nothing could have changed my decisions – everything you ever did, in fact, only made me put off separating longer. I think Cyril is right in a way – I don't think I shall ever be good at married life – which is the reason I don't try again. But it was lovely seeing you & do please come back soon & let us then arrange to have more time.*
>
> *I'm just off to Dumbleton with Graham for Christmas. I meant to write to you the day you left but felt entirely unable to*

& found every excuse – 'flu, Paris again to get my car, etc. Why?
the feeling one can never explain or say what one means, I
suppose.
  My best love
  Joan.[20]

Rayner stayed abroad for several more years in Australia and then returned to Singapore. Although he published a couple of books, he never returned to the world of journalism, and for the remainder of his working life he received a salary from the Foreign Office. Joan and he continued to meet and sometimes write to one another. Their letters were always warm and affectionate. John Betjeman, Tom Driberg and Costa, among others, remained mutual friends. In all John and Miranda went on to have four children.

In April 1948 Cyril Connolly suggested to the publisher Hamish Hamilton and his American associate Cass Canfield that they should let him write a travel book about Aquitaine, 'a very balmy and civilised region of France'.[21] Lacking money as ever, he persuaded Hamish Hamilton to give him an advance of £200 to help pay for the trip, which he thought would last for about two months. In return he would deliver 70,000 words for £350. Cyril's original intention was that Dick Wyndham would accompany him as his photographer, but following his death he felt that Joan would be the ideal replacement. Joan was more than willing to accept the commission and on 4 August she left for France.

They met at Valence, south of Lyon. Cyril was recovering from food poisoning and a temperature, although he feared that his sickness might have been prompted by feelings of guilt: he had begun to tire of his partner Lys Lubbock, who had just left him to return to England. Cyril and Joan drove to a two-star restaurant where he could only sit and watch while Joan enjoyed the specialities of the house – truffled *galantine de caneton* and *quenelles de langouste* and a delicious white Hermitage called Chante Alouette. The following day, there was another excellent lunch and Joan took lots of photographs of the chef in the kitchen as he stirred pans full of wonderful sauces. In her pictures it is as if Joan is seeing France through Connolly's eyes – market stalls laden with fruit and vegetables, a chef with a table of game spread out in front of him, a sideboard heavily laden with food sufficient for a banquet, and the restaurant itself, the tables, white tablecloths and cutlery all ready for the customers.

Paddy was already in France working on *The Traveller's Tree*. He was staying with Walter and Amy Smart, his old Cairo friends, who had a house in an apple orchard at Gadencourt,[22] a little village on the banks of the River Eure. Patrick Kinross was also staying. Joan sent her letters there. Her first was headed 'Grand Café de Paris et de la Poste' and written from Mende, a small town in Lozère.

> *I do miss you horribly – everything nice I see, eat, drink I wish you were here to share it. Lys is not here – for various good reasons she has gone back to London, & of course it is far nicer as it is, in a way. I was a little worried at first after all our talk, but I manage to keep my platonic travelling companion status with no difficulty; in which as you know I take great pride. And that tiresome old meddler Groddeck* has made me have the curse a week late for nothing [. . .]*
>
> *Now today, after an entire morning waiting for a train to go, we are in the first lovely town; squares, plane trees, cafés, fountains & thin grey semi-circular slate tiles, in heavenly country of small rivers, gorges & almost rounded hills; & this afternoon after a little sightseeing, we go to La Malène on the Tarn and start on the Gorges de Tarn. The end of next week our*

---

* Georg Groddeck (1866–1934), a pioneer of psychosomatic medicine.

address is chez Madame Riley, Chateau de Curemonte, Cor-
rèze. Everything is a bit slower as we have no car & we shan't be
at Bordeaux until about Friday 20th. Could you meet me there?
Cyril is all for it. There are lots of things round there in the way
of photographs & drinking but if you don't want to come I'll try
& hurry everything up as I really don't enjoy this separation.
What about it? it would be heavenly if you did come, but if you
think it's disastrous from the book point of view I shall under-
stand, although there really isn't all that terrible hurry, is there?
It's only in England one feels this terribly urgent rush. I hope I
hear from you at Roquefort but please, please don't say anything
nasty as I couldn't have it. I think every day that an island or
mountain in Greece is the only place for us.

C. is being very sweet & easy & is heavenly to travel with.
He really is hoping you come to Bordeaux & says we can all go
to Ch. Mouton Rothschild when you arrive (as an inducement).

I do hope, my darling angel, you are having a happy time.
Give my greatest love to Amy & Smarty – I am longing to be
there. I hope you are not staying with some horrible femme du
boulanger & darling, darling Paddy I am longing to see you
again. I've taken lots of photographs but it's been so far very
difficult country & I have little confidence in the new camera. It
should be better photogenically from now on.

Bless you my angel
All my love
Joan
Don't get worried about jobs and things. It's only in England
one has to spend so much & I'm sure I can never live there.
Forgive this untidy after-luncheon letter. Cyril sends love![23]

A week later Joan wrote again to Paddy from the Château de Curemonte in Corrèze. She was staying with Peggy Riley, the European

features editor of American *Vogue*. The previous year Cyril had met and entertained Peggy and she had invited him to stay with her in France. He had arrived at the chateau for the weekend and then, after a day or two, he said he had to meet a photographer on business. He reappeared with Joan. The weekend Cyril was supposed to stay turned into three weeks, and Joan was invited to stay too. She wrote:

> *This is the most heavenly place & I long for you to be here – it is everything you like. The house is small but built within the ruins of the old castle at the top of a very hand-knitted little village full of bearded women in fierce black shiny hats. Everywhere there is the most lovely view – wide rolling wooded hills, green lawn like fields, rows of flickering poplars, all very calm and happy. Today is boilingly hot and I am writing in the garden. No-one else is up although it is 12 o'clock. Soon I hope Peggy Riley will emerge with drinks and foie gras. She is extremely wise and you would adore her.* She is living here for 3 months with her lover, Georges Bernier, an ugly charming French intellectual of the best unboring French sort, a great gourmet . . . We have lovely conversations, arguments, discussions all day long & I seem to have talked more here than for the last two years and I wish, wish, wish you were here too. Incidentally the house belongs to the daughter of Collette, les mêmes moeurs as her mother and is full of sexy Lesbian books & pictures of snakes.*
>
> **Has lived for years in Mexico & sings lots of songs including Virgen de Guadaloupe. Aïe. Aïe. Aïe!*

Unfortunately, the week before their arrival had been a disaster. Cyril had exercised to the full his talent for making life complicated both for himself and for those around him. Having been more or less in love with Joan for years, he had made his feelings about her all too obvious and had made a pass at her. A week alone with her had been too much of a temptation.

> *The only blot on all this (& this, my darling, is for your ears alone) is that things are getting a bit strained – why do these complications have to spoil things so often? I feel like a boringly monogamous bourgeois bitch but I can't do anything about it. It seems so easy to make everyone happy but I can't, and I'm getting very nervous & we will probably end up bitter ene-mies**. It's not really as bad as all that but I feel gloomy & annoyed about it all & feel I should manage better than I do. Actually I think everything will be all right & I'm making a lot of fuss about nothing. Please don't let Patrick or Amy get hold of this letter – I can't imagine two worse people! Tear it up. We are staying here till Friday – they have a car and we drive about every afternoon & evening photographing & sightseeing, & then go to Bordeaux. I'm afraid now if you come there it will be rather hell for C., I couldn't disguise my joy at seeing you, as much as I should like it, unless you very much want to, it would be better not to come . . .*
>
> *Darling, what an incoherent muddled letter – worse than usual – but I haven't much time to write & all the plans are vague & the sun is very hot & the Larousse Gastronomique, on which I write, is slipping on my knees.*
>
> *Darling darling Paddy I do love you so.*
>
> *A huge great hug.*
>
> *Joan.*
>
> ***No this not true. C is sweet but sad.*[24]

In *Happy Deathbeds*, Connolly's unfinished novel from that time, Joan appears as 'Jane Sotheran'.

She had long legs, long ankles, toes like a Greek goddess, a neck that looked as if it had been artificially lengthened to support a princess's dowry of gold curtain rings and a face whose chief features were two enormous eyes of clouded violet blue, usually concealed behind dark glasses, a small fine nose, a slightly protruding lower lip, wrinkled brow and pelt of short blonde hair.[25]

Connolly had also told his mother that he wanted to marry Joan after her marriage with John Rayner had ended. He believed that she was the only person who could have helped him get over his first wife Jean – 'this Joan to end all Jeans'. Inconveniently, however, Joan was always away somewhere abroad because of the war and then in the Caribbean. During the week before Joan's letter he had been able to indulge his fantasies about her again, as she wandered beside him in her 'dark green cardigan and grey trousers, her camera slung over her shoulder and her golden hair bobbing as she walks, always a little fairer than you think, like the wind in a stubble field'. Although to please him Joan agreed to take part in a pretend wedding in a cave, during which they were interrupted by a party of boy scouts and some falling rocks, she had tired of being Cyril's 'lovely boy-girl . . . like a casual, loving, decadent Eton athlete'.[26]

Meanwhile, impervious to the upset he had caused Joan, Connolly spent his mornings in bed with maps and *Guides Bleus* working out ways in which Peggy and Bernier, who had a car, might entertain him. The trip to France eventually ended at La Rochelle, where Joan caught the train to Paris in order to meet Paddy. All that exists to show from the jaunt are a couple of envelopes of Joan's photographs: Cyril never wrote a line of his projected book on France for Hamish Hamilton, nor did he return his generous advance on his expenses.

10

Separation

After he left Gadencourt, Paddy spent a week in Paris with Joan, then, without making any advance arrangement, he took a bus to the Abbey of St Wandrille de Fontanelle in the Lower Seine. The relative seclusion of Gadencourt had helped him to write and he was making significant progress with the book. As somewhere quiet and cheap, a monastery seemed another ideal place to stay. For Joan, however, this meant further separation from Paddy, and she returned to London in order to look for somewhere to live. She had still not decided whether she wanted to live in London or in the country, and she clearly hated the search. A greater problem, though, was that Joan was desperate to have a family. In post-war Britain it was regarded as almost a woman's patriotic duty to have children; it was also her own experience of life. Joan had been brought up in a large, extended family and her two sisters had seven children between them. She was thirty-six when she returned from the Caribbean, and conscious that her chances of having a baby were receding. Prolonged separations from Paddy meant that opportunities for sexual contact with him were few. He had made Denise Menasce pregnant – all too easily – and Joan wondered if it was her own fault that she seemed to be unable to become pregnant too.

The June 1948 issue of *Horizon* had included an article by Lawrence Durrell, who was an enthusiast for the teachings of the

German physician Georg Groddeck. Groddeck, a proponent of psychosomatic medicine, taught that problems of health and disease were forms of self-expression. For someone so self-aware and so self-critical as Joan, such theories were tempting, as shown by her letter from Mende. Treatment could be effected, he suggested, by psychoanalysis, hot baths and massage. However, such therapy by 'that tiresome old meddler' proved fruitless for her. In her letters to Paddy, Joan wrote frequently about her desire for babies but her remarks brought no response. Paddy's only comment was unsympathetic and flippant – 'felt frightfully ill. It must have been Groddeck' – before going on to 'a wonderful party'.

For most of the months between August and December, and again for weeks on end while Paddy was in France, Joan and he were separated from one another. Writing *The Traveller's Tree* in order to make money and turn Paddy into a recognized author had to come first. They wrote affectionately to one another and Paddy's letters to Joan from the monasteries of St Wandrille and Solesmes later provided a framework for much of *A Time to Keep Silence*, his study of monasticism which was first published in book form in 1957. He writes to her as 'Angel', 'Mopsa', 'Pet', 'little mite', 'my tiny muskin', and the pages are embellished with pictures of little mice. Again and again Joan says how much she misses him. At the end of one of her letters she too drew a mouse but one with long-lashed eyes and blood dripping from its bleeding heart. Sometimes she enclosed 'Ds' or 'Benzers' – the drug Benzedrine, widely used at the time as a stimulant. There are many references to Cyril, or 'the H' or 'the Humanist', as Paddy and Joan called him, and his hopeless pursuit of Joan. Cyril wanted Joan to return to France to take more photographs but unfortunately, as Joan wrote to Paddy, his interest in her was more than just professional. In his letters Paddy comes across as both possessive and playful, anxious that in his absence

Joan might find another lover. Joan too was sometimes afraid that she would not see Paddy again. Neither had anything to fear.

On his arrival at St Wandrille, Paddy asked the black-robed monk at the gatehouse if it would be possible for him to stay. The monk went to speak to the abbot and returned smiling. He seized Paddy's heavy bag and led him to a cell. On the inner side of the cell door were the printed rules of the guest wing. They contained a mass of cheerless information. While the monks' day began at 4 a.m., a guest's began at 8.15 with the office of Prime, after which breakfast was served in silence. The rest of the day was laid out with meals, offices and duties until the service of Compline at 8.30 p.m., then at 9.00 the monastery once again fell silent. During the hours of night, when everyone else was in bed, Paddy continued to work. From his window, he watched the lights in the other cells go out and he settled down to fill the empty hours in front of his pile of manuscripts, maps of the Caribbean islands, and photographs of the Central American jungle and the faces of the Maya Indians. This was how it must have been to witness François Fénelon, the eighteenth-century divine. '*Rien ne change dans la vie monastique. Chaque jour est pareil à l'autre, chaque année comme celle qui la précédait, et ainsi jusqu'à la mort . . .*'[1]*

Paddy, who was not used to looking inward, at first found being alone with himself and his thoughts depressing, but his mood lifted. He gave the writings of Joris-Karl Huysmans as his excuse for his interest in monasticism. 'I was living a lot in France, much under the influence of Huysmans, and I haunted quays and bookshops and libraries,'[2] he wrote. The erudite and idiosyncratic novels of Huysmans are concerned with the spiritual progression which led to the French writer's own conversion to Catholicism. If conversion

---

* Nothing changes in the monastic life. Each day is the same as another, each year like the one which went before, and it will be so until death.

would have been a step too far for him, Paddy was, all the same, curious – like a little boy with his face pressed against a sweetshop window – to acquire what might be inside. Whatever his original purpose for staying in the monasteries, he was profoundly affected by the experience, yet found it difficult to say what his feelings amounted to.

The story of what happened over those months when they were apart from one another is best told in their own letters.

Paddy Leigh Fermor, St Wandrille, Monday

My darling Pet,

What a sweet funny letter. Oxford sounds as if it had been heavenly. I'm a bit more resigned to this place at the moment, and now that I've established my rights as a defaulter at Mass every day, it's not too bad. The weather has been perfect, and I have been writing away out of doors under a chestnut tree. But all the same, if I get the slightest excuse to come to London, I'm going to do so. Probably even if there isn't. There are tons of things I want to look up for the last three chapters, and I can't bear the thought of your (a) enjoying London like mad without me or (b) the reverse. I really do miss you like anything. At this distance you seem about as nearly perfect as a human being can be, my darling little wretch, so it's about time I was brought to my senses. So don't get too sentimentally embroiled for heaven's sake.

How kind these monks are! I'm not feeling an atom more disposed to religion at the moment, but the discrete [sic] and good manners and general aura of kindness and sweetness of nature of these people is something extremely rare. I wander about under the trees for ½ an hour after luncheon with the Abbé or the Père Hôtelier every day, talking about religion, philosophy, history, Greek and Roman poetry, etc. Very pleasant and satisfactory. The Père Hôtelier confided to me today that his conversion from atheism and monastic vocation was entirely under the influence of Huysmans, especially books like 'L'Oblat' and 'La Cathedrale'! V. interesting.

I feel such a relief having finished the Windward, Leeward and Virgin Islands. The Leeward Islands were becoming a positive incubus – exorcised now at last. Once I tackle a chapter I feel I'm alright. After a page. But what a tormenting accidie period of hesitation beforehand. I'm feeling much happier about this book now, and terribly excited. I'm longing for you to read and criticize the latest stuff. Must be going on scribbling now so good night my darling little mite! Please go on writing. I adore your letters and they stop me from feeling like Ariadne,

all my love P. xxxx

P.S. Compline takes place in broad daylight – 8.30 – and it's not dark for nearly an hour afterwards, which makes the evening seem very lonely and long. But it's rather like one's childhood, when grown-ups would still be playing tennis when one was supposed to be asleep. The trout rise in the Fontanelle and make little circles, and an old farmer has just ridden past on a huge cart horse to the thatched farmyard down the road. For some reason I hadn't noticed the first and last lines of compline till tonight. They are very fine, I think: (both out of Psalms translated by St. Jerome) or is it an Epistle of St Paul? I think it is.

Fratres, sobrii istate, et vigilate, Quia adversarius vester diabolus, tanquam leonem rugiens circuit, quaerens quem devoret, restitate fortes in fide.

Brothers, be sober, and watch, For your adversary the devil like a roaring lion ranges abroad, seeking whom he may devour, whom resist strong in the faith.

And

Sub umbra alarum tuarum protege nos!
Under the shadow of thy wings defend us!

18. Joan at the races, *c*. 1938.

19. Joan and John Rayner: they had in common a love of places
and nature, music, art, reading, wine and good food.

20. Tickerage Mill. Top row: Patrick Kinross, Constant Lambert, Angela Culme-Seymour, Dick Wyndham, Tom Driberg, Cyril Connolly, Stephen Spender; bottom row: Tony Hyndman (Spender's boyfriend), Jean Connolly, Mamaine Paget, John Rayner.

21. John Rayner, Tom and Isabel Delmer, and Tom Driberg at Bradwell Lodge in Essex. There were considerable tensions within this group: 'no two Toms could have disliked each other more'.

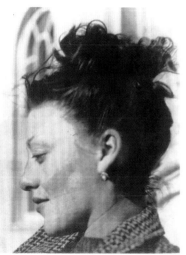

22. Isabel Delmer at Bradwell Lodge in 1940. An artist herself, she was a model for Epstein, Derain, Picasso, Giacometti and Francis Bacon.

23. John Rayner at the Political Warfare Executive in the early 1940s.

Darling – it is really affalling how quickly the Time goes here & it is with horror I realize I have been away 9 months now – I am filled with guilt at the easiness of my life here & at the thought of your starting a second winter coping with flats & rations etc by yourself. I do hope Is is staying with you – Anyway I really am about to make great dicisions & changes here* as much as Madrid grows on me it is a great waste (if situation allows.)

24. Letter from Joan in Madrid to John Rayner, 7 October 1943: 'Do you really want to start our same old life again?'

25. The National Buildings Record commissioned Joan to take pictures of bomb damage, including at Haberdashers' Hall.

26. 'One sees groups of Kurds dressed in their baggy trousers, long coloured sashes and fringed turbans.'

27. A Kurdish dandy,
May 1945.

28. Joan in Kurdistan,
May 1945, with Sheikh
Poosho Sayed Taha,
her host in the mountains
of Rowanduz.

334

335

336

337

338

Athens

339

29. and 30. Although Joan regarded her photographs principally as *aides-mémoires* for Paddy, these Athens street scenes of the early 1950s (some including John Craxton) show her great ability. The wording on the box of skulls reads 'Stefanos Takos, S T, 23 years'.

31. After Joan, Paddy Leigh Fermor (left)
loved Xan Fielding most of all.

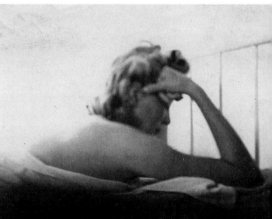

32. Joan in bed –
a picture taken for the eyes
of a lover in the late 1940s.

33. Paddy on a beach on Ithaca –
he was 'Byronically handsome'.

34. Paddy wearing a sunhat
in the Caribbean.

P.P.S. Important Darling, I've suddenly remembered that I haven't sent Mondi Howard's* brother £17 for the electric light. I'm, alas, £1 overdrawn. Do you think you could possibly send £18 to the Manager, Messrs Glyn Mills, (Holts Branch), Whitehall, S.W.1. and post the enclosed letter a day later. Darling, I know it's the sort of thing you loathe doing more than anything in the world (not the pennies, I mean, but writing to banks), but I do think it would be a good idea to give it back now. It might make all the difference between being allowed to live at San Antonio another winter, and not. There's still more trouble though. I've lost his address. But it is Dean Farm, I know, something-something, Glos. So could you look up Ld Howard of Penrith† in Who's Who in the London Library, and fill it in. Please, please, don't be savage with boredom at all this! It won't take long![3]

PLF, Abbaye de St Wandrille, Feast of St Jérome [30 September], Thursday

Darling Angel,
I've been wondering about what can be done about these silent meals in the refectory, and am just beginning to see daylight. In the library, piled up in a dark corner in a trunk and covered with dust, I've discovered a mass of 10th–16th century folios bound in vellum all dealing with the point where mysticism and necromancy merge. Chaldean magic, the Cabbalah, Hermes Trismegistus, astrology, the Rosy Cross, etc. I think that within a fortnight by dint of reading these books, by fasting and by prayer, and resort to the abbeys arsenal of flails and hair

---

* Edmund 'Mondi' Howard (1909–2005), diplomat and historian.
† Francis Philip Raphael Howard, 2nd Baron Howard (1905–99).

shirts, I ought to have mastered certain powers. I shall then initiate some of the likelier monks, beginning with the ones that look like Philip [Toynbee], Brian [Howard], Maurice [Bowra] and Cyril [Connolly] (no doubt more tractable in their monkish shape than I've found them in real life). Then, at a prearranged tap of the abbot's mallet, we shall all levitate ourselves three yards in the air, and no sharp words will bring us down in fact nothing will, until we obtain a number of concessions: no more reading aloud from the Doctors of the Church, an end to the rule of silence, half a bottle of wine with each meal and a glass of Benedictine afterwards; all very reasonable demands. It might be the beginning of reform for the whole order.

I got up at 6 this morning, and went for a long walk in the beech forest above the abbey. The valley was full of mist and only the ruined arches and gables and chimneys of the abbey stuck out. There are romantic rides running through the forest, carpeted about with rotten leaves and smelling damp and autumnal like your description of Haut Brion. Every now and then where the rides cross there is a pillar supporting a grey stone urn, or there is a rococo archway crowned with a scallop shell containing the lilies of France, or the mitred arms of the abbey. Squirrels are everywhere. I haven't drunk anything for 3 days and feel wonderfully clear-headed and light, the whites of my eyes are becoming as clear as porcelain, and bones are slowly emerging. I can't quite remember what a hangover feels like.

My darling pet, don't stay in England forever and above all, don't run away with anyone or I'll come and cut your bloody throat. This is on the road between Havre and Rouen. You might come and pick me up here, or we might meet at Amy's, or in Paris. All my love, dear little Joan, & kisses & hugs from Paddy.

p.s. I've forgotten which day my Voodoo broadcast is. Could you keep your eyes open in the Radio Times and wire me. I think it's October 12th.

p.s. I brought the 130 Journées* here by mistake, but sent it back to Paris by registered mail before actually entering the abbey. If I hadn't either the suitcase and I would have gone up in a sulphurous cloud, or the abbey would have come crashing down like Jericho.[4]

Joan Rayner, Dumbleton Hall, Wednesday

My darling Paddaki

I do love getting your letters so much. How fascinating the mystical mss. sound – do remember every word & tell me what they say. Would it be amusing to do an article on them for Horizon or Cornhill? Also would it be possible at any point for me to take photographs of the monastery for American or French Vogue?

I find your life very hard to imagine – I try to think of you tucked up in your cell at night or sitting silent and undrinking among the monks at meals, but it is difficult and it makes me feel very far away from you. God, I do hate not having you in bed with me – I suffer from loneliness, cold, the feeling of being unloved, angst, guilt & every form of fear from death to burglars.

I'm in a terrible muddle about my plans at the moment but I must see you SOON. The Colossus [George Katsimbalis][†] *is supposed to be arriving about the 16th, but everyone is very*

---

* PLF probably intends *Les 120 de Sodome ou l'école du libertinage* by the Marquis de Sade.

† So-called by Henry Miller.

vague & hasn't the slightest idea of how long he is staying. I would like to see him sometime. Then the H. wants me to go back to Bordeaux as some of the photographs were on a bad film & are all messed up. I wish it was June now – there seems to be so much still to do before the winter begins.

Here are some more Ds for you if you promise to take them only for work. I've stuck them up in this curious way as they are in a box and I thought they would get broken if I didn't.

I got the curse so late this month I began to hope I was having a baby, & that you would have to make it into a legitimate little Fermor. All hopes ruined this morning. I think perhaps you should rape me one day when I am all unprepared – Aquarians can never decide about their lives & like being forced into everything.

The H. writes daily, mostly very sweet & gay letters. He poured out his heart to Graham who takes no sides, but warned him, among other things, that I was as promiscuous as any homosexual. Not true at all. The H. apparently surprised G. a great deal by saying I was really incestuous & that all my troubles came from G. not having had an affair with me years ago!*

I'm going to London Monday or Tuesday – I may stay at Sussex Place† – it is safer than anywhere since Lys is always there – but I don't really want to if I can get anywhere else nice. I'll let you know as soon as I do, but write here until then as they will be sent on. I'll try to find Xan as soon as I get there.

Best love my darling Angel – I do so long to hug you again
Joan xxxx[5]

---

* Cyril used to say that such was the intensity of their relationship that Graham was the love of Joan's life.
†Home of Cyril Connolly and Lys Lubbock.

Separation

Paddy Leigh Fermor, St Wandrille, Tuesday

in a terrible hurry for the post

My darling Mopsa,

Just got your lovely two letters. Hooray! Darling, you have been efficient and brisk. The pullover is the smartest thing that has ever been seen in Saint Wandrille.

So the H. has been very attentive, eh? Hm. 'I-can-no-longer-exist-without-you' I suppose . . . well, bugger it, neither can I. Oh dear, what fun London sounds! I can't bear all these creatures having you to themselves. Late at night is a dangerous time. I wake in my cell at 1.a.m. when you are letting yourself into the flat for a last drink with whoever you have been dining with, and pray to Saint Wandrille to put the words 'thus far and no further' into your mouth . . . Grrrr! . . .

On Sunday, Christopher Buckley* (do you remember a tall, rather moose-like journalist in Greece?) and his wife arrived here and took me out to luncheon. (I had met him in the street in Paris, and told him where I was going.) I always thought him rather a bore but he is far from it.

This morning I bicycled down to the Seine to see the monthly tidal wave sweep up the river, a huge foaming well of water. Last night, the lights went out in the refectory. The pulpit had been fitted up with the electricity the same day so the solitary voice reading fell silent at the same moment, as if it had been the [unveiling?]. Very eerie. Dead silence except for munching and the swishing robes of the waiting monks. Huge candles arrived at last making the Norman room still more medieval.

---

* Christopher Buckley (1905–50), war correspondent and novelist. Killed by a land-mine during the Korean War.

Important. Do find out when my broadcast is. Could you possibly, my poor darling, ring up Miss Rowly, Talks Dept, BBC, and say how sorry I am not to be able to give a live broadcast, and explain. Longer letter tomorrow. All my love my darling pet from Paddy.[6]

Paddy Leigh Fermor, Saint Wandrille, 13 October 1948, 10 p.m.

Darling, I've just had the most frightful shock. After compline I went to the library to make some more notes about Stylites and stayed there till a few minutes ago, all the monastery being in bed and asleep. I put all the lights out, locked up, felt my way through the dark refectory (full of the noise of rats gnawing and scuttling), and out into the cloisters, a square pool of icy starlight. At the other side of the cloisters is a dark Gothic doorway opening into a passage that leads to my part of the abbey. Still thinking about the deserts of Chalcedon and Paphlagonia. I walked through the archway and happening to look to my left, saw a tall monk standing there, his face invisible in his cowl, his hands folded in his sleeves, quite silent. It was so frightening I nearly let out a scream and can still feel my heart thumping. Phew!

Sweet darling, thank you so much for your telegram about the broadcast. I managed to hear it on the curé's wireless set – there are more in the Abbey. I would never have recognised my voice if I hadn't known who it was. Does it really sound like that? I thought it sounded rather affected and la-di-da, and frightfully gloomy, as if I were about to collapse into floods of tears. Did you manage to hear it? I don't expect you did in London. You didn't miss a great deal. Oh darling, in case it came garbled by telegram, the Cephalonian Saint is S. Gerasimos . . .

I addressed my last letter c/o Cyril, as I knew you were having dinner there tonight. Is 56 Curzon Street nice? It must be the opposite end from our lovely nest. Has Isabel's flat petered out? I say, your dinner tonight sounds alright. You've probably just about got to the party by now. Do tell me all about it. Duke and baron indeed.

A curious thing que je constate is that the Humanist's devotion to you makes him much more sympathetic to me than before. It's about our only thing in common. But, please, my darling, I think it's absolutely essential – I'm studying his interests as a writer – that it should be an unrequited devotion . . . I wonder how it's all going. Any obstacles can be overcome by dogged perseverance. Parturit ridiculus mus et nascuntur montes.* And if not the Humanist, what about the tenebrous stranger? Eh? Do tell me about your London life. I'm afraid it's dreadfully exciting . . . Oh, oh, oh! And tell me about your new clothes. I wish you were in France . . .

The room is an extraordinary mixture of austerity and splendour – the tiles, the bare white walls, and then the four-poster, the arras, the peculiar column. It has some slight analogy to the disparate elements of some Guatemalan churches . . . It's a wonderful room to wake up in. The sunlight streams in through all those great windows, and from my bed, all I can see through them are layer on ascending layer of chestnut leaves like millions of superimposed green hands, and then the pale crystalline October sky, framed by thin reflected blue-white, or thick milk-white, or, where the sun strikes, white-gold surfaces of the walls and window arches in embrasures. A miraculous, feather-light, innocent, clear awakening!

My darling angel, I meant this to be a short, brisk letter. I see

---

* The silly mouse gives birth and mountains are born.

it's straggled over several pages already: I'm so alone here at
night, I can't stop talking to you, it's such a luxury. Darling, don't
feel ever obliged to write long letters, and put them off, in any
way, because you haven't got time to settle down to a whopper.
You're in a capital city, I'm in an abbey, don't I know what it
means! I do enjoy and look forward to your letters so – you've sent
me some lovely long ones. But do write often, even if it's terribly
shortly. I wake up in a dither about the postman. And don't you
think these accounts of cenobitic splendour mean I'm O.K. here
alone! I miss you the whole time my dearest angel and launch
armadas of kisses in the direction of Curzon Street, great hugs
and feverish clinches, and long, angelic, tender and gentle ones
as if we were on the verge of falling asleep tangled up together.

All my love to you, darling, mignonne, sweet Joan from
Paddy.[7]

Eventually, Paddy left St Wandrille de Fontanelle and its damp and
autumnal beech forests like Haut Brion. After all he had felt and
seen, he found his departure very hard.

If my first days in the Abbey had been a period of depression,
the unwinding process, after I had left, was ten times worse. The
Abbey was at first a graveyard; the outer world seemed afterwards, by contrast, an inferno of noise and vulgarity entirely
populated by bounders and sluts and crooks. This state of mind,
I saw, was perhaps as false as my first reaction to monastic life;
but the admission did nothing to increase its unpleasantness.
From the train which took me back to Paris, even the advertisements for Byrrh and Cinzano seen from the window, usually
such jubilant emblems of freedom and escape, had acquired the
impact of personal insults. The process of adaptation – in
reverse – had painfully to begin.[8]

In Paris, he met Joan for a few more days. After St Wandrille, Paddy was eager to experience another Benedictine monastery, so he went to Solesmes in the Sarthe. It was, however, much larger and more impersonal and he liked it far less. His and Joan's letters kept crossing.

Addressed to the Honble. Mrs Rayner, Dumbleton Hall, Evesham, Worcestershire; re-addressed to Flemmings Hotel, Half Moon Street, London, W1, postmark 6 December 1948 Paddy Leigh Fermor, Abbaye de St Jean de Solesmes, Sablé, Sarthe, Tuesday

Darling sweet little mite,

Thank you so much for your letter, and please forgive me for being so slow in writing. This is going to be in a terrific hurry, as the post is leaving the village in a few minutes. I'll write you a better one after Compline this evening.

Alas, I didn't get here till Sunday, as there was no through train on the day you left, and I didn't want another Rouen experience at the Mans, which sounds awful. On Friday Mr Kaye didn't appear at his office (ate and spent day on Thursday with the Pulhams', and bought the duffle coat for 3,000 but will send some more after your letter). Next day had lunch with Weingarten (author of 'pas de bon monture sans croisement de cheval.' Charming) and dinner with Lucienne. Saturday caught Mr K. But felt frightfully ill. It must have been Groddeck as I recovered at once on meeting François de la Rochefoucauld, who asked me to a St Germain-Balthus type existentialist party in his bedroom in the Montana, beginning at 1 a.m., if you please. Club St Germain then a wonderful party. He lives in a minute room with the beautiful Mlle. Schwob. 50 people came. (Please don't hate me.) He is our stern hostess's son, a great beauty and funny, and a capable musician. You will like him. (I repeat, rather timidly, no hatred, darling, please . . . !)

*Then here. A much dourer, more forbidding place than St W.
The plainsong is amazing, but, from every other point of view, it
is a dungeon compared to my old home. A lovely comfy room,
however, shaded lights, etc. But I don't want to stay long. Please
wire at once, my darling pet, and tell me any plans you have
made, and if I have time to stay 2 days at the Trappe. I can't
bear to stay away from you much longer. What about the
Betjemans?*

*My minute rodent, I love you and I miss you more than I
can say. Do let's get married and live happily forever. I simply
can't be without you. What a funny 3 months! You and your H.,
me and my abbeys, thank Heavens everything is alright now. I
wish this letter were not so hurried. Did you get my short letter
to Isabel Lambert's?* I do hope it went to the right number.
Write and [?] at once my dear little muskin.*

All, all my love to darling muskin & mopsa
From JEMY[9]

Paddy Leigh Fermor, Abbaye de St Jean de Solesmes, Sablé sur
Sarthe, Sunday night

My darling sweet angel,

*I'm feeling so gloomy tonight, I don't know why, and long to
be with you so that we could just curl up in a ball together and
snore our way through the night. It's frightfully cold and lonely
here, and I feel absolutely miserable [?] alone between these icy
sheets. Boo hoo.*

*I hoped there would be a letter from you and pelted down to
the gatehouse but only got a bill from London. I've been mon-
strously bad about writing, darling, and please forgive me. The*

---

* Isabel Delmer married Constant Lambert on 7 October 1947.

trouble is that the post goes at 3.30 in the afternoon, and as I'm
writing like anything, I always think that it's earlier and the
bloody thing has left by the time I get ready to write, so I put it
off till tomorrow thinking 'I'll write to the Rodent a really long
and fruity one tomorrow morning' etc. After this I'll send you
something every other day at the very least, and please, please,
darling, write to me absolutely constantly or I'll only get terribly
downcast, and you wouldn't like that.

Darling, what an unmitigatedly happy time we had in
Paris. Scarcely a moment of guilt or saturation or high-
town-blues. Once or twice at the very most, but the rest of it
sheer heaven. You were so sweet, my angel. I really could eat
you.

Do you remember, darling, Mr Monk talking about an
English trappist, ex-R.A.F. monk that he saw in Brittany? *
Well, he arrived here 3 days ago, an extraordinary man, about
my age, very slightly insane and absolutely enthralling. He got
shot down at Danzig, imprisoned, studied for the Anglican
church after his release, went over to Rome, and finally went to
the worst Trappe of the lot, Thermadenc in Brittany. He was
there for a year, couldn't stand it, and is on his way to the
Benedictines in the Isle of Wight. It wasn't the dead silence for
12 months that got him down, so much as the gruelling hard
work in the fields, digging up carrots, smashing stones, sorting
turnips, living the life of a navvy without a single moment's
solitude; and with monastic discipline from the dark ages. No
meat, fish, only veg. for meals, scarcely any sleep. He looks a
nervous wreck, wild eyes, chapped hands and broken nails, talks
the whole time – terribly well – and can't believe he's out of it.
He's a fascinating boy, extremely sensitive and well-educated, an

---

* The name of the monk was Henry Joseph Campbell.

omnivorous reader, a sculptor, a musician. He felt he had to go
to the furthest extreme in the Catholic faith 'to do penance' for
the misery of the world. His reading in Christian mysticism
carries him to all kinds of miseries and ecstasies. He is at the
moment gobbling up the works of St Dionysius the Areopagite,
his lips mumbling away and his eyes rolling. He has the most
dreadful doubts every now and then and careers into my cell to
ask for my advice. He told me the dream he had last night: 'I
was in a stable somewhere, they were saddling up a horse for
me. But the saddle hadn't got any stirrups! And by God! I
noticed the horse was getting smaller and smaller – shrinking
and shrinking until it was the size of the dog that pulled the
little milk-cart at the Trappe. I got on the thing, we set off at a
gallop. No stirrups and the horse shrieking all the time. Hell of
a job to stay on. Faster and faster. Then I noticed we were
heading for a small hole, about the size of a mouse's. I was still
hanging on somehow, and we were going like the wind. The
horse shoots through the hole and disappears and BANG! I
crash into the wall, knocked myself silly, and wake up. What do
you make of that?' What do you? Has it got a psychiatrical or a
mystical exegesis? Good old womb stuff, or headlong [into] the
mystic's inner chamber of one-ness with Godhead supported by a
diminishing spark of faith?[10]

I am working like anything at the moment and in spite of
Benzers feel absolutely exhausted. The books I read in the
intervals are a Flemish mediaeval mystic called Ruysbroek and
St Angela of Foligno who even surpasses Marie de l'Incarnation.
I would like to have a year doing nothing except read in an
enormous library with you somewhere. I feel I might use it
properly at last, instead of mucking about in the manner I have
done all my life so far. The time I have wasted makes me

shudder with horror. No hope, I'm afraid! Anyway, one would need 5 years.[11]

Joan Rayner, Hotel Normandie, Knightsbridge, S.W.1.

My darling sweet Paddy,

Thank you so much for your two lovely letters I got this week-end what a long time they take to come. This is not a proper letter because I very much hope that you will have left before it gets to you. Of course you were quite right to stay on as we can go to the Betjemans any time, and she was so busy this weekend you would hardly have seen her anyway. Do stay if you are enjoying yourself as I don't think you'll enjoy London much, but of course I am longing for you to come back selfishly. I have lots to tell you about houses, flats, friends, etc but I won't until I hear [what] your plans are & whether you are likely to get any more letters.

I've been really very bad about writing but I really thought you were only going to be a couple of days in Solesmes & I didn't know where to write to & I rather hated you for not sending me one word for so long.

How fascinating the RAF monk sounds – I'm longing to hear all about the Trappe. I'm so glad you are writing so much & I can't wait to see the Mayas. Darling, do you think you could get the book done by the end of Feb? Please try as then we could have the most wonderful Mediterranean spring (and summer?) bowling down in a tiny car to Sicily to meet Peter [Quennell] there about March 10th. Then Sicily for about 3 weeks (this is your holiday) then back slowly, you staying at all the places we want to see, you writing articles (Mr. Weiden- felt's[sic] idea) & me snapping. Then of course we might try to get to Greece. But if the book is not finished we won't be able to do all this. I intend to wall you up as soon as you arrive here in some terrible flat. As soon as we come back from our Mediterranean jaunt we sink into our own Georgian country house & I shall have tiny Fermors every year (if we ever get married). Oh dear, how nice it all sounds & now I've got to go to the Gargoyle to meet the H., Robin C. [Campbell] & Philip [Toynbee].

Christmas is always hell, & I shall have to go to Dumbleton, which is worse but if you came too it wouldn't be so bad & you could scribble away in comfort at least.

I may get Ian Fleming's flat on Jan 1st & that ought to be nice, but it's not certain yet.

My darling, darling angel I do love you so much & I am dying to see you & I don't want to see anyone else at all.

All my love from Joan.[12]

After leaving Solesmes, Paddy made for the austere Cistercian monastery of La Trappe, which he found far stranger. His curiosity had been aroused by its history but also by the ex-RAF postulant. A place of almost Kafkaesque inaccessibility, he was taken there through dark, drenching rain in a butcher's van which broke down twice in the middle of a moor. When he arrived, his cell was freezing cold and, apart from a bust of St Bernard, quite bare. The monks, including the abbot, slept in cubicles in a dormitory on palliasses of straw stretched out on wooden planks. They led lives of the utmost harshness and often, in the morning, High Mass was replaced by the Office of the Dead. 'In the daylight that followed my arrival,' Paddy wrote, 'the pale grey Trappe resembled not so much an abbey as a hospital, an asylum or a reformatory. It dwindled off into farm buildings, and came to an end in the fields where thousands of turnips led their secret lives and reared into the air their little frostbitten banners.'[13]

Monks communicated in sign language, but there was a special dispensation from the rule of silence for the monks who dealt with the abbey livestock when they were addressing their dumb charges. As the winter air grew colder and the puddles creaked with the first ice of winter, their world – 'Nordic, haggard and frightening' – became like that of Grünewald. Of the vows of poverty, chastity and obedience, Paddy felt that of chastity must be the hardest – although he was told by a Benedictine monk that hair-shirts, which were intended to quell desires, fell into disuse largely because they sometimes encouraged the dangers they were supposed to allay. Paddy did find, however, that all seemed quiet and peaceful, and the privacy of the individual silences was bridged by an authentic, brotherly love. Despite his initial revulsion at the 'sepulchral sadness' of outward appearances, the abbot and the two monks Paddy was able to speak to seemed disconcertingly normal and friendly. All had an indefinable air of benevolence and happiness. At the end of his stay he accompanied the abbot by bus to Paris, said his goodbyes to this dignified and completely unaffected man outside the doors of the Convent of Notre Dame de Cluny, then headed – profoundly mystified – through the rainy streets towards the Hôtel de la Louisiane in the rue de Seine.

'You are a beast not writing even a post card before,' Joan wrote to Paddy. 'I was beset with doubts & gloom & thought you must be concocting some appalling letter saying you never wanted to see me again. London is hell, of course, but I'm seeing a lot of nice people, although I feel very anti-social and really only want to settle down in the country.' Cyril had held a dinner party for the French artist Jean Hugo, whom Connolly had commissioned to do work for *Horizon*; afterwards they had a 'nice bitter conversation about religion'. He also gave a great party for Stephen Spender's return from America and T. S. Eliot's Nobel Prize. Seventy people were present (Paddy had been invited).

*Darling angel, I am longing to see you again so much and I do
think it would be lovely to get married awfully soon – I don't
think we will ever get anywhere the way we live at the moment
and I'm sure that we shan't feel any more tied than we are
already. So please come back soon – I'm very lonely without
you. Could you send me a telegram so that it arrives not later
than Monday morning c/o Betjeman, Farnborough, Wantage,
saying when you think you will be coming back and I'll try to
have somewhere nice for us to stay.*[14]

In December, Joan went to stay with her sister Patricia at Upham
Cottage, her new house in Hampshire (which despite its name had
eight bedrooms). She was married to Peter Kenward, the former
husband of the society columnist Betty Kenward, and Patricia's first
son, Robert, was now a few months old. When Joan left she put
simply a question mark as her address in the Upham Cottage visitors' book. It would be another twenty years before Joan and Paddy
married, and Joan never found a house in the country. However
many she saw, there was always something wrong: they were on a
railway line, or beside an aerodrome, or too poky. Although they
always had a home in Dumbleton, from 1949 on Paddy and Joan
lived either in London or Greece. And although both a caring aunt
and an affectionate godmother to the daughters of John Betjeman
and Cyril Connolly, Joan was never to have children of her own.
Some years later, when long past child-bearing age, she was introduced by Maurice Bowra to Alan Pryce-Jones's son, David, at a
cocktail party. 'You could have been mine,' she said to him.

11

Family Affairs

Even if he was yet to earn much money, Paddy was at last beginning to make a name for himself. In the summer of 1949, an article by him about the monastery of St Wandrille appeared in the *Cornhill*, a magazine edited by Peter Quennell and published by John Murray, and a second article, 'From Solesmes to la Grande Trappe', appeared in the new year. After his visits to the French monasteries, he wanted to visit monasteries further afield, and this became possible in 1950, when he and Joan were in Greece.

> Passing through Turkey some time after this expedition to the Trappe, I learnt that the remains of the old monastic community of Urgüb were only a few days' journey away. The site had been abandoned for centuries but, having always longed to see one of these desert monastic establishments of the Levant – so different from the convents of Western Europe but from which, after all, the whole of monasticism stems – I decided to see what it was like. The friend with whom I was travelling was equally eager for the journey, so, postponing a dozen alternative plans, we caught the train and set off.[1]

The 'friend' was Joan, and her photographs of the abandoned monasteries and the harsh, bleak landscape in which they were situated accompanied a third article, 'The Rock Mountains of Cappadocia', when it appeared later in 1950. Having at last abandoned the professional title of Joan Rayner, they were accredited as being the work of 'Joan Eyres Monsell'. She was delighted to have her work accepted but she would have liked to have been paid more: 'I had lunch with Peter yesterday after arranging about the snaps for the Urgub article, they are printing ten of them. It is rather maddening to think that if they were published in Picture Post I should be getting about £150 instead of £20.'[2]

In December 1950, *The Traveller's Tree* appeared at last, to considerable acclaim – it won the Heinemann Foundation Prize for Literature. When Joan wrote to Paddy in early January 1951 the book was already being reprinted, and Costa was going round rubbing his hands, saying he was going to be a millionaire. Harold Nicolson in the *Observer* called Paddy 'a natural romantic, having in his veins the ardour of the buccaneer'.[3] According to Alan Pryce-Jones, the review in the *Times Literary Supplement* was all the more extraordinary, as it was the only complimentary review its writer, Edward Cunard, had ever written – he was always 'crabbing'.[4]

Joan and Paddy fell into a way of living which required them to be separated for long periods. Paddy rarely seemed to stay anywhere for more than two months at a time at this period of his life: he seemed to need this stimulation. And so Joan was leading her own life. However in the summer of 1949 Joan found a flat to rent at 76 Charlotte Street in Fitzrovia. Her landlady was the mother of Barbara Warner, who was married to Rex Warner, Paddy's old boss in Greece. She felt she had a home there for the first time since leaving both her marriage and her flat in Palace Gate six years earlier. No doubt Joan found the long separations harder to accept than Paddy but she respected his urge to travel, which she shared, and his psychological need to write. And she wanted to encourage him. She wrote to Paddy who was in Cyprus with Lawrence Durrell:

What are you up to? I am dying of envy thinking of you all
staying with Larry – drinking in the sun – while I shuffle up
and down Charlotte Street in the rain with my shopping bag.
Do let me know how long you think of staying as I wouldn't
mind at all coming there myself a bit if I wouldn't spoil all your
fun . . . Should we take a great house together somewhere or
have you other plans by this time? I do long for a huge library
& not to have to pack every week. I really think I wouldn't be
too bad-tempered & nagging if we had enough rooms to our-
selves & it would be a good thing for you to have somewhere to
settle down and write. We could always try and see anyway. I'm
all for the country but Greece or England? I feel like staying 6
months in one place & then travelling. Anyway my darling, will
you please promise that you won't get tied up with journalism
with the Sun. Times. Everyone thinks that is sheer madness –
that you write far too well – it's the one thing that you should
try and avoid – how do you think Sir Thomas Browne would
have written if he had spent his days composing 'Leaving
soonest Athenwards etc.'[5]

Although willing to support Paddy's writing, Joan was still a professional photographer. In 1952, her pictures for Peter Quennell's
Spring in Sicily were published. 'A good number of excellent photographs,' wrote Edwin Muir in the *Observer*, but neither Rose
Macaulay in the *Listener* nor the anonymous reviewer in the *TLS*
mentioned them. A group of pictures Joan took of fire dancers at the
Anastenaria festival in northern Greece – old ladies and men holding bibles dancing on hot coals – also found a publisher, but some
of her photographs seem to have been done speculatively. A batch
of photographs of dusty statues taken in a cemetery in Genoa probably did not find a buyer, despite the scene catching Joan's eye and
imagination. The rather wonderful oddness of a roadside junk

dealer in Normandy, who sold uniformed mannequins, clearly delighted Joan, but unfortunately she does not seem to have found an outlet for their sale.

Photography, for Joan, was always a means to an end, preferably that of making an income, so she felt obliged to take whatever work came her way. In January 1952 she was offered an assignment in Ireland to take pictures for the Economic Cooperation Administration, the agency set up to implement the American Marshall Plan, which provided aid for the rehabilitation of post-war Europe. The project was going to pay her £200, money she regarded as useful, but in every other way the work lacked any job satisfaction whatsoever, let alone aesthetic gratification. After her arrival in Ireland, she wrote to Paddy from the Shelbourne Hotel in Dublin.

> *My darling Paddy*
>
> *What I am doing here, God knows. Nobody else does, apparently. How I wish you were here which you could have been, and then it would have been great fun. But as it is I am gloomy without you & it's no good trying to be alone in a town. I expected to be whisked off by my reporter at once but nothing seems to be arranged at all & I shall linger here for days. Derek Jackson asked me to stay for the week-end but it seems too complicated to arrange & I shall probably stay with Cracky Wicklow for Sunday. I was met at the aerodrome by Mr. Taft's large car – he seems very nice, tall, gangling, spectacled, entirely uninteresting & unattractive & not Mr. Right (or Wrong, for that matter). The same goes for the reporter Mr Brown. (NOT a drink even from either of them.) After long, pointless conversations & buying films etc. it was too dark to see much of Dublin but what I did see looked too lovely – Everyone talks with an Irish brogue too – I thought they only did that on the stage now – and is charming in shops etc. I had a room booked (small but*

a bath) in the grand hotel & was rather pleased to go to bed early. Of course the one thing I long for is your guide book – in fact I spent hours looking for a second hand book shop with one like it – no good of course – what a lunatic I am.

I spent all today photographing a drain being laid in a bog in a thick mist, & was driven about by Mr. Taft's fat Irish chauffeur who insisted on giving me a huge glass of whisky at every pub we passed with lots of winks & nudges in the ribs – I hope he's not going to get more familiar. We had lunch together in the back of a draper's store – tea and tinned salmon – & when we got home tonight he presented me with a quarter bottle of whisky to drink when I went to bed! Tomorrow I spend the day with Mr. Taft, a poultry farm first & then a place called Trim (oh for the guide book) where there are some ruins & a nice priest apparently whom he wants me to snap though what that has to do with ECA I don't know – it looks as though there is an ECA boat coming in then & they want pictures of it unloading. I don't know yet about Paris – if I have to go for money & photograph reasons it will save trouble to go from here but I shall only stay a few days so should be back anyway in England the beginning of the week after next – about the 6th. Do please give me the Abbé's address in case I go.

Darling sweet Paddy I do wish you were here –
All my love
Joan[6]

Paddy's reply came from Kent. He thanked Joan for her 'heavenly' letter – Paddy's language was typically effusive. 'Dear little muskin, what fun Ireland sounds. I'm reassured about Mr Taft and the ECA newshawk. I hope all your acquaintances achieved the same satisfactory level of dowdiness and non-glamour – though I suppose I ought to wish you the reverse under our new pact of liberty. But I can't quite manage that yet. The whisky swilling driver sounds heaven.'[7] The 'pact of liberty' implies that Paddy and Joan now had an agreement where each could take lovers should they wish, although this agreement had yet to be tested. In his letter, Paddy went on to say that he had just finished Patrick Kinross's latest book when the telephone rang, and a female voice asked for Joan. 'It turned out to be Angela ex-K. [ex-Kinross], asking you and me to a party that evening. I went, of course, and wish you'd been there, because there were Patrick and Angela laughing away in front of the fire with their arms interlocked like the most inseparable friends. It was a problem to know whether to press her hand in silent commiseration or to wring Patrick's in congratulation.' While Paddy and Joan had just made an arrangement for an open relationship, Angela – for whom no marriage had ever been closed – was, as ever, in between lovers.

One of her future lovers was the same Derek Jackson that Joan had been trying to meet in Dublin. Jackson was a brilliant physicist who was able to fund his own research into spectroscopy from his considerable personal wealth. During the war he had been made chief airborne radar officer of Bomber Command. In all he flew 1,100 hours on active service and was subsequently awarded an OBE for valour. However, being by disposition fiercely independent, in 1943 he offered his home in Oxfordshire to his brother- and sister-in-law – Sir Oswald and Diana Mosley – on their release from internment. Diana Mosley was the sister of Jackson's wife, Pamela Mitford. In 1947, Jackson moved to Ireland to avoid what he saw as the punitive taxation imposed by Clement Attlee's incoming government. In 1951, his marriage to Pamela dissolved, he married Janetta Kee – the former wife of the journalist Robert Kee – but left her, too, to live in Paris with Janetta's half-sister, Angela Culme-Seymour.

Joan wrote again from Shelton Abbey a few days after her first letter to Paddy. The Abbey was the home of 'Cracky' Clonmore, the

8th Earl of Wicklow, a jovial Catholic convert as well as an old Oxford friend of John Betjeman and Evelyn Waugh. It was the Abbey, Betjeman claimed, which had made him interested in Gothic revival architecture.

Darling Moleskie Paddakimou

Thank you for your sweet telegram. I do wish you were here – I seem to have got stuck in Ireland now but really am dying to leave. The trouble is that planes go direct to Paris on Weds & Sats only – couldn't catch last Wednesday & then longed to come here (Shelton Abbey) to stay with Cracky Wicklow so now shall have to leave Wednesday – I'm sick of Dublin but luckily Derek Jackson will be there on Monday & I shall be able to have a rich meal with him. I stayed with them last weekend after all (this is their writing paper) & it was quiet & pleasant. Then all the week I've been photographing bogs, peat moss, factories & nearly going off my head with the horror of it all. It's the last time I do anything like this. Luckily Mr Brown the reporter (whom I've only been out with 3 days) dislikes the whole thing as much as I do & we drink a lot of whisky to get through the day.

I've had some good meals in Dublin & been to the Abbey Theatre & a nice music hall with Cracky – The Abbey[Theatre] so boring – a modern Irish small town comedy – that we left after one act. Do you know Henry Clifton? He is in Dublin, raving & nearly dangerous, but luckily seems to be bedridden at the moment. He sends me flowers and telephones me at 8 in the morning spiritual messages.

This is a wonderful house – Strawberry Hill Gothick – enormous – which Cracky turned into a hotel about 2 years ago when his father died, to be able to keep it up. Freezingly cold at the moment as no central heating but nice fires everywhere.

I'll see you at the end of the week or the beginning of next, I

pray – it does seem a long time somehow – please don't disap-
pear altogether, my darling.
Best love & hugs & kisses xxx xxx[8]

Among Joan's Irish photographs there are pictures of a couple of country houses which have fallen on hard times, a drainage works and a woman driving a pig along a street. Shortly after her stay the hotel failed; Cracky was declared bankrupt and moved to a flat in Dublin. Shelton Abbey and its contents were sold, and the Irish state turned the Strawberry Hill Gothick masterpiece into an open prison.

If she was in London by herself without any plans for the evening Joan would go round to Graham's house, play the gramophone, and drink his excellent hock – Graham prided himself on his knowledge of white wine. Since Paddy was so often travelling – as if to stay in one place too long was some kind of psychological impossibility – Joan's visits to Graham were likely to have been frequent. On many other evenings, however, there was a cocktail party or a dinner party to attend and her letters to Paddy include lists of fellow guests and who she saw or what she talked about:

> *Annie [Fleming] is about to leave for Jamaica. She had a nice*
> *small supper party last weekend after Freddie's [Frederick*
> *Ashton] two new ballets on Thursday; Lucian [Freud], Pandora*
> *Jones, Ann Norwich's sister who he appears to be having an*
> *affair with while Caroline is still in Ireland, Margot [Fonteyn],*
> *Fred, a few of the ballet, Willie Walton, Evelyn Waugh who I*
> *talked to most of the time, mostly about the time he went mad*
> *& all his voices – fascinating.*[9]

She apologized for gossiping, but Paddy's letters to Joan also included similar lists. However much they wanted peace and silence, both were social creatures, and although self-effacing, Joan enjoyed good company.

Often her evenings ended up in the Gargoyle Club in Dean Street – the heart of Soho – which was only a short walk away now that she was living in Charlotte Street. Entry to the Gargoyle, which had been opened at great expense in the 1920s by David Tennant, was by a rickety lift no bigger than a telephone box. The lift led to a bar, a coffee room and a drawing room, and then, down a rather precarious staircase, there was a ballroom. The band was not very good, but it played continually and with enthusiasm tunes like 'Bye-bye Blackbird' or 'Melancholy Baby'. Membership cost three guineas, but if you were penniless you could probably get in for free, and no one minded what anyone wore: what mattered was that you were interesting. The Gargoyle was a resort of artists, writers and their friends, and the atmosphere was distinctly raffish. It had been decorated by Matisse, who had covered the walls with fragments of eighteenth-century mirrors and hung two of his own paintings. 'There used to be something marvellous about the Gargoyle,' Francis Bacon said.

When people came down the staircase the broken mirrors made them look like birds of paradise. The Gargoyle was a place where people could let their hair down, and it was famous for its rows. It was a place made for rows, and some of the members would come back every evening to continue their row or to listen to someone else's. Of course the rows were usually to do with unhappy love affairs, and what is more fascinating for onlookers than what's called other people's unhappy love affairs?[10]

As Joan wrote:

I went to the Gargoyle Club several times, of course, & now never want to go again. David [Tennant] very drunk, Pauline

[Tennant] having a tremendous affair with Micky Luke, Julian
Baines with a black eye Natalie had given him for talking to
Pauline, Ann Dunn tearing Sally Newton's hair & eyes out
because she was talking to Cyril & having her dress torn off by
Mr Blackburn – all very much the same, but enjoyable, as I was
with Graham one night, then Barbara and Rex [Warner], &
Jeremy for one moment, & then the next night with Peter Q. I
saw Xan & he seemed quite well.*[11]

Francis Bacon was a new friend – Paddy always sent him his books
in the years to come. In the spring of 1950, Paddy had gone to Portugal and, only an hour after his arrival, he found himself in a wine
shop off one of the minor squares of Lisbon – 'an atmosphere,
sympa (as they say), and promising', where he started drafting a
letter to Joan. The evening before his departure from Liverpool, he
had been drinking brandy in David Tennant's flat with Philip Toynbee, Derek Jackson and Francis Bacon. Paddy began to draft a letter
to Joan in his notebook:

*David was entirely un-boring and informative about Spain, we
were all rather drunk. Derek and Francis exchanged pecks
between drinks like two bullfinches in a cage. It was rather
sweet, and utterly un-rebarbative. Derek (all of us drunk) [After
this the conversation must have turned more intimate and
personal, for Paddy has heavily crossed through some of the lines
which follow. From what one can make out Derek seems to have
told Paddy that he found Joan very attractive . . .]
    (So different from your smarmy-hostile humanist). I said of
course I understood, and I do. You can't own somebody. And, my*

---

* Michael Luke (1925–2005), habitué of the Gargoyle Club and author of *David
Tennant and the Gargoyle Years* (1991).

darling, your minor-planetary beams are not the fault of you, or
of the fellow stars they illuminate, and turn into satellites –
anyway, the mists and monsoons and upheavals are only for the
closest of them, the ones in the position to see the mutual craters
and deserts and blank stellar cordilleras. I see yours as plainly
as you see mine, and love you very much.[12]

Bacon also met Isabel Delmer at the Gargoyle. Isabel's relationship
with Giacometti had only lasted a few months, and she had returned
from Paris to London. She and Giacometti remained friends, and
she introduced him to Bacon – he was one of the few living artists
Bacon would admit to admiring. Isabel became part of Bacon's close
circle and he painted her often. Like other artists before her, he
found her an excellent model and, in his work, she became one of
the twisting, screaming, tormented figures pressed up against the
glass which he painted; contorted images of a former lover which,
as it happened, John Rayner always hated. Isabel and Francis even
tried having sex together but, predictably, this was a failure. Aged
thirty-five and looking around for another husband among her
circle of friends, in late 1946 she met Constant Lambert in Paris –
she had been introduced to him at Sadler's Wells by John Rayner.
He had been having an affair with Margot Fonteyn, but the following October he married Isabel. Fonteyn was on tour when she found
out – and, later, rarely spoke about her past relationship. Years
afterwards Isabel said, 'Constant thought if he married me I would
bring him back to life. His friends thought so too. He was a sad man
and a sick man. He had been a public figure since a very young
man, had acquaintances of all kinds, only few close friends.'[13] But it
was too late to save him from himself. 'Constant is back on the
bottle and is an intolerable bore. I think poor I. is getting quite fed
up although she behaves angelically towards him,'[14] Joan wrote to

Paddy. Constant Lambert died in August 1951, two days before his forty-sixth birthday, an ill and prematurely aged man.

By the late 1940s, Cyril Connolly had fallen out of love with Lys Lubbock and was looking around for someone new. He became besotted with a young painter called Anne Dunn, but in 1950 she married Michael Wishart, another artist (the party for the wedding took place in Francis Bacon's studio and lasted two days and three nights: 'I was *immensely* drunk, and I found myself reclining in a pool of vomit,' wrote Paddy). However, around the same time Barbara Skelton re-entered his life. During the war, at the suggestion of Donald Maclean, she had been a cipher clerk in Cairo; King Farouk had been a lover and used to whip her with his dressing-gown cord. 'One glance explained the abundant notches in her tomahawk,' wrote Wishart, with whom she also had an affair. 'As feline in appearance as she later proved in character, she had a tantalising quality of needing a tamer, while something indefinable about her suggested she was untameable.'[15]

The relationship between Connolly and Barbara, or 'Baby', as she was known, was often unhappy but always eventful and, as an intimate of Cyril, Joan kept Paddy informed about the convolutions of the affair. In July 1950, before they had started living together, Barbara wrote in her diary that Cyril had rung her early in the morning to say that he had spent the greater part of the night allotting marks to all the women of his circus, according to their suitability as wives. 'I, of course, got fewer than any of them for spirituality, but had top score for sex appeal, followed by Sonia Orwell, who had tremendous appeal in a blowsy sort of way when blotto. Lys and Joan got top marks for loyalty and giving him a sense of security.'[16] Joan and Barbara were never to get on. Over a couple of pages in her published diaries she complained that Joan 'groans and sighs', is 'grumpy as hell', 'gets whiney', 'looks cross'. In the photograph of

Joan she used for the book, Joan is on her knees with her bottom in the air and her back to the camera.

In October 1950, Cyril and Barbara married in Kent, where Barbara owned a cottage between Canterbury and Folkestone. They had a row in the car on their way home; Barbara was late for a dentist's appointment. A couple of days later she went into her bedroom to find Cyril staring into space. 'What's the matter?' she asked. 'It's marriage,' he answered. 'I feel trapped.' In January 1951, Joan invited the couple to a dinner party she was holding for the Berniers in Charlotte Street. Afterwards she wrote to Paddy:

> *I think they enjoyed it very much, everyone stayed for ages, nice and tipsy but no one terribly drunk. The last left about five – Robin [Ironside], John Russell and [Denys] Sutton, Derek and Johnny after masses of bacon and eggs and religious conversation. Skelton left before C, the only one not to enjoy it in a furious temper of course, although C could not have been kinder to her, and when he got home about 4 she had locked him out of the flat. It took him about an hour to get in after nearly being arrested, and then apparently he socked her good and proper and slept on the sofa in the sitting room. Robin [Campbell] and I were going to lunch there but C met us at an exhibition in a frightful state, asking us what he was to do, longed to leave but nowhere to go, couldn't be alone etc, Barbara was still in bed crying so C went home to lunch alone to make up his mind and Robin and I went to Smidts* to join Mary and Donald Maclean.*[17]

Paddy replied from Greece: 'Poor Cyril, it sounds a bloody life. The more I think of it, the more suitable (in a way) it seems, from Cyril's

---

* Schmidt's Restaurant, Charlotte Street.

Roman Silver Age point of view. There must be a lot in common between Skeltie and Catullus's Lesbia and Prop.'s Cynthia.'[18]

At the end of December 1953, the Connollys went to stay at Stokke near Great Bedwyn in Wiltshire, the home of Robin and Mary Campbell, for the New Year. Frances and Ralph Partridge and Janetta Jackson* came over on New Year's Eve. Afterwards Barbara wrote:

We have just spent four horrible days at the Campbells. I never wanted to go, but was tricked into it. The other guests, Joan and Freddie Ayer. Vast unheated house like a boys preparatory school, a twin-bedded room with a two-barred fire giving out no heat. No privacy and Robin bursting in at all hours without knocking, bringing someone with him to inspect his dead father's suits, a chest of silver and a cupboard full of shoes [. . .] Robin, who doesn't like me, is all the time on the nag. To make conversation, knowing Joan to be interested in cooking, I say, 'Do you ever use any cooking GADGETS?' She gives me a cold stare and drawls, 'Only a FORK.' In order to rouse them, I suggest the inherited silver tea caddy (left by Robin's father) would be pretty gilded; Joan does not approve of any metals being made to seem what they're not. I think to myself that she should be made to take a course of cleaning silver solidly for a year [. . .] What is it? Conceit? Complacency? Just don't feel I've got anything to say to anybody. Robin's puritanism a drag. Seems to disapprove of all his friends' wives; in fact he's uncharitable about most women. Joan, though, is sacred (well-bred, intelligent, has a private income, is a generous provider of food and drink. Has the right friends . . . Maurice Bowra . . . Cyril . . . is also considered to be a beauty! And is too bluestocking to take an interest in CLOTHES!).[19]

* Janetta Woolley (b. 1922); m. Humphrey Slater; Robert Kee; Derek Jackson; Jaime Parladé.

Frances Partridge said that Barbara could be 'aggressively silent'. In 1955, Barbara, who liked fat men, began an affair with George Weidenfeld, Cyril's new publisher and also the publisher of Barbara's first novel (which was dedicated to Cyril). Cyril was devastated and the affair became the talk of literary London. Joan wrote:

> *Weidenfeld has got cold feet & says he will not marry Baby so she has gone scuttling off to Tangiers to meet Cyril there. I'm sick to death of the whole thing but I do give her top marks for determination, not only for making Cyril thoroughly miserable & stopping him writing, talking & seeing his friends but also making him not enjoy anything & stopping other people enjoying anything too.*

Eventually Cyril and Baby divorced, naming Weidenfeld as co-respondent. She and Weidenfeld did marry, but that marriage did not last either and Barbara took other lovers; Connolly was named as co-respondent when Weidenfeld and Baby divorced. (In 1966 Barbara became Derek Jackson's sixth wife but the marriage only lasted a year.)

In the circles within which Paddy and Joan moved divorce and remarriage were commonplace. Divorced couples might resume perfectly amicable relationships afterwards. Homosexuality was also regarded as a perfectly acceptable way of life. In 1954 the trial and conviction of Peter Wildeblood, Michael Pitt-Rivers and Lord Montagu of Beaulieu for conspiracy to commit acts of gross indecency (the first use of the charge since the trials of Oscar Wilde) had become a cause célèbre, which attracted both sympathy and abuse, and a considerable amount of sanctimonious press coverage. Paddy published a letter in the *Spectator** advocating homosexual toleration and hoping for a change in the law: 'There are three

---

* So ardent was the *Spectator* for homosexual reform that it was accused of being 'The Buggers' Bugle'.

prerequisites to most reforms: the maturing of public opinion, a sort of tribal guilty conscience and a courageous legislator.'[20]

While such liberal attitudes were taken as a given by Paddy and Joan, Paddy was also at heart a traditionalist and a romantic royalist. He adored pomp and circumstance, uniforms, titles and honours, together with all the weight of history they carried, as well as all the flummery and fancy dress that went with them – the more exotic and ludicrous the better. After the death of King George VI in February 1952, he wrote to Patrick Kinross from Gadencourt, where he had listened to the funeral ceremony on the World Service. As Baron Kinross and a member of the House of Lords, Patrick was entitled to attend the coronation of Queen Elizabeth II the following year.

> I listened in most of yesterday to the Royal Funeral, and for someone like me who reacts to these things exactly like a scullery maid, it was almost too much – a knot in the throat for 6 hours on end. Bosuns' pipes, cannon booming, the sound of horses' hoofs, clink of bits, muffled drums and distant pibrochs . . . Phew! The mention of the emerald Henry V had worn at Agincourt glittering on the crown on the bier was a dangerous moment. You'll have to be shaking the moths out of your ermine soon if, as I hope, you're taking part in the Coronation. You really mustn't miss it.[21]

Joan was much more sceptical. She wrote to Paddy:

> The King's death was taken in widely opposite ways by our friends – some in deepest mourning & behaving as though they had lost a relation & others, alas, with ribaldry. For me it doesn't make the slightest difference materially to life here – it was only maddening that the whole time I was at [Dumbleton] the 3rd programme was stopped – what balls – & the scherzo was cut out of Vaughan Williams' 4th symphony. I didn't see

any processions or even the lying in state, though if I'd known
that (daughter of a lord!) I could have walked in at the side
door & not have to wait in the queue I would certainly have
gone. Annoying not having taken advantage of a rare privilege.[22]

Although strongly anti-communist, Paddy was not otherwise political and he probably never voted in his life. He and Joan had friends
of all political persuasions, and of none, but of Paddy's close British
friends only George Jellicoe and the Duke of Devonshire were
politically involved (both served as Conservative ministers, although
Andrew Devonshire later joined the Social Democratic Party).
People were always interesting, however. Paddy once wrote to Joan
from Lismore, the castle the Devonshires owned in Ireland: 'Sir O.
Mosley arrived unannounced. He has an alarming, perhaps uncon-
scious, perhaps would-be hypnotic, characteristic of suddenly lifting
his upper eyelids so that a white rim appears over the pupil. Thank
God, no politics [. . .] A v. quiet, charming manner and style; but
curiously eerie. I'm glad to have seen him.'[23]

The social and political changes which affected the nation came –
literally – close to home in other ways. Throughout the years of
Paddy's roaming in the late 1940s and the 1950s and her own travels
for work or to see Paddy or visit friends, Dumbleton Hall had always
remained very much part of Joan's life. Yet if she had sought in it
permanence or refuge she would have been disappointed. Indeed, as
she must have known, its sale was already being discussed before the
end of the war. In June 1945, Joan's brother-in-law, Colonel Tim
Casey, was in Schleswig in north Germany dealing with the German
Air Force. He wrote to his wife Diana that 'Yes Dumbleton should be
sold, really hard as it may be for you. It belongs to a different age, not
in the world we are going to be left. I fear most soldiers and airmen
will vote Labour and I shouldn't be surprised to see Labour in at all.'[24]

This opinion was widespread. In the same year, Evelyn Waugh published *Brideshead Revisited*, when it seemed to him, as he added in a later preface, 'that the ancestral seats which were our chief national artistic achievement were doomed to decay and spoliation like the monasteries in the sixteenth century'. Although Dumbleton Hall was not exactly an ancestral seat – the Eyres Monsells had only lived in it for sixty years – it remained the heart of a family estate. Like Waugh – and many others – Casey imagined that an incoming social-ist government would tax such houses out of existence: sentiment alone would not be sufficient to save it. During the Second World War country houses were at a premium, because they were found to be adaptable for so many other uses, but that brief period was at an end.

Graham had ended the war as a lieutenant colonel. In September 1943 he was mentioned in dispatches and had been recommended for an MBE for his services during the planning of Operation Torch. He had also been awarded the United States Medal of Freedom with Bronze Palm. Five years later he was still in the army, serving in intelligence with the British troops. He wrote to Alan Pryce-Jones, who had just been appointed editor of the *Times Literary Supplement*:

> *Vienna was drab and full of displaced persons and were it not for the music life would be unbearable. It is all 'married families' now and there is very little fun. I find as I get older I am less and less dependent on gaiety but I do like to see a pretty face from time to time.*[25]

Alan and his wife Poppy never went back to live in Austria. Poppy's family failed to recover most of their property – the Fould-Springer lands and houses in the east were confiscated by the communists.

Graham was also involved with the repatriation of POWs to the Eastern Bloc – many to their deaths – which caused him lasting damage. The emotional ordeal brought about another nervous breakdown, from which he never fully recovered. When he at last returned to England in the late 1940s it was to take on his duties as the only son and the heir to the Dumbleton estate. His father – once universally regarded in the press as – 'the best-looking and best-dressed man in Parliament' – was a serial womanizer. By the end of the 1940s, his marriage was over, and he had moved out of the Hall. Joan wrote that she and Graham were there alone with their mother and it was very pleasant. In May 1950 a decree nisi was granted on the grounds of adultery, and after forty-six years of marriage, Bolton and Sybil divorced. Two months later, in July, Bolton remarried. His new wife, Essex Drury, a divorcee, was a granddaughter of Sir John French, who had been ennobled after the First World War as the first Earl of Ypres. Essex had been a contemporary of Diana at St James's School in the 1920s – both Diana and Joan detested her. At Christmas, however, she always gave her husband's grandchildren boxes of chocolates, so they appreciated her rather more. Bolton's family regarded the divorce as a great scandal and they sided with Sybil. She, however, would never have a word said against him.

Straight after the divorce, Joan wrote to Paddy from Dumbleton: 'Mummy went to Scotland after the case – it's all rather difficult & I have such a violent reaction I find it hard to be kind & polite. Oh dear.'[26] After years of trying to have as little to do with her family as possible, Joan now found herself taking on responsibilities. The next year she wrote again to Paddy, who was in Greece:

I had meant to set off about the end of this week but my poor mama has fallen down and cracked two bones in her back and so has to lie in bed without moving for three weeks. It's all very difficult and a ghastly bore especially for her, but I must stay on for a week or two longer to be able to go and see her and not leave it all to Graham. It is really too depressing for him being there all alone at the weekend and having to sit with her. Oh dear, and I

*am longing to see you again and think of retsina, sun and flowers
which I'm terrified of missing. Do, my darling, write at once and
tell me where you are and if you are going on any journeys.*[27]

While she became more protective towards her mother and sometimes referred to her in her letters as 'Mummy' instead of 'the
Viscountess', she could still find her trying.

*The V. is in a terrible state about servants etc. The cook's hus-
band has been badly burnt in a factory explosion, the chauffeur's
wife has gone mad, Spenser [sic] has got a septic leg after the
removal of a 1914 bullet, the Spensers [sic] want to leave because
the housemaids are black, & the housemaids want to leave
because the Spensers [sic] tell them they are – Oh for the
Greeks.*[28]

When they were at Dumbleton Joan and Paddy stayed in bed until
11.30. The staff did not approve. Joan's attempts at keeping up a
relationship with her father remained difficult. He called to see her
one evening while Betjeman happened to be visiting. When Bolton
left they all fell about laughing. In January 1955, Paddy received a
typed letter from Dumbleton. Typed, Joan said, because she found
it quicker than writing.

*TYPEWRITER? There is not much time. And do get all your
reading done in Athens (if any) before I come as I don't think I
shall want to be there many days but you must promise to meet
me as I couldn't bear to be alone there. Do write soon and send
it to 20 Chesham Place, SW1, as I shall be there until I go, with
weekends here of course. I haven't yet told my mother that I am
coming back as she seems in a dreadful state about everything
and we have lots of hysterical conversations about selling*

Dumbleton because no-one wants to be here etc . . . Mr V
[Viscount Monsell] seems to be behaving even more shittishly
than was predicted. Needless to say he is the only one not losing
any money, but he also seems to be arranging things so that
everyone else loses a great deal more than they need. He appar-
ently has a kind of charmed effect on even the toughest lawyers
and Graham seems the only one who can contradict him at all.
G. says he's quite mad and the lies and crookedness which he
thinks he can get away with are unbelievable. ALL THIS IS
STRICTLY CONFIDENTIAL.[29]

However detached Joan felt from her family, and however little they
seemed to share her interests, she was bound to them all the same.
Paddy was so rarely in England, that the family must have seen very little
of him, if at all, which can hardly have increased their confidence in
Joan's elusive lover. Paddy himself was not the most attentive of sons or
brothers. He wrote regularly to his mother and his sister Vanessa but did
not see much of them. Joan, despite her complaints, was more caring.
'I am not going to [Dumbleton] this weekend as Mummy will be away;
rather a waste of virtue but I am acquiring some more but getting off a
whole lot of family,' she wrote to Paddy at the beginning of 1956.

Lunch with Bridget (Diana's second daughter) today & a film
'Bel Ami', rather good & Bridget enchanting; so pretty & gay &
having a wonderful life with swarms of young men. Lunched with
Patricia & Robert [Patricia's eldest son] on Thursday & a morning
with them at the Natural History Museum. Robert very intelli-
gent, knowing everything about fossils. Far more interested by that
than the circus we went to in the afternoon. Wednesday Graham
& I took Sir B. to Brown's for lunch & we went to Les Diaboliques
after. Very good. Did you see it? Tomorrow lunch with Aunt

Molly! Rather wonderful isn't it? I've still got Anna to get through.[*][30]

So, unable to be a mother, Joan could at the very least be a good aunt. In 1957, Joan's younger sister, Patricia, died, leaving a husband, Peter Kenward,[†] and three young sons, and the following year Tim Casey died from a heart attack while out riding, and Diana was left a widow with a son and three daughters. Peter Kenward and Diana had rowed and did not speak to one another. Kenward, whose father had been a brewer, was a heavy drinker. He married again but his new wife showed little maternal feeling towards her newly acquired stepchildren. It was Joan who encouraged her young nephew Robert in his interest in natural history, an interest she shared, and fossils became a standard birthday or Christmas gift. They also went collecting – on a trip to the island in the middle of the lake at Dumbleton Hall, Joan distracted the swans by feeding them while Robert raided their nest. (He was only allowed to take one egg.) To Robert's older cousin, Michael, Joan was always the wonderfully exotic younger aunt who periodically drifted in to stay with the family in Rutland. She dressed in a fashion not seen in the country and looked amazing, not at all like his mother, Diana, who he was more used to seeing feed the hens. All too soon Joan was gone again, but not before they had all received some beautiful little present.

Eventually it was agreed that the Hall should be sold, and in 1959 it was bought by the Post Office Fellowship of Remembrance which, as a memorial to the fellow workers who had died during the two world wars, provided holidays and convalescence for Post Office workers. Graham moved into the Mill House, which had formerly

---

* Aunt Molly was an unmarried younger sister of Bolton, much loved by all the family. Anna was Diana Casey's eldest daughter.
† Peter Kenward's first wife was Betty Kenward, who wrote 'Jennifer's Diary' in *The Tatler*.

been occupied by the estate's land agent. The house was to be shared as a country home with Joan and Paddy. Joan wrote:

> *As you see I have a new & glorious Olivetti. I thought that one between us might lead to trouble. Goodness how I want to come and join you in your castle when you get there. London seems more and more depressing for words. If it was only nice weather I could live in Mill House for ever, it's going to be so nice and cosy. I am longing for you to see it though I'm afraid it may be pretty funny with Graham's and my despair at decorating and the occasional obvious help of G's smart London interior decorator. But I shall have to be here a bit longer as I think G would really give up altogether if left alone with MH, Dumbleton and the V and it would be too unkind. It has all been absolutely dreadful, the V getting desperately ill just in the middle of moving, refusing to give up, rushing up and downstairs sorting out 80 years of rubbish, saying there was nothing the matter and then being carted off to Cheltenham Hospital. Ivy [Compton-Burnett] mixed with Chekhov. She is better at the moment and we are having a badly needed rest in London but I fear it may all begin very soon. Two more weekends at D then we shall have to picnic in the MH to get things sorted out. I think it will be a very good place to work if you want to be in England.*[31]

After she left Dumbleton, Sybil moved to Weymouth Street in Marylebone, but died in hospital a few months later, on Christmas Day 1959. Graham and Joan were 'oddly shattered', Paddy told Annie Fleming, 'mostly, I think, through feelings of filial duties left undone in the past; completely baselessly. If you didn't see, do write two lines to Joan, as I overheard a conversation between them say-ing they wished they had always written to people in the past in like circumstances, because – against all their principles – it gives tremendous pleasure.'[32]

12

In Love with Greece

In 1949, the civil war in Greece came to an end. Although the country was far from healed, it could begin to recover. From 1950 onwards, Paddy and Joan spent as much time as possible travelling around the country; it was as if they felt drawn back – whether stated or not – by the urge to live there permanently. In 1951 they explored for the first time the Mani, the central of the three peninsulas which stretch down from the Peloponnese. They came upon Kardamyli – this little castellated village by the edge of the sea was unlike anything they had seen before. The upper village enclosed the remains of a Venetian castro built high above the dry river bed, and inside its walls there was an eighteenth-century church with a tall, steepled campanile and houses which looked like miniature castles built of golden stone with medieval-looking pepper-pot turrets. The whole village was a fusion of Byzantine, Venetian and Turkish styles. Great whitewashed amphorae for oil or wine stood at the doorways of the houses. At the water's edge, among the fishermen's homes, there were high rustling groves of calamus reed and fishing nets looped across the trees. Joan took photographs of the skeletons of boat hulls under construction, as well as of the men drinking in a bar. According to legend, Kardamyli was one of seven cities offered by Agamemnon to Achilles to induce him to rejoin the fight during the Trojan War. And it was here that Neoptolemus, the son of Achilles, landed on his way to Sparta, to ask for the hand of Hermione, the daughter of King Menelaus.

To their surprise, Paddy and Joan found an acceptable small hotel in rooms over a grocer's shop. There was a comfortable bed and some wicker chairs. The owner, Socrates Phaliréas, was a gigantic man but a civilized host, and it turned out that he was the cousin of a sculptor friend in Athens. The little town of Kardamyli felt welcoming and leisurely; the weather was temperate, protected from the harsh northern winds by the screen of the Taygetus mountains. The following morning, as he was drinking his tea outside in the street, Paddy was thinking of the Mourtzini and Palaeologi – the ancient hereditary rulers of Byzantium. He asked when the last of the Mourtzinos family had died out. He was informed that, far from being dead, the last of them, a fisherman named Strati, lived down the street. Indeed, Strati was sitting in his cottage doorway, busy making a fish trap. From this a conversation ensued – from which Paddy built up an exotic fantasy about returning Strati to his rightful place as Emperor of Constantinople: 'the generous strength of a second glass of ouzo accelerated these cogitations.' By the end of the discussion the bottle was empty and the caïque for Areopolis was leaving. Paddy said that he already felt inclined to settle in the small hotel with his books and his papers. Too remote to fear an influx of tourists, this would be a good place to live and to write. In his notebook, he wrote that the pillows on the bed were unlike the usual cannonballs and that Kardamyli, in its own quiet way, was perfect. He also wrote that when they left that afternoon a slow drizzle had begun and Joan and he quarrelled. ('I grumbling because she grumbled so.')

The caïque disembarked at the little port of Limeni. To reach Areopolis, they ascended winding steps 'through olives, angle after angle, till at last a straight road led into the little Maniot capital . . . Cool mountain, heady air. "Welcome" from everybody. (Police at once appear with telegram: "O.K!").' He continued:

Airy feeling of a plateau town like Guatemala City and amazing one of remoteness. Stroll along gently sloping cobbled main street, murmurs of welcome from groups sitting out round tables. Joan's eye caught by a big round wicker hat. Woman behind counter beckoned her in.

JOAN: 'How much?'
WOMAN: 'Ten . . . twelve . . . fifteen.'
DEEP MAN'S VOICE BEHIND COUNTER: 'Ten.'
A bit of tape was fitted on to tie under the chin.
JOAN: 'Well how much now.'
WOMAN: 'Ten for the hat . . . let me see . . . and then with the tape.'
MAN, gruffly: 'Ten.'[1]

Greece had taken hold of Paddy and Joan's imagination but it would take more than a decade, during which they were often separated for long periods and leading very different lives, before they could settle there permanently.

Paddy's notebooks came in all shapes, sizes and covers, and in them – amidst lists of names and telephone numbers – he noted down private thoughts, reflections and fragments of conversations. In a diary he kept at Gadencourt, dated December 1951, he wrote 'Girl in the Pergola: Presque tous les noirs sont dérogés. [illegal] ??? What does she mean?'

Paris. How I hate it all of a sudden.

The aim of climbing: to appear to take for granted what you don't at all take for granted. Remedy [sic] for success: (a) Charm and an innate lack of cynicism. (b) I have awareness that I hardly believe in.

Get the French book about Greece from DIVAN.*

See FREYA in Paris.

In the looking-glass room. 'What are you doing?' 'Sucking my breath in so the ribs will show.'

How badly translated slang and banter comes off. All except originals alas. The cliché doesn't survive translation.

So-and-so is a good old-fashioned bigoted atheist, so please keep off the subject. You know how susceptible people are and it's so easy to hurt his feelings. It gives him something to hang on to – an anchor in life, you see.[2]

Occasionally, although not often, Paddy mentions Joan. Relations between them were not always easy, in this period and throughout their lives. There are allusions to rows and arguments in Paddy's journals, but not their causes. Perhaps because they were apart so often, when they were together there were sometimes difficulties in adapting to one another. They were, after all, very different people. Paddy sometimes roused Joan from her natural reserve into powerful emotion. In the autumn of 1950, for example, they were exploring northern Greece. One evening in October, they had come from a village lived in by Pomaks or Slavic Muslims and arrived in Xanthi, a large city close to the Turkish border. Paddy wrote:

Lute-playing Turk. (Gypsy?) Strangely renaissance-looking instrument. Pleasant sitting in muleteers café – vine trellis outside, smell of cooking. Sunlit dust through the windows with waggons, saddlemakers, branworkers' rope, harness shops – then poplar trees and the limestone mountains, with the white monastery on its flank.

---

* Bookshop, Librarie le Divan, rue de la Convention, Paris.

Lonely walking in Xanthi. Tap of the coppersmith's hammer. Spotless sky over the low semi-circular roofs, and mountains clustering in great lumps of limestone. Outside a café, a vain old Turk, with a rainbow-coloured turban, beautifully embroidered bolero and short shalvar, a military band playing. The thousand-strong ambulatory crowd, the strings of electric light, the crowds drinking. A metropolis. The silent, stone-roofed Pomak world a whole world away, lunar or martian experience. The bus driver helps with the luggage to the hotel. Terrible row with Joan, like a storm breaking after oppressive day, with only a lovely moment of happiness drinking and then driving on from Porto Lago. Now I'm alone in the square, she in tears in her room, both utterly miserable.

2 October Lying reading Martin Chuzzlewit. Sky gets overclouded all of a sudden, a desperate downpour, the knell of summer. Walk with J. – all happy now after a tremendous mutually vituperative blow off – through the narrow streets to the stadium for the scratched football match. The river in sudden spate – brown, roaring, turbulent.

Up, as dusk fades, to the monastery. Up, up. Four young boys with a rifle each, 2 tommy guns and a bren gun (Note: Communist leaflets), and an eldritch man who has served with Force 133 & blown up railways with Miller, a sailor kitbag. As we left, youngest and prettiest, sighing deeply, lifted his trilby, saying, 'There you are, you lucky things. You travel all over the world – look at you, miles from London. Whereas me, all I do is stay in Xanthi.' Immense, friendly, dolorous grin. Night quite fallen as we descend. Twinkling galaxy, the roar of the brown river and the tangos ascending through the dark.[3]

It is as if Joan's feelings, and Paddy's own, were registered by him as yet more sensory experience – another part of the environment he was moving through. It is an effect he achieves again when, in another notebook, he writes about leaving Gadencourt. The extract is dated 3 May [1952]:

In Tôtes, Normandy. Gloom of returning to England tomorrow. . . . J. and I lie on our beds in a dark bedroom, looking forward to what is going to be a tremendous dinner. Paté with truffles, then either quenelles de brochet or a lovely trout with almonds, followed by an entrecote or a chicken . . . Oh, sadness, sadness of uprooting after my long Norman winter at Gadencourt. Lovely moment, sitting under the apple tree in the garden last night, heavy smell of the mown grass lying round in swaths, the shadows deepening under the branches, the leaves swallowing up the mistletoe in all the trees a few gnats in the air, all the sadness of spring, navy blue swallows playing and wheeling, a blackbird singing . . .

Or just walking in Parga on Yanina Island:

The lovely lemon groves of Anthousa. Slow walk back with Joan in happy silence – talking now and then, below the path, the – to me – most beautiful sight in the world: pale blue late afternoon sea seen through the twisting trunks and leaves of olive trees. The women carrying loads of sticks and thorns on their heads, smiling and wishing good evening, stopping to chat, 'Won't you take us to England?' 'if you are with a pretty girl,' the old ones croak, 'Take care they don't steal her!'[4]

Paddy wanted to meet all that life had to offer. Many years later, Xan Fielding was asked by *The Times* to draft an obituary of his closest friend. Paddy's appetite for life, he wrote, was in Paddy's own phrase, 'that of a sea-lion for the flung bloater'.[5]

Xan and Daphne were very much part of Joan and Paddy's lives. Daphne was fourteen years older than Xan. They married in 1953 after a prolonged divorce from her first husband, the Marquess of Bath. 'When I first knew her,' wrote Deborah Devonshire, '[Daphne] was synonymous with enjoyment, laughter and high jinks. She was one who lifted the spirits with her energy and overflowing good nature . . . Daphne alone and in the prime of life meant lovers; one or two serious, some here today and gone tomorrow. Her admirers were legion.'[6] Her husband, who was also promiscuous, wanted a divorce because he had found someone he wanted to marry. By this time Daphne had fallen in love with Xan. ('Daphne told Peter [Quennell] that she's never been in love with anyone like this before – so it all sounds wonderful,' wrote Joan.) Xan agreed to marry her but broke down in tears in front of Paddy, his best man, the day before his wedding because he did not want to go through with the ceremony.[7]

Xan could not bring himself to tell Daphne his feelings. The wedding went ahead and Xan and Daphne started their married lives in Cornwall. Paddy went to visit them while working on the proofs for *The Traveller's Tree*. He had started his journey in London and arrived at the station in Looe:

> His suitcase had fallen . . . open and its contents scattered. The floor and seats were littered with his clothes, a dispersed ream of foolscap paper, a ship's compass, several boxes of Swan Vestas, the remainder of a bag of toffee and a score or so of loose cigarettes which had escaped from the big blue box of fifty Players constituting his minimum daily ration. 'I was looking for my sand shoes,' he explained. 'I couldn't very well start off from Paddington wearing them – ah good, here they are – but I wanted to arrive at the seaside appropriately shod.'[8]

Both Xan and Daphne intended to write for a living but when Daphne's first book of memoirs, *Mercury Presides,* was published in 1954, Joan was unimpressed by her talents. She wrote to Paddy: 'Have you got Daphne's book? I must say it's far worse than I thought it would be. I really thought she was quite literate – I thought the first few chapters must be a skit on "My Royal Past" sort of thing but apparently not.'[9]

In 1954 their landlady gave up the Charlotte Street tenancy and so, after five years, Paddy and Joan were obliged to move out of the flat they had been renting and found themselves without a London home again. However, their friend the Greek artist Niko Hadjikyri-akos-Ghika offered them his family summer home on the island of Hydra as somewhere to live, since he and his wife Antigone – 'Tiggy' – rarely went there. Paddy wrote to Ann Fleming:

> . . . *it's a large house on a slope with descending terraces like a Babylonian ziggurat, a thick-walled, empty thing surrounded by arid reddish rocks and olives and almond and fig trees, and the mountainside goes cascading down in a series of tile roofs and a church cupola or two to the sea . . . The sun sets in a most spectacular way over these mountains and the sea, and every night Joan and I watch it from the top terrace drinking ouzo, then eating late – about 9, when it is dark – by lamplight at the other end of the terrace.*[10]

Everything looked 'insanely beautiful', he added.

Among the friends who came to visit them during their time on Hydra was Maurice Bowra, who stayed with them on two occasions, both for long periods. Bowra felt at home in the Mediterranean. 'Joan, oh dear, Joan has got a house on an island,' he wrote to their mutual friend, Billa Harrod. 'It sounds bliss to me. Dear Paddy will be there and I have decided to be angelic to him and treat him like a great writer . . . though of course one sees his toes more.'[11] Bowra's visit coincided with one by Ann Fleming, who first got to know him well there. She reported to her brother, Hugo Charteris:

> *The conversations were largely on events before the birth of Christ so I have become a good listener! Although Maurice and P. are supposed to detest each other they appear to have totally similar tastes including Joan Rayner – they both love Greeks, Greece, talking, reciting, war, medals and royalty; I had not realised Maurice had enjoyed 1914–18, and staggering up the hill from harbour to home we invariably sang 'Keep the home fires burning'.*[12]

Paddy told Lawrence Durrell that it was 'the best bit of high level cadging [he had] done for years, a real haul . . . It's a perfect Shangrila for work, and at last I'm getting a move on.'[13] At the time he was working on both *Mani: Travels in the Southern Peloponnese* and *The Cretan Runner*, George Psychoundakis's account of his time helping British forces around the villages of Crete during the war. The book was published in 1955. That summer Maurice Bowra came back to Hydra, this time bringing with him the historian Eka Kantorowicz, a close friend from Harvard. They were joined by Cyril Connolly and Giorgios Boukas, a photographer. Boukas took a number of pictures, including one of Joan playing chess with Kantorowicz on a whitewashed terrace while Maurice sat behind them looking 'jovially radiant' (in Paddy's words), together with Connolly and Paddy standing at the rear. Connolly called the photograph 'one of the key-pictures' – the fact that he was in it being, of course, a mere coincidence.

Eventually they had to leave – in part because Paddy was beginning to feel restless again but also because of the political situation in Cyprus. Because the British were resisting calls for *enosis* – the unification of Cyprus with Greece – there was growing anti-British feeling in the country, and Paddy and Joan began to feel uncomfortable. If they entered a bar or a cafe, it fell silent. When George Katsimbalis refused to dine with them, Joan was in tears. Paddy, in fact, supported unification with Greece but they were very deeply hurt. In the autumn they packed up and left.

Joan loved Hydra. She would have stayed indefinitely, as Ghika wished them to. Not long after, however, the house was burnt down – by the gardener. Ghika had left Tiggy for Barbara Warner and the gardener found this unpardonable. Years later, Paddy recalled how 'this lovely house was white and grey-shuttered at the top of a steep escalade of terraces with crags above it and gorges shooting down to the sea. In summer it was so hot we had luncheon in a sort of cellar dining-room and dinner under the stars or the moon on one of the terraces or in the port. The scenery was exactly like one of Ghika's pictures.'[14]

Now that she had to return to London, Joan persuaded the trustees to buy her 13 Chester Row near Sloane Square, which would serve as a base while Paddy and she went travelling. However it was only a house, never a home. Unquestionably they remembered Hydra when several years later they built a house of their own at Kardamyli. It was more modest than Ghika's, but Joan's sole requirement was that from it she must be able to watch the sun go down over the sea.[15]

At the time of the first of his two visits, Bowra, who had been Warden of Wadham College since 1938, was also Vice Chancellor of Oxford. He was a complex, difficult man and often emotionally out of his depth, but he appreciated the company of warm, intellectual and witty women. Although predominantly homosexual, he also had strong feelings for women and, after she was widowed, he claimed to have got down on one knee and proposed marriage to Ann Fleming. However, as Noel Annan wrote, 'Perhaps most of all he loved Joan Eyres Monsell.' The philosopher Stuart Hampshire said that they enjoyed 'a short fling', and Bowra himself openly suggested that their relationship might have been more than platonic.[16] He felt physically for her and she was willing to listen to him. Early in the 1950s Joan wrote to Paddy after a weekend when he had been staying with her at the Mill House.

> He really is fantastic. He talked from 5.30 till 12.30 without drawing breath, eating and drinking enormously. Primitive people, languages and songs, Shamanism, politics, the first war, guilt, old age, death, homosexuality (or, rather, lack of it) at Oxford now, Eliot, Yeats, Valery and Rilke. The whole of the next day was just as good. He is full of ideas about new books to write and has nearly finished one about the songs and poems of primitive tribes. It sounds fascinating. He has got stuck with the Greek one he is meant to be doing. It seems so frightful with that tremendous brain and all that intellectual curiosity should not live forever.[17]

Paddy, however, had got in the way of Bowra's pseudo-romance. Indeed, anyone who came into Bowra's circle was a potential threat. When the economist Roy Harrod told Bowra that he intended to marry, Bowra replied that he was 'strongly in favour' of his marrying, 'provided 1) It is not into the upper classes 2) she has money 3) you are prepared to go through [. . .] the revolutionary changes it means in your life. Write me a full account at once.'[18] As it turned out, Harrod's bride had turned out to be Billa Cresswell, of whom Bowra strongly approved, and he was delighted. But when it came to Joan, for whom his feelings were intense and possessive, men were more of a problem. In the habit of composing satirical verses about both his friends and his enemies, he included both Paddy and Joan among the subjects. In 1950 he had written a poem about Paddy called 'The Wounded Gigolo' (Bowra said that Paddy and Xan Fielding were 'hero gigolos') in which he made references to Paddy's affair with Balasha Cantacuzene. Bowra imagined Paddy, 'The Wounded Gigolo' of the title, as having been cast out of her house by Balasha, and he was desperate to get back in. 'He will not admit he's been beaten/While there's money to be made.' The truth, as Bowra must have known well, was that Paddy left her to join the army. For 'Balasha' read 'Joan', however, and the attack is even more wounding.

> *O Balasha Cantacuzene,*
> *Hear the war-cry of the Gael!*
> *In his last fierce fight, but he will fail.*
> *Cruelly his lady spurned him,*
> *Struck him when he asked for more,*
> *Flung him down the stairs and turned him*
> *Bag and baggage from the door.*
> *Oh unhappy gigolo*
> *Told to pack his traps and go;*
>   *He may mope and he may mow, Echo only answers 'No'*

It was as if Bowra was unable to direct his emotions openly to Joan, and instead turned his resentment against Paddy, who was deeply hurt by the attack when he read the poems. 'There's lots to be said about him, most of it v. good, but spoilt by a streak of v. bad,' Paddy wrote in a letter to Deborah Devonshire. 'My own private conclusion is that Maurice *could* become very faintly cracked for as long as it took to write a poem, then stepped back into being a marvellously funny fellow.'[19]

Around the same time, Bowra also wrote a poem called 'On the

Coast of Terra Fermoor'. In it, Bowra pictures Joan as she sits wondering whether she should have chosen Paddy as a lover when he
was so frequently absent and unreliable:

On the coast of Terra Fermoor, when the wind is on the lea
And the paddy-fields are sprouting round a morning cup of tea
Sits a lovely girl a-dreaming, and she never thinks of me
No, she never thinks of me
At her morning cup of tea,
Lovely girl with moon-struck eyes,
Juno fallen from the skies,
At the paddy-fields she looks
Musing on her Tibetan books
On the Coast of Terra Fermoor high above the Cretan Sea.

Melting rainbows dance around her – what a tale she has to tell,
How Carmichael, the Archangel, caught her in the asphodel,
And coquetting choirs of Cherubs loudly sang the first Joel,
Loudly sang the first Joel
To their blessed Damozel.
Ah, she's doomed to wane and wilt
Underneath her load of guilt;
She will never, never say
What the Cherubs sang that day,
When the Wise Men came to greet her and a star from
the heaven fell.

Ah, her memory is troubled by a stirring of dead bones,
Bodies that a poisoned poppy froze into a heap of stones;
When the midnight voices call her, how she mews
and mopes and moans.
Oh the stirring of the bones

And the rumble-tumble tones,
How they rattle in her ears
Over the exhausted years;
Lovely bones she used to know
Where the tall pink pansies blow
And her heart is sad because she never saw the risen Jones.

Cruel gods will tease and taunt her: she must always ask for more,
Have her battlecock and beat it, slam the open shuttledore,
Till the Rayners cease from reigning in the stews of Singapore.
She will always ask for more,
Waiting for her Minotaur;
Peering through the murky maze
For the sudden stroke that slays,
Till some spirit made of fire
Burns her up in her desire
And her sighs and smiles go floating skyward to the starry shore.

The verses include a number of allusions: Joan had taken lessons in Tibetan before the war; 'Carmichael' refers to members of the Cretan Resistance using 'Kyr Michali' ('Mr Michael') as a code name for Paddy; 'Joel' is a fusion of 'Joan' and 'Noel'; 'Poppy' is a reference to Thérèse 'Poppy' Fould-Springer, the wife of Alan Pryce-Jones; and in 1950 John Rayner was living with his wife Miranda Lampson in Singapore. What reaction Bowra hoped to invoke in his muse is unclear, but we do know that Joan burnt her copies of the poems.[20]

By the time of his visits to Hydra, there was less coolness between Paddy and Maurice Bowra, but they were never close. Nor did Bowra always fully understand how to behave with Joan. In August 1954 they had spent a fortnight travelling around Italy together. 'I keep feeling he must be so terribly bored and that makes me worse a conversationalist than ever – but he seems to want me there the whole time and won't see anyone else even here,' she wrote. Bowra often behaved like a man obsessively in love, unaware that the object of his feelings could not return his devotion in the same way; despite being over sixty, he was too ignorant and inexperienced to realize how intimidating he could be.

As Paddy had claimed in his letter to Durrell, being in Greece really did help him get 'a move on' with his writing, or at least as much movement as he ever managed in that regard: *The Cretan Runner* followed two years later. In 1957 his essays on the monasteries of France and Cappadocia were collected in one book, *A Time to Keep Silence*; the latter he saw as a companion piece to *The Violins of St Jacques*, his short novel inspired by his Caribbean travels published in 1953, spiritual searching as opposed to worldly pleasure. *Mani: Travels in the Southern Peloponnese*, which was dedicated by Paddy 'with love to Joan' was published in 1958. It was illustrated with Joan's photographs and with drawings by John Craxton. In the preface to the book Paddy wrote that at the end of 'this long and fascinating journey' he had realized that the number of dog-eared and closely written notebooks was such a forbidding sight that to reduce all this material to a single volume was plainly out of the question, and so there would have to be a series. 'Thus I could allow myself the luxury of long digressions.' And few writers could be more digressive than Paddy. Even so, he regretted, he had to thin out material to prevent ballooning, and there were many omissions. 'The most noticeable of these is vampires, their various nature and their origins, to which many pages should have been devoted [. . .] But fortunately, or unfortunately, vampires exist in other regions, though they are less prevalent than in the Mani; so I will be able to drag them in else-where as a red herring.'[21] A few months after its publication, *Mani* won the 1959 Duff Cooper Memorial Prize.

In the spring of 1960, after a decade of wandering, Craxton would finally find a small and dilapidated house to rent in the Venetian harbour of Chania, on the northern coast of Crete. Once settled he invited Joan – although, as things turned out, she did not enjoy her first holiday which was all the worse, as she wrote to Paddy, 'as everyone is so disappointed when I turn up without you'. She was staying at the Plaza Hotel which was more modest than its name suggested.[22]

Darling Paddy,

This is a bit different to my other Cretan lives &, alas, not a millionth part as nice in spite of the agony one sometimes went through. Also I feel all wrong here without you.

It was very exciting arriving Easter Saturday (no seats on boats or planes before that) & seeing the peacock blue green purple of the sea round the cliffs of the Akrotiri so far intenser than anything in Greece. A glorious sparkling day after muggy cloud in Athens. And the wild flowers – waist high white and yellow daisies, marigolds, gummy aromatic pink or white cistus, poppies, broom, gorse, every kind of purple, mauve, pink, blue, red, yellow flower you can think of – far better than anything in Sicily or Morocco.

I stay at this still primitive hotel wth a wonderful view of the port opposite Johnny's still more primitive house, where Charles Haldeman lives too – He is extremely clever & nice, I think, full of ideas & words & a great friend of Larry's. another friend, also in the parea,* is Alan Bole, gentle & civilised, who has a friend in port. But I'm afraid the sailor life is too much for me. Johnny is literally entwined with them at every

---

* A Greek word in common use meaning a group of friends who meet regularly for discussions and an exchange of ideas.

meal, the only times I see him as he is occupied otherwise.
Really rather embarrassing & makes me feel de trop to say the
least . . .

   Bless you my darling angel & do feel terribly missed & loved
   Huge hugs & love
   Joan

Joan had fallen in love with Greece and she wanted to live there permanently – but with Paddy. She was now nearly fifty and, aside from the few years of her brief, failed marriage, she had never had her own home. She must long ago have given up hope of having children but now, at last, she wanted certainty. The next couple of years were spent looking for somewhere to live. Paddy's intended series of books on Greece only had one successor, *Roumeli: Travels in Northern Greece,* and, because Paddy was a painfully slow writer and always happy to be diverted in his researches, *Roumeli* took eight years to write. The book was finally published in 1966 although far from being a long volume, it was only half the length of *The Traveller's Tree.* Its introduction includes both the book's raison d'être and excuses for the way it has been written. 'Roumeli,' it begins, 'is not to be found on maps of present-day Greece. It is not a political or an administrative delimitation but a regional, almost a colloquial, name; rather like, in England, the West or the North Country, the Fens or the Border. Its extent has varied and its position has wandered rather imprecisely.' In fact, the book is more a series of reflections inspired by random journeys round northern Greece either by himself or with Joan, and sometimes with Joan and John Craxton, both of whom again illustrated the book. At the end of the introduction to *Roumeli,* Paddy listed the eight places in five countries where the book was written: St Fermin, Passerano nel Lazio, Forio, Locornan, Lismore, Dumbleton, Sevenhampton (the home of Ian and Ann Fleming) and Kalamitsi. The last of these,

Kalamitsi, was a strip of land by Kardamyli, the village he and Joan had fallen in love with in the early 1950s. By the time *Roumeli* was published, it was Joan and Paddy's new and permanent home.

13

Kardamyli

When Paddy and Joan came to live in Kardamyli in the mid 1960s the war still stirred up deep emotions. The British Military Mission to Greece was not a glorious episode, and it ended in chaos and confusion in Kalamata, a town of strategic importance just to the north of where they were intending to live. British and other Allied forces had been forced to flee the region in 1941 in the face of an overwhelming German invasion force, abandoning the Greeks. Those who could slipped away in all sorts of vessels to the ports of Crete during the hours of darkness before they were spotted at daylight by the German bombers. The British troops who failed to escape were marched north to POW camps in Austria and Germany. The Battle of Crete was comprehensively lost. In the 1980s Paddy became involved in this still very contentious issue, when he supported the erection of a monument in Kalamata commemorating those who had served and lost their lives in the Allied evacuation forty years earlier.[1] Ironically, it was the fact that Paddy had not been involved during the war in mainland Greece which made it easier for him to live there. Given their ties and the island's familiarity Crete would have been the most obvious place for Paddy and Joan to build a new house, but for all its attractions it was impossible. They knew too many people and Paddy would forever have been interrupted in his work by visitors: 'any passing Cretan

– damn it,'² as Joan said. Nothing would ever have been written there, and so they chose the Mani peninsula.

After the death of her mother at the end of 1959, Joan came into a substantial inheritance, so she and Paddy were actively able to start looking for somewhere to live. In June 1962 Paddy found the perfect place when he and Ian Whigham – a friend of Graham's – came upon a mule track leading to a little cove, about twenty minutes' walk from the southern end of Kardamyli. There was not a house to be seen anywhere, just two rocky headlands and an island a quarter of a mile out to sea with a ruined chapel, and a vast expanse of glittering water. 'Homer's Greece, in fact,' Paddy said. The land around the site was nothing but olive terraces, thistles, asphodels, thorns and pine trees. Kalamitsi itself means 'the place of reeds'. Paddy and Joan had been hoping to buy one of the towers which were distinctive of this region, but that had proved impossible, and land was their next preference. They had sufficient funds, but first of all the current owners of the land had to be persuaded to sell. Angela Philkoura, who lived on the property, said 'she couldn't sell the land [. . .] sadly, money's just bits of paper. It flies away like birds. But if you have land and olives and vegetables and chickens, you'll never starve.'³ Confident all the same that he would get his way, and before any money had changed hands, the walls of the house were rising in Paddy's imagination:

Darling! I wonder how you feel about the Kardamyli project? It seems to me a criminal act to let it go. One would rue it for the rest of one's life. (If we can get it that is!) [. . .]

If we built it, I think it should be exactly as the locals build, same size and materials, but with bigger rooms and thicker walls. If it turned out too much at first one could simply proliferate into other rooms – there's masses of space. Local stones & tiles, with those lovely Mani arches over doors if necessary, a loggia and balcony. Anything but abundant simplicity would be jarring in such surroundings – only I think we ourselves should be able to come down to ground level to be able to go in wet and barefoot from the sea, and there should be a vast comfortable main room, full of sea and sky, books, gramophone (when electricity comes), comfortable chairs, divans, a hearth, stone floor, a Ghyka or two (except they cost more than the whole outfit by now!) [. . .] I could go on writing about this forever, but it only delays this letter, so I'll knock off now, with apologies for delay. My darling Joan, imagine the most beautiful place in the world and multiply it by ten! Heaps and heaps of fond love, my darling angel.[4]

Nearly two years passed before contracts were finally exchanged and the building work was ready to start. In June 1965 the foundation stone was laid. The mason placed the head of a cock on the stone and cut it off with his trowel. The priest sprinkled holy water and chanted prayers – and everyone ate and drank a great deal. Joan and Paddy pitched their tents suitably, even symbolically for a house which was to be dedicated to books, in the exact place where the library would be. Gradually, walls, doors and window holes were made, rafters began to sprout and tiles to pile up under the olives, but it would be many months before the house could be occupied. The first visitors were invited even while Paddy and Joan were sleeping in the open air. In 1965, Deborah Devonshire visited at a time when Paddy was alone and Joan was back in England. Paddy wrote to warn her: 'You could either doss down in Joan's evacuated tent, or stay at the tiny hotel in the village (terrible loo but otherwise nice. No rot of that kind up here; we cut out the middleman and vanish into the middle distance with trowel and scroll.) [. . .] My theory is, there must have been a time when Chatsworth was only holes in the ground.'[5]

For several years during the winter months, while the work continued, Paddy and Joan stayed in a hotel in Kalamata. Paddy, as ever, was gung-ho. Joan, who after all was paying for everything, was anxious. She wrote to Maurice Bowra.

It was nice getting your letter, a lovely undeserved present in the midst of all the anxieties & frustrations here. I wanted to write to you ages ago but one is always either in a state of elation or despair, both cases impossible for letters. Things have been more difficult than one feared, starting with the architect breaking his leg the day he was first coming here. That does seem like bad luck & not his own hopelessness, but perhaps it is worse. Then the extremely expensive local topographer from here proved completely incompetent and we have only just been able to persuade another to come from Athens. Everything, as you can imagine, takes endless hours of discussion and unless one is there ceaselessly nagging & urging nothing at all gets done. We are getting on slowly, though the temporary road for building materials has been arranged. As it passes over at least ten families' land that took a good deal of intrigue. And now the water pipes are ready to be laid, stone & workmen are waiting so it shouldn't really take long once it gets going & the final plans are decided.

Another cause of despair (but more mine than Paddy's as he doesn't think it will interfere with us) is that they intend to build an autostrada all down the Mani. Of course they will never finish it. The vast amount of wasted money will run out, and the bits that are done will remain, with the crumbling concrete and rusting iron frames of giant tourist hotels as fitting monuments to the Tourist Age in Greece. But they plan to start it at Kardamyli, ruthlessly pulling down Byzantine chapels, Turkish bridges. All the feeling of peace and remoteness will go by the time you see it, I hope next summer, it will probably rival the Côte d'Azur. It's depressing trying to live in a Greece being developed by scheming philistine politicians. The latest law is that all tavernas, cafés, wine cellars with whitewashed vaults or wooden beams should have to have a wooden ceiling underneath [in case] (it seems never to have happened) a flake of whitewash should fall into a tourist's glass. A more lasting law, alas, & almost as silly as the one in Hydra in force for our summer, making all the mules & donkeys wear sacks to catch the shit, in case the tourists disapproved of seeing it in the streets.

In the meantime everything is extremely beautiful as it always is at this time of year, a washed & limpid golden look, mountains & islands & peninsulas appearing which had before been hidden by hazes, carpets of flowers & bright green corn coming up under the olives. Most days it is baking & swimming is still glorious. We go to Kardamyli two or three times a week, & come back total wrecks each time. Turned out of our tents by the equinoctial gales and rain. We found a curious but light & sunny jazz vorticist flat on the sea front here, above an avenue of jujube trees. Although it's lovely still having summer I'm rather pining for civilisation again, & we've seen no-one since a heavenly visit of Barbara & Niko [Ghika], three weeks ago. I dream of food & all my delicious wine waiting in England. (By the way I've left that, & there's quite a lot, to you & Graham & Cyril in my will.) I want to come back soon but must wait for the sacrifice of the cock when we lay the foundation stone, but will be back anyway before Christmas & am dying to see you again.[6]

Joan's anxieties, as often, were exaggerated, and Paddy and she survived them all.

The axis of the whole house was planned so that the windows of the main room – which was referred to variously as the library, the drawing room, the great room or the salon – caught the very last rays of the sun, winter and summer. As Joan had wished they could watch the sun go down into the sea. An eight-arched gallery led from the great room to a loggia with bedrooms, bathroom and a kitchen to one side, and to the south there was another wing with two more bedrooms and bathrooms, and an outside staircase led down to another bedroom and bathroom below. (They expected a lot of visitors.) Jasmine from in the courtyard filled the house with its scent. Paddy and Joan had separate bedrooms, as he was never fully house-trained. In a letter to Lady Diana Cooper, Evelyn Waugh referred to the 'Nicotine maniac and his girl', and it was always possible that Paddy – who was a heavy smoker – might set his bed on fire or pour red wine all over the sheets. Or flood the bath. Joan filled her room with cats, which Paddy did not much care for, and there was even a cat flap in her bedroom door. Her bedroom had the best view, over the sea to the south. On one wall there was a Giacometti still life. She kept a photograph of Cyril and a silhou-ette of Patrick Kinross – people who mattered. The back of the door was covered in postcards. Both the bedroom and the kitchen were private: no one was allowed to enter unless they knew Joan well; one might have to wait for years.

By September 1966, Paddy felt so confident that he wrote to Patrick Kinross, inviting him to come for Christmas. The house was now roofed over with tiles bought cheaply from the wreckage of a recent earthquake in Kalamata: 'D.V. it'll be ready by Christmas and it would be marvellous if you were here to help inaugurate a gigantic fireplace that's now going up!' Two months later, the house was still unfinished. Joan wrote to Kinross:

I do hope the house will be ready, sometimes one feels it never will, but if not the hotel is charming. We rather forgot what a time the inside of a house takes & now doors, windows, floors,

ceilings, sinks, baths, kitchens, plumbing, plastering are all
being done at once & as we have to see to & get everything we
are nearly mad thinking of door knobs, lavatory seats, taps,
hinges, designing fire places, doors, shutters, etc, etc. It's beauti-
ful though and we long for you to come and see it.[7]

He came for the New Year instead but the Greeks did not make much
of the event. A year later, at the beginning of January 1968, Joan wrote
to John Banting, who had sent a picture as a house-warming present:

It's a very anti-festive season here, I'm afraid, even in Kalamata
our favourite tavern, usually full of caique captains, spivs &
tarts from the port clip joints was empty. However we had
lunches in the sun & lit a roaring blaze in our new fireplace
with pruned olive branches in the evenings. Now we spend our
evenings painting tiles as they are so hideous to buy here.[8]

Some of the tiles were painted with mandala shapes, a remembrance of Joan's interest in Tibetan studies.

When the house was nominally finished, it is hard to say, as the
building work was never-ending; in March 1968, Paddy returned to
Greece after a trip to Spain:

We found Kardamyli emerging from the worst winter in recorded
history – snow a foot deep even on the island. We just missed
this amazing vision, alas. Meanwhile our old pals the workmen
have taken possession again. I don't know what we'll do when
they finally clear off, and the patter of hobnailed boots falls
silent.[9]

By then the house was up and standing, and the limestone from
which it was built, roughly cut from the foothills of the Taygetus

mountains, had weathered. Standing as the focus of an untouched coastline, it looked, Paddy said, like a monastery which had been crumbling there for centuries.

The fact that the house was finished certainly marked a staging post in Joan and Paddy's life, and on 11 January 1968 there had been another, when they married at Caxton Hall in Westminster. Paddy likened the ceremony to buying a dog licence but Joan had broken her family mantra that while one might sleep with or have an affair with anyone, one must only marry someone in similar financial circumstances. Niko Ghika, his wife Barbara and Patrick Kinross were all present at the wedding. After a pick-me-up drink in a local pub, Barbara Ghika provided a lunch and Patrick Kinross provided the dinner. Why Paddy and Joan should have decided to marry at last is difficult to say. Probably, it just seemed the right time. In her commonplace book Joan noted down a passage from Rilke in his *Letters to a Young Poet*.

> [. . .] the good marriage is rather one in which each appoints the other as guardian of his solitude & shows him the greatest trust that he has to confer. A togetherness of two human beings is an impossibility and, when it does seem to exist, a limitation, a mutual compromise which robs one side or both sides their fullest freedom & development.

An epigram by Jean de la Bruyère:

> Etre avec des gens qu'on aime, cela suffit; rêver, leur parler, ne leur parler point, pauser à des choses plus indifferentes, mais auprès d'eux, tout est égal.*

---

* Being with those you love is enough; dreaming, talking to them, not talking to them, stopping to think about unimportant things, when you're near them it's all the same.

And a single word from the Fuegian language of South America:

> mamihlapintafoi means 'looking-at-each-other,-hoping-that-either-will-offer-to-do-something-which-both-parties-desire-but-are-un-willing-to-do.'
>
> (Jane Harrison, Prolegomena)

These thoughts must have echoed her private feelings. It was nearly twenty-nine years since Joan's first wedding at Caxton Hall to John Rayner. The affairs she had had during her marriage to JR had caused her unhappiness and guilt; at the back of her mind there must have been Cyril's comment that she would never be good at married life. Paddy and she had been together for over twenty years, so she had proved him wrong. Joan once surprised Janetta Parladé by telling her how many lovers she had once had,[10] but, despite her agreement with him that they would have an open marriage, there is no trace in her papers of her ever having been tempted by another relationship, or even so much as a passing sexual encounter, with anyone other than Paddy.

Paddy's affairs, on the other hand, were scarcely covert – and by nature Paddy was very far from secretive. He had had a brief affair with the daughter of the journalist Tom Hopkinson, Lyndall Hopkinson, who was working as a proofreader at the time. She was inexperienced, and the affair ended in her hurt and disappointment. In 1960, shortly afterwards, he became involved with Enrica 'Ricki' Huston, the fourth wife of the film director John Huston. She and Paddy first met when she rescued him from a fight after a hunt ball in the early hours of the morning, although the affair started several years later. Among Paddy's papers was the start of a draft note or a letter to Xan and Daphne. It was written at half two in the morning as he was sitting over his drink in the Bag O'Nails, a nightclub in Soho.

I suppose this is alright. Slight solitary gloom tonight. This is
not a letter, just kakography over bumf because all the available
soulmates are being wooed in flat high class tones by junkers at
neighbouring tables, wretched early birds, lovely worms in their
beaks . . . Most of them are like genteel Clarissas one Doone
(already seized); a near-Ricky (Glory on her – on Ricky). O, the
beauty of the sway of skirts, that heavy delayed-action sway after
the particular movement has been completed and superseded,
like a silk echo; this gratuitous corollary to the sway of dance
steps. Round they go, and round, half an instant later, goes,
that pleated, ironed, goffered and ruched slack that somewhere
in its volutes hides bums. [but not, the way things are going so
far, for me].[11]

Ricki was very much in love, and although the affair did not last
long they remained friends. In January 1969 she was killed in a car
crash near Strasbourg while on the way to see John Huston. It was
Joan who told Paddy – in a short paragraph at the end of the fourth
side of a letter of six sides, as if the death of Paddy's former lover was
only a matter of passing interest. She mentioned what arrangements
had been made for Ricki's daughter by John Julius Norwich – with
whom Ricki had also had an affair – 'so she is all right but poor
Ricky. It *is* sad.' Many years later, when Paddy found the letter he
had begun writing a quarter of a century earlier, he added a note,
'The man's drunk P.L.F. 21.7.87.' Whatever the drawbacks of marriage and Joan's reservations, they wanted to be with one another so
all was passed over.

Although they had lived together for years, marriage also gave
Paddy and Joan an added respectability and security – perhaps
useful in an increasingly paranoid Greece. In the spring of 1967
there had been a military coup. The junta – or the 'Revolution of
21 April 1967' as it called itself – proclaimed its mission to be the

defence of the traditional values of 'Helleno-Christian civilization'. This, of course, meant whatever they wanted it to. John Craxton was already suspected by the chief of police in Chania of espionage. The fact that such a cultivated man who had a house by the harbour had a liking for sailors surely signalled an interest in naval intelligence – this raised a laugh from the suspect. Then the fact that Johnny rescued antiquities from roadside heaps, which were about to be turned into building foundations, led to charges of looting the national heritage. During a police search, an owl he had constructed was pronounced ancient treasure. So Craxton dismantled the bird and said, 'Look, it's made of brick, just like this.' He tapped the policeman on the head with one of the pieces. The policeman festered a grudge. He was promoted and eventuallly he forced Craxton to leave the country.[12] Paddy and Joan Leigh Fermor, however, were able to see the junta through.

14

Friendship and Loss

Joan's father, Viscount Monsell, died in March 1969, aged eighty-eight. His ashes were scattered at sea from a warship. In accordance with his explicit wish there was no memorial service, but in 1974 a window was installed in his memory in the south aisle of St Olave's Church, Hart Street, a church with many naval connections. The window displayed the Eyres Monsell arms; three woolpacks in the top right-hand quartering represent the source of the family's prosperity. At the base of the window the text reads, 'So much one man can do that doth both act and know.' Graham now inherited his father's title and became the 2nd Viscount Monsell, but he never took any active role in public life, nor did he take his seat in the House of Lords. He had already inherited the Dumbleton estate of some 5,000 acres from his mother's trustees, and over the coming years he sold off the odd cottage and building site to provide himself with an income. In the early 1950s, the Corporation of Leicester had already acquired land that the estate also owned in the southern suburbs of the city by compulsory purchase, in order to build a greener and more attractive council estate. The family name which was created on the marriage of Sybil Eyres and Bolton Monsell is still carried by the city's Eyres Monsell estate council ward.

Throughout his life, Graham could be quite intimidating; if one said the wrong thing one would be made to feel a fool. He was kindly, but it was difficult to be intimate with him. While Paddy was outgoing and friendly, Graham was always fastidious and fussy. He was wary of Paddy, and it took a long time before he believed that his motives towards his beloved Joan were more than mercenary. His reserve eventually broke down, and there came to be more mutual regard and affection: Paddy was not just an adventurer and Joan was not letting the side down by marrying outside her class. Paddy described Joan's brother as a 'very intelligent, very retiring, literary-musical hermit'.[1] But Graham was no hermit; he was loyal to his small number of very close friendships – including Joan's first boyfriend, Alan Pryce-Jones, to whom he wrote in November 1961 after Alan's recent move to the USA:

> It is angelic of you to ask me to come for a visit . . . [but] my dancing days are over, old rocking chair has got me and I must say I love it. I emerge each summer to plunge into the Mediterranean, hear a little music in Germany or Austria, eat some delicious food in France, and then come home to prepare, like an ageing bear, for winter hibernation.[2]

One man very much outside that circle was his old school and university contemporary Jim Lees-Milne. When they encountered each other at a theatre having not spoken in years, Graham made an overture of friendship, but it was rebuffed. Lees-Milne was unforgiving, and he recorded in his diary how his feelings of resentment had not lessened over the decades:

> He held my hand and said how delighted he was to see me and would so much like us to meet and talk over old times. Old times, my foot! I was terrified of Graham as a boy [. . .] At Oxford he was considered extremely dashing, the 'fastest' man

in the university, wore a black polo sweater and allegedly took drugs. Was exceptionally supercilious, rich and disdainful. Now he is bent, blind, sallow, dusty and diffident. How the late worm changes places with the early birds.'[3]

In fact, Graham continued to lead a full life. The estate was well run and he was both active and conscientious in his duties towards his tenants; at harvest he would help out by driving a tractor. He also continued to travel a great deal. On a visit to Bali Graham wrote to Joan to tell her that he had encountered the Balinese queen in her palace at Solo. Graham bowed low, only to then feel self-conscious about the holes in his socks. Another time, Joan and Paddy went with him. On her return to Kardamyli, Joan wrote: 'We are still in a daze with all the glories we have seen – Taiwan, Angkor even better than I imagined, Bangkok, Bali, the dancers wildly exciting & not spoilt yet with tourists, Java, Singapore, India, Nepal. Such beauty all the time, especially of people. One felt ashamed of being huge pinkoes.'[4]

For most of the time Graham lived in Dumbleton, but on Wednesdays and Thursdays he came up to 9 South Eaton Place in Belgravia, his London home (the old family house in Belgrave Square had been bombed during the war). The house was theatrically decorated with dark paintwork. On the hall landing there was a golden table held up by a golden cherub, a couple of exquisite chairs, and a huge bunch of flowers standing on top, silhouetted against a window which was swathed in rich velvet curtains. The drawing room was murky red, so dark you could hardly see, and the walls were packed with pictures by Robin Ironside, including a painting called *The Flaying of Marsyas*, which had the god Apollo preening himself in the background.

Ironside himself was a sort of *fin-de-siècle* figure. He painted two pictures of Graham: in one, the more conventional, he is lying on a sofa, a music score laid out before him; the second, *en grisaille*, mimics a Roman tombstone. He also drew decorations and a map of the imaginary island for the endpapers of Paddy's 1953 novella *The Violins of St Jacques*.

Eventually Joan, who inherited Robin's pictures, gave them to the permanent collection of the Tate Gallery, but the gravestone portrait always hung in her bedroom at Kardamyli.

From 1967 onwards there were hundreds of entries in the calf-bound Kardamyli visitors' book; it reads as both a catalogue of the owners' rich lives and a who's who of mid-twentieth-century society. The first name to appear is that of Magouche Phillips. Magouche was born Agnes Magruder, and was the daughter of an American naval officer. Her first husband was the Armenian artist Arshile Gorky, and it was he who called her Magouche, an Armenian term of endearment. After his death she married Jack Phillips, an American painter who came from a family of Boston Brahmins. She had two daughters with each husband. When her second marriage failed she came to live in Europe with her children. She was very beautiful and had thick dark hair, a low, rich voice, a warm smile and large eyes. 'Quelle belle invention!' said the Romanian sculptor Constantin Brancusi, when she was introduced to him in Paris by Alexander Calder. Soon, this beautiful invention became very much part of Paddy and Joan's innermost circle.

Both the company and the location doubtless made invitations hard to refuse. On 1 September 1968, Freya Stark wrote to Gerald Brenan from Kardamyli:

> *Here I have been for three days, & three days more, just breathing air & sea. The mountains are dove-grey in the sky & red like foxes as they run along the shore. They push & shoulder one another till the sea wraps them in light & here, among the*

*cypresses & olives, Paddy & Joan have built themselves a house
of the hillside stone, quite unimaginably solid & beautiful.
Arcades & a great roomful of books & steps down to their little
pebbly bay. They are very happy & theirs is a lovely atmosphere
of leisure with space & sunlight running all through it.[5]*

The very last signatures of all were written in the summer of 2011, just
after Paddy's death. Across the intervening decades, visitors had
included: Niko and Barbara Ghika; Nancy Mitford; Diana Cooper;
Tom Driberg (who forgot to sign his name, so John Betjeman was
asked to forge it); George Seferis; John Betjeman and Elizabeth Cav-
endish; Cyril Connolly; Ann Fleming; Bruce Chatwin; Janetta
Jackson and her new husband, the Spanish decorator Jaime Parladé;
Xan and Daphne Fielding; Gerald Brenan; Isabel Rawsthorne
(Isabel had married Constant Lambert's friend, Alan Rawsthorne, in
1954); John Craxton (who had a beautiful signature but whose spell-
ing was appalling – he boasted that he had never passed an exam in
his life); Jock and Diana Murray; Frances Partridge; 'Billa' Harrod
and Dorothy 'Coote' Lygon, who usually travelled together; Stephen
and Natasha Spender; Roy and Jennifer Jenkins; Steven Runciman;
Deborah Devonshire; Joan's sister Diana Casey (who Paddy
described as 'very nice, but has not a single interest in common with
Joan or Graham, and is v. unlike: shy, tall, correct and well dressed
in a not very imaginative Knightsbridge way and stitching away at
gros-point. I think Joan finds her heavier going than I do!'[6]); and very
many others.

Annie Fleming visited Kardamyli in the summer of 1969. She wrote
to the diplomat and writer Nicholas Henderson from Greece about
dining on the terrace, 'where Paddy's experiments with lighting
coincide with peasants bearing food, and we are all suddenly
plunged in Stygian dark,' while Joan shrieks 'Oh, Paddy'. On her

return to England, she also wrote to Aline Berlin, the wife of Sir Isaiah Berlin. 'The Leigh Fermors' house is a triumph. Paddy is a much better architect than writer. The stone, the wood, the water, and the marble come from vast distances and a mini Xanadu constructed. It includes stone tables under shady olives designed to inspire a spate of writing but Paddy is only inspired to further visits and fountains, and Joan wails at approaching bankruptcy.'[7]

Despite his early visits during the building work, Sir Maurice Bowra never saw the house once it was finished. He claimed that he refused to go back to Greece so long as the Colonels of the junta were in charge but, as Ann Fleming continued in her letter to Aline Berlin, he no longer had the physical health for so arduous a journey. Buses and taxis served Kardamyli – the first private car in the village belonged to Paddy and Joan – but from then on one had to walk through olive groves, scrub, and along a narrow cliff path; 'the descent to the beach [is] 24 uneven stone steps and though the bathing is perfect I suspect he prefers a table where he can shout *"Vino subito"*.' And there were problems with the water; Peter Quennell complained that there was hot water only once a week. Paddy suggested to Jim Lees-Milne that he might like to stay but admitted: 'It's not very inviting at the moment as there is a water shortage, and Joan, Graham and I pour cupfuls of water over ourselves, then leave them standing in the bath for later use. Pretty disgusting.'[8]

Xan and Daphne Fielding were always welcome. One August in the early 1970s when Paddy and she had gone home to Dumbleton, Joan wrote to welcome them to Kardamyli. They were using the house in Joan and Paddy's absence:

Darling Daphne & Xan,
    I'm not going on apologising for not being there as it's always as nice staying in houses when the owners are away & I

*feel we are the real sufferers being deprived of you. I do hope
everything is all right & that they have finished whitewashing
the rooms, usually left until the last moment & nothing ready
when one gets back. As you will have realised from the first
moment Lela is a wonder & will order you better chickens etc
from Kalamata, fish etc & I hope look after you marvellously.
Let her have an evening off occasionally if Daphne can cook
some eggs or something or go to the tavern run by great friend
Pavos Poneireas & nice family, the son Nico was our sort of
foreman; or the new smart restaurant, quite good food, Belgian
wife. There is a glorious beach with icy fresh water springs in the
sand & sea about 4 or 5 miles on, just before Stoupa (nice
tavern for lunch). There are roads everywhere now.*

*Paddy & party are back from the dangerous mountain peaks,
all very successful & exciting. I've just had a wonderful 19 page
letter from him. He should be here just before I leave. Li-lows
[sic] are in the cupboard in the bathroom, & goggles. Whisky &
vodka in the cellar. Don't play the gramophone as it needs a
new needle which I'm bringing out. There's a wireless in my
room but needs new batteries. Be kind to the forty cats. Do
please manage to stay on your way back. Surely you could leave
a few days earlier. I do so long to see you.*

Very much love
Joan[9]

Joan always apologized in advance to visitors about her cats, in case
guests did not appreciate her passion. Wherever one went on the
premises a cat or kitten would suddenly appear, all of them
descended from a single Abyssinian which had mated freely with
the village toms. Joan wrote to John Banting in 1971: 'Cats multiply,
a beautiful mixture of Abyssinian and Maniote, but too many now.
Graham says they're like having crabs.'[10]

Although there were fewer in later years, at one time, when Janetta Parladé was staying, she counted seventy-three of them living
in warring families. Since local veterinary services were lacking, if
Joan had to put them down she used strong sleeping pills.[11] Sometimes, although not often, they annoyed her: 'The cats have killed
the red rump swallows just as they had finished building the enormous miraculous nest just inside the front door. You can imagine
my rage and despair.'[12] However, the 'down-holsterers', as Paddy
called them because of the harm they caused to the furniture, were
part of Kardamyli life: 'It's been wet and cold and if my writing is
worse than usual it's because I'm sitting in the sun with eight cats
on top of me. Paddy has been and is working like a demon, all day
& a lot of the night. He is very pleased with himself, for that &
keeping thinner, & it makes me very happy.'[13] Photographs of the
cats were turned into postcards. One showed a cat asleep on the
open pages of Rudyard Kipling's *Kim*, a favourite book which Paddy
and Joan read in alternate years. 'Overleaf is a little cat, which I'm
sure you knew ("Tiny Tim"), great favourite of Joan and mine, now,
alas, mousing above the clouds . . .'[14]

Joan herself was not always the perfect hostess. She admitted as
much to Patrick Kinross:

*I loved your letter & the eavesdropping remarks about my
behaviour. It was a trial & I'm afraid I was often impatient &
irritated with everyone. Thank goodness you were here but it was
rather bad luck for you & I longed for you to be here too with
Dadie [Rylands] and Raymond [Mortimer]. That restored one's
faith again in conversation. Paddy was upset about it especially
as he had been looking forward to it tremendously. They were so
nice but I am afraid they will tell Balasha I am even more cold
and aloof than Bridget Parsons.*[15]

And there were sometimes guests who could begin to outstay their welcome, or prove trying in other ways, none more so than her old friend Eddie Gathorne-Hardy. Eddie's selfishness was phenomenal, although, as Heywood Hill wrote to Nancy Mitford, 'Joan . . . said that she likes having him because he is so selfish that there is no doubt what he wants. A point of view, I suppose, though charitable.'[16] After working for the British Council in Athens, Cyprus and Cairo, Eddie had retired to Athens, but was in the habit of making extended visits to his friends and family, whom he treated like members of his personal staff. Even Joan's charity could be exhausted.

> *Eddie is here and driving me mad with his continual banter about food: 'I suppose, my dear, you are giving us pheasant to-night, my dear. Oct 1st, my dear, I have to have a pheasant my dear.' 'I don't think this is any good, my dear, without at least a pint of cream in it, my dear.' 'I hope you have stuffed the chicken with foie gras, my dear.' On and on and on, after a week one really doesn't know how to answer.*[17]

Not that Eddie was completely unfeeling. When Bowra died in 1972, he wrote to Joan with his sympathy – and then told her about his own medical problems.

Eddie's sister Anne was married to the bookseller Heywood Hill. In the Leigh Fermor archive there is a letter from Heywood Hill to Robin Fedden:

> *Dearest Robin,*
>
> *Pardon for using my Jumbo Economy Scribbling Pad upon you. It's a bad sign when one starts to stinge on writing paper. But I have not yet got to my late father's stage of counting the sheets in a toilet roll. I suppose these days Andrex would win – according to telly adverts of Bonzo getting mixed up in it and*

rushing downstairs and out onto the patio (all anathema to you, I guess).

If I sound in cheery spirits, it's because Eddie has been safely got away. I had an awful fear that he might be stuck here. If he had I think Anne would have gone round all the bends. He became more violently demanding as time progressed. Two days before he left he shouted at her I WANT YOU AT MY DISPOSAL THE WHOLE OF TOMORROW. 'But Eddie I can't,' said Anne, 'it'll take me 3 hours to cook the pheasant which I've been keeping for you – deeply frozen – as a treat for your last day.' FUCK THE PHEASANT, he shouted, I WANT YOU TO PACK. Jonny came down for the last two nights & cheered us up. Then on Friday morning he drove Eddie off among a welter of pee bottles, syringes & Andrex. Jonny* told us when we rang him up that evening that only the bottles had been needed. When throwing the contents of one out the window, it all blew back in Jonny's face. Sister Anne's sisterly love was fairly dried up by the end though absence is making the heart grow fonder . . .

*   With love from us both*
*   Heywood*[18]

When Eddie died in 1978, Paddy wrote a typically generous, unpublished obituary:

Time gradually changed [Eddie] into a Peacockian figure – for bookish analogies are inevitable – a sitter for the Dilettanti portraits with a dash of great Whiggery, a sceptic Voltairean aristocrat but not a stoic for tedium, humbug, bad scholarship, and, indeed the recent handicap of ill-health, could set the air crackling all around him with oaths and groans. He demanded much of his

---

* Jonathan Gathorne-Hardy (b. 1933), biographer.

friends and got it, by cutting through their quandaries by never doing anything he didn't want but repaying their troubles many times over by the charms and surprises of his company.[19]

At Kardamyli there were thousands of books: in the library, the studio, in all the bedrooms (one of which had a set of unbound copies of *Horizon* – the defining magazine of its time – on its shelves), and on the shelves fitted into the largest bathroom. There were cookery books in the kitchen, and, because there was no room for them anywhere else, there were more piles of books in the basement. Joan kept her copies of Paddy's books in her bedroom. He decorated their inside front covers and flyleaves with drawings of seascapes and seagulls. But it was the library, the great or the big room, which was at the centre of Paddy and Joan's lives. The seating was arranged so that they could gather with guests in little groups to talk, or sit by themselves and read or write letters at the desk, or retreat to the *hayáti* – a seating area at the end of the room – in order to play chess. Joan loved chess, and spent hours over the board, either with an opponent or just playing against herself. She bought a small computer with chess programs when they were introduced. She also loved Call My Bluff. After dinner, the Oxford English Dictionary was taken from the shelves and the players would take it in turn to find a word no one knew; everyone had to guess which concocted definition was true, for a point, then it was the turn of the winner, if there was one, who would choose another word. When players lacked inspiration, they suggested 'A small Mediterranean fish' as a definition and so 'A small Mediterranean fish' became a kind of family joke. But, as Paddy wrote in his entry in a book of essays and photographs entitled *The Englishman's Room*, books were the raison d'être of his house:

Where a man's Eleventh Edition of the Encyclopedia Britannica is, there shall his heart be also; and, of course, Lemprière,

Fowler, Brewer, Liddell and Scott, Dr Smith, Harrap and Larousse and a battery of atlases, bibles, concordances, Loeb classics, Pléiade editions, Oxford Companions and Cambridge histories; anthologies and books on painting, sculpture, architecture, birds, beasts, reptiles, fishes and trees; for if one is settling in the wilds, a dozen reference shelves is the minimum, and they must be near the dinner table where arguments spring up which have to be settled then or never.[20]

Many of the books on the shelves had been given to Paddy and Joan as gifts. Among the poets were two books by Tristan Tzara (who composed a poem for her) and six by John Betjeman. No two poets could be more different. After his first visit to Kardamyli, in September 1969, Betjeman thanked Joan and Paddy individually, writing to Paddy:

> *What is time for? To make things as beautiful as possible as you*
> *have. I suppose that big room – the big room is one of the rooms*
> *of the world. What is marvellous about it is the arc of light*
> *– daylight or evening light. It charms and is perfect in each. It*
> *is something to do with proportion or you have an instinct . . .*
> *I doubt it comes from books.*[21]

And to Joan:

> *Darling Joanie,*
> *   Oh I did enjoy myself at Kardamyli. Of course that big room, as*
> *I've written to Paddy, is one of the rooms in the world. It is the*
> *thought in everything you ever look at which delights me about the*
> *house(s). In that way Paddy is like Butterfield.* *In proportion and*

---

* William Butterfield (1814–1900) was one of Betjeman's favourite architects; he built Keble College, Oxford.

35. Fishermen at Kardamyli.
Too remote to fear an
influx of tourists, it seemed
a good place to live.

36. The ecstatic Anastenaria
fire-dancing ceremonies
are performed in northern
Greece during religious
festivals.

37. Niko and Barbara Ghika,
John Craxton, and Paddy
and Joan Leigh Fermor on
the terrace of the Ghikas'
house on Hydra, 1958.

38. While their house was being built, Paddy and Joan lived in tents on what was to be the site for the library.

39. and 40. Paddy and Joan during a stay in Nauplia when they were still looking for somewhere to live. They had to row across to an island for breakfast.

41. Both of Joan's weddings took place at Caxton Hall in Westminster; she married John Rayner in July 1939, and in January 1968 she married Paddy Leigh Fermor.

42. Janetta Parladé at Torre de Tramores, Malaga, Spain in the late 1960s.

43. In the early 1970s their new house was far less accessible than in later years and could only be reached by walking through olive groves.

44. Graham Eyres Monsell, Diana Casey (née Eyres Monsell), Paddy and Joan Leigh Fermor at Kardamyli. Graham is 'a very retiring musical-literary hermit' and Diana is 'shy, tall, correct and well dressed'.

45. Joan and Diana, early 1970s.

46. Joan and Paddy picnicking.

47. Joan and Paddy
at Kardamyli
in the 1970s.

48. The house at
Kardamyli was
alive with cats, mice,
insects, scorpions –
and the occasional
donkey.

49. Joan at Kardamyli, 1981: 'even in a crowd she maintained a deep and private inner life'.

50. In 1978 Xan and Magouche Phillips married and moved to Ronda in Spain.

51. The Mill House, Dumbleton, was an old farmhouse surrounded by fields of sheep and an orchard. Inside the house was a mixture of shabby elegance and bohemia.

52. Joan, late in life.

*use the garden is part of the architecture, he is less Lutyens and Jekyll – all the time he is himself. I've never seen you so beautiful, not even when with eyes as big as your cheeks and downy soft and straight, you stood in the Ritz. I've written to Jock [Murray] a long letter giving him news of George [Seferis] and telling him also about the house – how it is really a book of Paddy's and more lasting.*²²

But on his return to England Betjeman also wrote to Wayland Kennet:

*Greece was enchanting as scenery and as siting for temples, but the atmosphere of not being able to speak freely was markedly noticeable. Even I noticed it. I don't think it could ever be like that in Italy. I don't think it was even like that under Mussolini . . . The nastiest man I ever met in my life was the Chief Reception Clerk at the Grande Hotel in Athens, never go there.*²³

When Brian Howard died from a drugs overdose in January 1958 Cyril Connolly gave Joan a copy of *Wheels*, an anthology of poems edited by Edith Sitwell and published in 1921 when he was still at Eton, young and full of promise. The anthology was dedicated to 'Joan with love from Cyril in memory of Charles Orange'. *Wheels* included a poem by 'Charles Orange', Howard's pseudonym which he used because he feared he might get in trouble with the Eton authorities. Howard's great talent was later dissipated in drink, drugs and idleness but his name runs like a thread through the memoirs of so many of his generation. John Banting wrote to Joan about his death, which he said was an accident: 'He wanted to die in my arms and he did – held tightly encircled – with no murmur – and then I reached desperately for the heart beat which had stopped [. . .] He told his mother "If John can't come – then Joan *must*". He loved and admired you steadily.'²⁴ Cyril Connolly also gave Joan his own books, as well as volumes by others. A *Study of Charles Baudelaire* by Arthur Symons was dedicated to Joan from Cyril 'with love, love & love, 1964 June'. Tennyson's *Maud, and Other Poems* was inscribed 'Joan's Book – O, why should Love, like men in drinking songs/Spice his fair banquet with the dust of death?' Cyril's last book, a collection of essays called *The Evening Colonnade*, appeared in 1973, when he was seventy. By then his health was failing. In November 1974, Joan received a telegram in Greece saying that Cyril had had a heart attack and was seriously ill. She flew to England immediately with Graham, who happened to be staying at Kardamyli. Paddy wrote to Balasha: 'I drove them in, J. very upset and anxious, and saw them off at the aerodrome. I *do* hope he'll be all right, but there's not much hope it seems.' As Cyril would have expected, and as he would have done himself, his friends kept an account of the following days in their letters and diaries. On Saturday 3 November, soon after she had arrived, Joan wrote to Paddy:

> *[Cyril] is getting weaker and weaker & it can't last long now, though he is still completely lucid at times. I tried to telephone you today but the international operators this end could only say loive dint . . . & had so much trouble spelling Teddington I gave up & will try from London. I go back to-morrow as though there's little one can do but hold C's hand & be an extra nurse I feel so anxious away for more than a day.*[25]

Joan organized the traffic around Cyril's bed in the Harley Street Clinic. His complicated emotional life meant that a lot of friends and lovers came to see him but did not necessarily want to meet one another. John Betjeman wrote to Penelope:

> *Cyril is dying very fast. I went to see him today. Liver and no hope. Joanie and his new girl called Sheila, and Deirdre, take it in turns to*

watch by his bed. He sent you his love: 'Give my love to Penelope.' I
am very proud of how much you are loved by our friends.[26]

Connolly's then wife, Deirdre Craig, was in love with Peter Levi, a
writer and former priest. Cyril's own last affair, which not all his
friends were aware of, was with a woman called Shelagh Levita.
Barbara Skelton came over from Grimaud in the south of France,
where she lived:

> When I first visited the Harley Street Clinic, the first thing that
> struck me was the dust and the array of dead flowers, cluttering
> the room. Why had no-one bothered to throw them away? My
> visits could not coincide with Deirdre, Sonia [Orwell], Joan or
> Janetta's. But Shelagh was always there until my last visit, when
> C. was alone. He was studying a medical encyclopaedia, when
> two doctors entered who were doing their rounds. Cyril
> addressed them querulously, 'Why is it I'm not getting any
> better?' The doctors seemed to be baffled as to what was the
> actual cause of his illness. 'Was it a heart or liver complaint?'
> 'Have you ever lived in the tropics?' one of them said. Cyril was
> pitifully thin but could be persuaded to drink a little glucose . . .
> I left the clinic crying and soon after returned to Grimaud.[27]

Cyril died on 26 November. His funeral took place a few days later
at Berwick Church in East Sussex, a small twelfth-century church
famous for its wall paintings by Duncan Grant and Vanessa Bell.
Grant, who lived at Charleston nearby, came to the service and was
seated at the back of the church together with his daughter. Anthony
Hobson, a bibliophile and head of Sotheby's book division, read one
of the lessons. Stephen Spender wrote in his diary that it somehow
did not seem to suit Cyril that both the lesson and psalm should be

about the resurrection of the body – he was so famously dissatisfied with how he looked.

> The vicar who had a stick, without which he can't stand up, talked very briefly and understandingly about Cyril and his work. We stood around the flower-covered grave, in the wet and windy cold weather, just a tarpaulin of some kind over the coffin. The person who seems most stricken is Joan Leigh Fermor. I held her arm a moment but didn't dare speak to her. She looks 20 years older.[28]

Joan was named as an executrix, and Deirdre his legatee; Coutts Bank were fellow executors but, aside from his library and his papers, Cyril had nothing to leave, except his considerable debts. At four in the morning on 27 December, a month after Cyril's death, Paddy awoke from a dream which he recorded in his notebook:

> The decor of the room was very elaborate and among charming details were two enormous pink and grey poppies, in and on each of which, by an old Chinese process had been recorded a poem, and also a review by Cyril Connolly so that people sitting near the table and the vase containing them could hear snatches of both: 'The moths turning alone on ears of rye . . .'; 'a misplaced adjective here and there'; 'transparent skiffs . . .'; 'imprint limited to five copies . . .'; 'stalks disappearing swamp . . .'; 'Sir A. Douglas-Home' . . . 'each eighth pearl being black'. Unfortunately both flowers were thrown away next day by mistake, the petals of one of them were already coming loose. Saw them with the crinkly chocolate papers so their contents are now lost to us. Off to sleep now.[29]

In May 1971, two days before his sixty-ninth birthday, John Banting wrote to Joan from his home in Hastings: 'Darling Joan, I often think of you in your (I hope) glorious reclusiveness. You once said to me "I know *enough* people". I too treasure my six or seven chosen ones but I do sometimes meet some good new ones – usually much younger and far more intelligent.'[30] Banting had long since ceased to be the dangerous, shaven-headed young artist of his bohemian youth, and his political views were no longer so violently left-wing as they had been in the 1930s, although he still counted Tom Driberg, another ex-communist, among his friends. 'I saw Tom D. last year in the House and his false eye was unnoticeable and he looked very well and handsome.' In her diaries, Frances Partridge calls Banting 'a genial slow old duck'.[31] His letters to Joan are meandering and written with a shaky hand – he was frequently drunk. Joan wrote inviting him to Greece – 'It's blissful here & we live on our own eggs, garlic, veg. salads, bread, oil & fish straight from the sea' and suggesting how he might get a cheap flight, but Banting pleaded ill-health and the fact that because of his youthful political affiliations his name might yet be on some list which would prevent him from ever travelling again. Less than a year later, Banting – another of Joan's friends from the 1930s, the painter who had once offered to decorate her bedroom ceiling – was dead.

Time continued to take its toll on Joan's friends throughout the 1970s. In January 1976, Tom Driberg was made a life peer. His introduction to the House of Lords was a grand affair; John Rayner called it his apotheosis. In August, however, Tom died of a heart attack while in a taxi on the way to the Barbican from Paddington station – taxis played a large part in his life to the very end. The following day his obituary in *The Times* described him as 'a journalist, an intellectual, a drinking man, a gossip, a high churchman, a liturgist, a homosexual [. . .] an unreliable man of undoubted distinction. He looked and talked like a bishop, not least in the Bohemian clubs which he frequented. He was the admiration and despair of his friends and acquaintances.'[32] He was the first man *The Times* ever outed in its obituary columns, although it would have been dishonest to write about him without mentioning the fact. The obituary writer also mentioned his wife, Ena, whom Tom had married for the sake of respectability. Joan wrote to Rayner asking him for any press cuttings about the memorial service and the funeral: 'I wish I could be there & that I could write something about Tom, but not being a writer I find it impossible to say anything about one's greatest friends.'[33]

John Rayner administered Tom's will, and it took him several years to settle his old friend's affairs: his duties included the publication of Tom's autobiography, which made no mention of Ena. (Future royalties from Tom's books were divided between JR and the anti-apartheid movement.)

Tom had sold Bradwell Lodge in 1971, on account of his considerable debts, and moved to the Barbican. Joan and John Betjeman were among twelve friends who were each left £50, two pictures and a dozen books. They went together with John Rayner to collect the books and pictures. 'I did not often go to that flat of his,' Betjeman wrote to Ena. 'Only someone as eccentric and individual as Thomas Edward Neil would choose to live in such a frightful, lonely, hideous bit of housing. I always told him how awful it was but he didn't seem to notice it. I collected an Edward Lear of an Italian tree, a drawing of the old portico at Euston and a Nonsuch Milton. I find Milton heavy-going and thought he might be easier in that beautiful edition.'[34] Joan lost her two pictures, along with much else, almost immediately, as Paddy and she drove back to Greece via Italy together with Coote Lygon, who was then also living in Greece.

At Brindisi Coote's car was stolen, just before we got on the boat
[?] found unharmed next morning on a vast rubbish dump
outside the town (so like the beginning of Italian films) with all
our cases bust open & everything new or of any value gone. We

picked up some old clothes, hairbrushes, pills, papers, books, etc.
out from the refuse, watched by jeering children, but the miracu-
lous loudspeakers & amplifier, the Graham Sutherland drawing
& Toulouse Lautrec lithograph, silver spoons & forks, all
Paddy's suits and shirts & new suits, all mine too & leather
coats, jerseys, all those presents bought after hours of silent
screams at Marks & Spencers, rugs, sheets, lamps, everything in
fact that she wanted & was bringing back at last for the house
disappeared for ever I'm afraid. I only have now the oldest shirt
& skirt I was wearing at the time & can't even go to Athens.
Think of the hours of ghastly shopping ahead of one, I feel I
shall stay here for the rest of my life.[35]

As some sort of recompense, John Rayner wrote back to Joan to tell
her that while emptying the Barbican flat he had found a portrait of
Tom when young by John Banting, 'in the style tho' not so good as
his portrait of Eddy Sackville-West. You will have it.' The £50 Tom
had also left her Joan spent on the complete ten-volume
Mahabarata; JR also sent her, as gifts, Darcy Thompson's *Greek
Birds* and *Fountains in the Sand* by Norman Douglas. He himself
bought a mourning ring. Joan wrote to thank him for the books:

It is very kind of you to bother. I feel in a selfish rage about not
seeing Tom when I came to England. He never signed our
visitors book when he was here, a space was waiting. Have you a
signature of his anywhere I could stick in? Otherwise Betj is very
good at forging them.[36]

Although Joan might claim to have 'enough' friends, every death
was a break in the circle.

15

A Time of Gifts

In 1973, John Betjeman wrote to Cecil Beaton recommending both Penelope and Joan for inclusion in a book on the history of photography which Beaton was writing. If Joan was, by then, a suitable candidate for a retrospective she would have been the last person to have pressed for it and would probably have hated the idea. The publication of *Roumeli* in 1966 had marked the end of Joan's career as a photographer. Afterwards she might sometimes take photographs, but living in the Mani meant that it was no longer feasible to work as a freelance photographer. Besides, she now had her inheritance, the new house gave her other interests, and Paddy himself was making an increasing financial contribution from writing. The subject matter of Paddy's two late works – *A Time of Gifts* (1977) and *Between the Woods and the Water* (1986) – is the writer's search for lost time, a time that was both real and imaginary. These were books which could not be illustrated by photography. The passing of time, and the violence caused by war and politics, had brought down barriers across the frontiers of lands where Paddy had wandered as a young man with a rucksack on his back. Half of Europe was virtually inaccessible. Many years later, when at last the Iron Curtain had been removed, Joan and Paddy went to Bulgaria:

I'm just returned from our Bulgarian battering, long car jour-
neys & sight-seeing get more exhausting, but it was well worth
it. Of course Paddy looked in vain for his old towns & villages of
over 50 years ago, now concrete industrial messes, & the beauti-
ful footpath he took for days through dense forested cliffs along
the Black Sea coast now nothing but high rise hotels & millions
of East German tourists.[1]

Joan teased him by calling him Rip Van Winkle, but Paddy was
close to tears.[2]

By 1976, the studio at Kardamyli was finished. It was separated from
the house by a path through a small grove of lemon trees. Its single
storey was square in shape, with a flat roof and vines growing up the
walls. There were three rooms – a bathroom, a small bedroom just
big enough for a single bed, and the main room, Paddy's study,
which was 'lovely & large for striding up & down between sentences'.[3] On two sides there were French windows, and there were
further windows at the back and side. Here, Paddy could compose
his sentences and paragraphs, pick out books for reference and
inspiration, and turn the words around and around in his head or
on the page until they were satisfactory. The books on the study
shelves had an organization of sorts – even if it was only theoretical.
Dictionaries in various languages, guidebooks, Oxford poetry
anthologies, books on Hungary, Bulgaria and Romania and some
books bequeathed to Paddy by Sir Aymer Maxwell stood on the
shelves closest to him, behind his desk. Books relating to the Second
World War were placed on either side of the back window. A set of
Dictionary of National Biography volumes was arranged along a low
bookcase built for Paddy by a friend called Jon van Leuven. There
were yet more books in piles on tables and on the floor. Foreign
translations of his works were on shelves in the small bedroom,

where cats slept on the bed during the daytime. Paddy's own desk was an adventure in itself. It represented his own special kind of personalized disorder, with the drawers labelled to give some idea of the contents. Aptly, one of the labels read 'Total Confusion'. Another drawer was labelled 'Vol III', but all the drafts for the successor to *Between the Woods and the Water* were in folders on the shelves, and the drawer's true contents were a mixture of broken spectacles, empty envelopes, pads of paper used and unused, stray photographs, pencils and postcards. Paddy also kept wads of small printed notices saying that he was very busy and unable to answer his correspondents, although these failed to stop anyone from writing.

A tin trunk contained typescripts of *Roumeli*, some travel brochures and a copy of *Architectural Digest*. At the very bottom of the trunk were two pennants from General Kreipe's staff car, snatched as trophies, and on a table stood a box marked 'KARDAMYLI. A CHAOS OF PHOTOS. & GENERAL MANI. Work for a rainy day. (Mostly Crete).' A rainy day which never arrived.

In one corner of the room stood a tall, narrow set of drawers. These were full of blue airmail envelopes into which letters had been sorted by correspondent in alphabetical order. (Previously the letters had been stored in the roof space of the house, but the mice had found them.) All manner of people used to write to Paddy, so many that sometimes he did not bother to open the letters. The correspondents varied: there were old and intimate friends, unknown fans, an academic researcher who wanted a detailed analysis of Barbara Skelton's charms. There was an Austrian who, using a multicoloured pen, kept sending instalments of a long, somewhat manic account of his own walk across Europe, until Paddy eventually wrote back and asked him to stop. Paddy also kept scores of coloured files on shelves built on either side of the back-wall window. The files were arranged in no order whatsoever, but stood up against one another, leaning this way and that. The information written on the covers as to what they contained may or may not have been accurate or helpful. One said 'Interesting papers on Items'. On another was written, 'Prints, reproductions, can't bear to throw away'. The file contained early-nineteenth-century prints of molluscs, a random Christmas card and a watercolour drawing of an Indian scene. A green file, 'Mummy', was full of letters from Paddy's volatile but loving mother.

The bedroom cupboards were also filled up – boxes of files and letters, two typewriters (one bought by Jon van Leuven in Kalamata, the other Bruce Chatwin's, although Paddy never really learnt to type), pairs of sandals, photographs, a broken lamp, a pack of tarot cards. Here and elsewhere there were piles of books and bundles of papers. Somewhere, amidst all this disarray, was the story of Joan and Paddy and their lives together.

One January day, after surveying the state of the studio, Joan wrote to Patrick Kinross that, 'It rains more here than it does in England & Paddy can't work in his studio for the soaking walls. I'm writing a piece called "Portrait of the Artist as a Bower Bird".'[4]

Paddy's income as a writer had been satisfactory but not more than that. In April 1959, Hambro's Bank informed him that they had received 'a cheque for £1,217.17.4d from your publisher, John Murray [. . .] I trust you are having a happy and profitable time on your present journey.' But gross royalties from 1976, 1977 and the first months of 1978 were only £1,417.87. Between *Roumeli* in 1966 and *A Time of Gifts*, eleven years passed. 'We used to be famous once,' Joan complained. In early 1976, Paddy at last handed over the manuscript of *A Time of Gifts* to Jock Murray – 'What a sigh one heaves when that barrier is passed! It's like going through the Looking Glass, and all looks different. I wish I were a better concentrator: feel like a grasshopper harnessed to a plough'[5] – but he continued to make endless changes to his text to the very end. Murray once showed Jim Lees-Milne one of Paddy's manuscripts. 'A spider's nightmare of corrections which he goes over and over again,' Lees-Milne said. Murray told him that Lord Byron's were just the same.

Over the years Paddy produced a considerable flow of articles, essays, obituaries, book reviews and pen portraits. They were less hard work than the slog of writing full-length books, and probably what he enjoyed doing best. Whatever Paddy wrote, Joan heard first. Joan was a good listener and a good reader, and she became Paddy's sounding board. Paddy would bound triumphantly back into the house straight from his desk in the studio with papers in his hand and give them to her. Not immediately, but perhaps two or three hours later, Joan might say, 'Haven't you missed out the part about . . . and isn't that the point of the story?' Paddy would mouth an 'oh', turn round again and go back to work. For all his writings, it was Joan who provided judgement. She had an innate expectation of excellence, both for Paddy and for others. She was always encouraging and always tried to get the best out of people. Without Joan, there would have been even less writing.

A *Time of Gifts* was finally published in September 1977, over a decade after Paddy had started writing what he had intended to be a 2,500-word magazine article. The title, suggested by Sir Aymer Maxwell, came from 'Twelfth Night', a poem by Louis MacNeice: 'For now the time of gifts is gone – / Oh boys that grow, oh snows that melt, Oh bathos that the years must fill'. The cover illustration by John Craxton depicts a young man in the foreground, his feet in snow while black birds wheel about him. He watches while the sun rises over distant peaks, Schlösser yet to be visited and a golden River Danube yet to be conquered. (The original sketches were actually made on Hampstead Heath, and young 'Paddy', the archetype of youth, was Craxton's partner, Richard Riley.) From its first publication, A *Time of Gifts* was a tremendous success. 'This glorious peregrination across Europe,' wrote Philip Toynbee in the *Observer*, 'is a reminder that the English language is still a superb instrument in the hands of a virtuoso skill with words, a robust aesthetic passion, an indomitable curiosity about people and places; a rapturous historical imagination. A writer, in fact, who is a dangerous mixture of sophistication and recklessness.' Gabriele Annan in the *Listener* was equally effusive: 'This is very rich stuff [. . .] It is rich, not like chocolate truffles, with a homogenous texture, but like a terrine of game where resilient chunks of bird and beast alternate with layers of creamy pâté and fortifying jelly, and where you come upon the occasional crunch of an exotic pistachio nut or a spicy juniper berry.'

In November, Jock Murray reported to Paddy that 'all goes spiffingly (forgive schoolboy language, but I am just back from giving a lecture to undergraduates at Oxford, where I rather overdid it)'. In 1978, *A Time of Gifts* won the W. H. Smith Prize, which was worth £2,500 and not taxable. Paddy's income rose accordingly. His work was published overseas: *A Time of Gifts* even had a Norwegian translation. Among his financial papers there is a note to say that, after commission, his Dutch publishers had brought him an income of £73.76 for *The Traveller's Tree* and £1,087.55 for *Mani*. Before long, all of Paddy's back catalogue was republished and was to stay in print.

It was another nine years before the publication of *Between the Woods and the Water*. After the publication of *A Time of Gifts*, Paddy received a fan letter from Rudi Fischer, who lived in Budapest. A polymath, linguist and historian, Fischer was born in Kronstadt in Transylvania, the son of a Hungarian-Jewish father and a Saxon-Lutheran mother; he was, however, raised in Australia, where he was taken as a youth to avoid conscription in the Second World War. In his letter, Fischer pointed out a number of inaccuracies and misspellings, which he hoped was constructive criticism. Paddy was delighted, and a long friendship resulted. Rudi Fischer's erudition was remarkable, and his knowledge of both Transylvanian history and the genealogies of Hungarian families was vast. In many ways, *Between the Woods and the Water* is the fruit of the friendship of Paddy and Rudi. Paddy wrote in his introduction, 'My debt to Rudolf Fischer is beyond reckoning. His omniscient range of knowledge and an enthusiasm tempered with astringency have been a constant delight during all the writing of this book.' But all the poetry was of Paddy's own making, and his portrait of the Hungarian aristocracy just before their way of life was about to be obliterated, is a wonderful piece of literature.[6] Just as with *A Time of Gifts*, the sequel was met with tremendous enthusiasm; it received the Thomas Cook Travel Award and the International PEN/Time Life Silver Pen Award.

In many ways, Paddy's greatest collaborator was always Joan, and her influence on his next book would be even more direct than usual. In 1971, Paddy had gone to Peru with a group of friends in order to walk and climb in the Andes: Andrew Devonshire; André Choremi, a French lawyer; Carl Natar, who had been manager of Cartier's in London; and Robin Fedden, who was now the deputy Director General of the National Trust, and his wife Renée. Twenty years after this expedition to South America, Paddy turned the letters he wrote to Joan in his absence into a slim book, *Three Letters from the Andes*. The book begins:

CUZCO August 3, 1971

At last the morning of departure arrived in Little Venice, but no sign of the ordered car. We dialled and dialled for a cab, everywhere was engaged, so in despair I started lugging my stuff to the pavement while Patrick Kinross stood in the middle of Warwick

Avenue in his Persian silk dressing-gown waving and to some purpose. A taxi stopped at once.[7]

In a note serving as an introduction to the book, Paddy wrote that he had made only minor changes before the publication of the original letters, cutting out one or two irrelevant passages, topped and tailed it a bit but not much, and generally tidied it up to make it more presentable as a kind of memento of the journey. This was nonsense: as ever, Paddy was incapable of preventing himself from tinkering, and the original letters were in fact completely rewritten.

But it was not only Paddy who continued to travel. Joan shared his extraordinary wanderlust and just as he returned from South America, she went off to Samarkand:

Darling Paddy,

A rushed word, written with trembling hand before catching train to sister Diana, to say I suddenly seem to be going to Samarkand with Patrick [Kinross] and Alan P.J. on the 3rd. I feel a proper swine doing this without you but you know how I've always longed to go & God knows if there will ever be a chance again. God knows if it will be nice anyway as a dreaded package tour, 25 people organised by Connoisseur, so it should be cultured at any rate. Alan P.J., his Swedish boyfriend & his next potential American millionairess, Gladys Charles, who unlike the other one is charming by all accounts, & Patrick are the only ones I've ever heard of. Patrick said, 'Why not come?' & I of course longed to but of course no place as filled up months ago & then someone yesterday chucked & so P has arranged for me to go. Can you forgive me? We should go to Persia next in any case . . . Long to see you. The rumours are that you and Andrew leap to the top of every peak leaving others gasping below.

JOAN

*Tons and tons of love my darling & I'll write a newsy little
letter but must get this off by London post. xxx Joan*[8]

They had barely got back to Kardamyli before they left again, this
time for Turkey. 'Our fleeting visit to Turkey was glorious & we pine
to go back & see more,' Joan wrote to Patrick Kinross on their
return. Patrick had made innumerable visits to Turkey and knew the
country well. In 1964 he had published a biography of Ataturk. As a
result of his writings and his knowledge of the country he came to
enjoy a reputation in Turkey almost unique for someone British.

Old friendships meant a tremendous amount to Joan – she almost
lived through her friends – yet she had already lost so many of her
generation. When Maurice Bowra had died in 1971, John Betjeman
wrote to her. Joan replied, 'I am most touched by your writing to me
when you must be so miserable yourself. Of course life without
Maurice will not be the same, something so good and vital and strong
has disappeared as well as one's oldest friend and I think of him
the whole time.'[9] John Betjeman had unveiled a plaque to Auden in
Westminster Abbey's Poets' Corner only a month before Cyril Connolly's death in November 1974. Now, in June 1976, shortly after
Paddy and Joan had returned from Turkey, Patrick Kinross died unexpectedly. Joan wrote to Janetta who had briefly, by Patrick's
marriage to Angela Culme-Seymour, been his sister-in-law but was
always his friend.

*It's so dreadful about Patrick. I feel utterly sad & miserable. He
was really the last rock left in London, always so welcoming &
generous & a marvellous friend all one's life, never changing
except to get nicer & nicer. I can't bear the idea of never being
in that lovely grubby friendly house again with Patrick bursting
into one's room in the morning with plans for the day [. . .]*

*Paddy was on his way to stay with him but was intercepted at
the airport by the kind thoughtful Coote who rightly couldn't
bear the idea of Paddy arriving at the house to find Patrick lying
in state [. . .]*

*I will quote what Paddy says about Patrick. Masses of
people came (you probably saw in Friday's Times). Bier
covered with flowers & such a beautiful Palladian church inside.
I was shoved in a front box pew with John Betjeman; sun
pouring in through leafy ivy-laced windows. John's address from
the pulpit excellent, a bit wobbly but v. moving. I'd been asked
to choose the lessons: first Isaiah 35, read by P's brother, second
(by me) that lovely passage from the Apocryphal Gospel of St
James that George Seferis loved so much. I got permission from
the Vicar to read anything so uncanonical. Everyone said they
were bowled over by the strangeness of it & the aptness [. . .]
motion, then stasis, everything seized up like a fresco on a
trecento Sienese religious pastoral: then released into action by
the last verse; & all thought Patrick would have liked its lack of
orthodoxy . . .* After the church, Lucy Lambton drove Coote &
Miranda & me to Kensal Green, where the cremation seemed to
be over in 5 minutes; then back to P's house where he had left in
his will that a party should be given for all his close pals, &
there they all were & it was great fun, just as he would have
liked.*

The thing that worries everyone a bit is that he has left the

---

* Joan was to request the passage from the Apocryphal Book of James for her own
funeral: 'Now I, Joseph, was walking, and I walked not. And I looked up into the air
and saw the air in amazement. And I looked up into the pole of the heavens and saw
it standing still, and the fowls of the heavens without motion. And I looked upon the
earth and saw a dish set and working lying by it, and their hands were in the dish and
they that were chewing, chewed not . . .'

house & its contents to Constance McNab* (why not Coote or
some other deserving old pal?) who bores everyone stiff. It's
thought to be out of guilt for some passing affair he broke off 25
years ago [. . .] Anyway what a shame.
   *A dreadful woman.
   Very much love to you & Jaime
   Joan.[10]

'For all of us here, Patrick was chiefly a friend and mainstay of our happiness. At his table I met friends I've known for the rest of my life,' said John Betjeman at Patrick's service.[11] One of those lifelong friends – of both Patrick and John – was, of course, Joan. John himself had not only a bottomless need for love but also to share it, and he did so with the Leigh Fermors:

Dearest Joanie and Paddy,
   Your ingenious lines in that gloriously complicated metre
have cheered me up a lot.† I hear the waves of the Aegean softly
lapping against rock, and I picture Groundsel at Dumbleton
striding over his acres. And I long to put into such catching
rhyme and rhythm my memories of Sir Bolton and the Viscount-
ess and the terrified children. To-day is like Siberia and there's
every chance of Feeble [his mistress of thirty years, Lady Eliza-
beth Cavendish] and me being sent to Gothland in the Baltic to
look at the old churches there. What a life you and Joanie have

---

* No one had ever heard of Mrs McNab, who was probably as surprised to learn about the legacy as everybody else. She quickly sold the story of her supposed great love affair with a Scottish lord to the *Sunday Express*. A couple of months later, Joan wrote to Paddy: 'That terror Mrs McNab has written you two complaining letters but saying we can have the desk. I've answered her and said at the end: "I'm so sorry the house is a burden to you. What a pity Patrick didn't leave it to someone else."'
† PLF had recently sent JB his lines about swimming the Bosphorus.

had, and how wisely and well you have spent it, where the
orthodox saints look down with olive shaped eyes from the walls
of the basilica and the goats leap from crag to crag and the
olives are silvery. Penelope comes to luncheon to-day and I have
ordered chocolate éclairs for her but not for
 Yours with love, John B.[12]

In the late 1940s, just as the Betjemans moved to Farnborough, strains began to show in their marriage. John was decidedly Anglican, and although he had religious uncertainties, he had no doubt about belonging to the Church of England. Penelope, on the other hand, had long been attracted to the Church of Rome, and in 1947 she began to receive formal instruction in Roman Catholicism with the Dominicans in Oxford. Betjeman was deeply hurt. Relations with Penelope grew more and more distant. This was almost literally so, for while Betjeman was insular, almost xenophobic, Penelope travelled widely. Joan once dined with both Betjeman and Penelope together after he had visited Kardamyli with Feeble. Joan told Paddy that she was paralysed with horror when Penelope turned and said to her, 'But however did John get to you? He's so hopeless at travelling abroad alone.' Since the mid 1950s, Betjeman had a house at Cloth Fair, close to St Bartholomew's Church. He kept up old friendships – Alan Pryce-Jones, Osbert Lancaster, John Rayner (whom he asked to help his son Paul find employment). And he kept up with Paddy and Joan. Alan ('the Captain') married again, Mary Jean Thorne from Galveston, Texas, but neither Betjeman nor Joan was impressed. However John's feelings for Joan were now touched with regret. After all these years whenever he met Joan he would still start singing the first lines of one of the hymns written by her great-grandfather, 'Oh worship the Lord in the Beauty of Holiness (Bow down before Him His beauty proclaim)', but change 'Him' and 'His' to 'Her':

Darling Joanie.

It was nice to see that country-house, relief-nib handwriting of yours even though on Greek paper. I saw Paddy at Patrick's. We met the Captain's new bride. She seemed to rule the roost but I think the Captain will escape. I can't tell just from our dinner party what she was like – whether there was any love there. I have an idea that the Captain is very kind and very weak. I would very much like to have far closer contact and of a physical nature, with you. But then, as you know, in letters to Abroad, one gets very indiscreet. I went and filmed at the Ritz in colour lately. I thought of you. I wish I had realised I could have spoken then. Look at me now, fat, bald and finished and knighted like Sir Henry Newbolt (good) and Sir William Watson (less good) and Sir John Squire . . .

Darling Joanie, ta ever so for writing. Hope you'll forgive my bad handwriting.

Love, John[13]

What Joan thought of this late declaration of love we cannot know but doubtless she had always been aware of his feelings for her and was touched.

There were not only old friends to entertain at Kardamyli, but new ones too. As one generation of bohemian travellers had begun to die out, Paddy and Joan found kindred spirits in the next. Bruce Chatwin was already famous in his twenties for his golden looks, his flamboyant manner, his long walks and his conversation. Jim Lees-Milne, a neighbour of Chatwin in the Ozleworth Valley in Gloucestershire, described how Bruce 'came in like a whirlwind, talking affectedly about himself'. He had no modesty and he showed off, but he also bubbled with enthusiasm, 'still very young, not self-assured'.[14] All the same, at the time, Lees-Milne was impressed and liked him. Although he was married, Chatwin thought he was homosexual, because of the way he had been brought up by his 'unwise mother'.

It was Magouche Phillips who first introduced Bruce to Joan and Paddy in 1970, arriving together at Kardamyli from Patmos. Chatwin wrote to his wife, Elizabeth:

> I am sitting on the terrace of Paddy and Joan Leigh Fermor's house in the Mani. Quite heavenly here. The whole Taygetos range plunges down into the sea and eagles float in thermals above the house – a low arcaded affair of limestone beautifully marked with red karst. Olives and pencil thin cypress clothe the terrace between the mountains and the sea.[15]

Joan grew very fond of him. She saw 'the point of him': the phrase Paddy and Joan liked to use to show approval of someone. For Bruce, the attraction was not only that Paddy was a great walker, but also that both he and Joan had known Robert Byron, one of Chatwin's heroes; *The Road to Oxiana* was very high on his list of great books. Chatwin had theories about the importance of walking; for him man's restlessness was a natural condition. For a long time he had been working on a book he called *The Nomadic Alternative*, which was to be his great masterpiece, proving all his speculations and philosophies. When his agent Deborah Rogers read the indigestible, leaden prose her heart sank: the book, as delivered in the early 1970s, was unpublishable. It would be more than a decade before his great idea would be ready for print.

As Paddy's success had grown, Xan Fielding had continued to struggle to establish himself as a writer, and now saw a younger generation begin to surpass him. By 1975, Xan and Daphne had been married for twenty-five years. After Cornwall they had lived in Portugal, Tangier, and in France both in the Cévennes and near

Uzès in the Languedoc, close to where Lawrence Durrell lived. Over the years, however, their marriage had become more and more unhappy – not least because they never made much money. In 1977, Janetta invited Magouche to spend Christmas with her and Jaime in southern Spain, and she suggested that she pick up Xan from the south of France on the way. Daphne, meanwhile, returned to England to see her family. Daphne phoned Xan every morning, not realizing that Xan and Magouche were by then in bed together. When Xan and Daphne saw one another again, he told her that he was leaving her.

In 1978, Xan and Magouche married, and moved to live in Ronda in the south of Spain. (Daphne chanced to meet an old friend, an American millionaire, and moved with him to Arizona.) Now that he was married to Magouche, Xan had fewer financial worries and, rather than working as a translator, he was able to do something more satisfyingly creative. He began writing a book about the influence of the winds on man, and wrote to Paddy:

> [Magouche] generously gets on with almost all the chores
> while I try to get on with the winds. I came back with another
> briefcase-full of notes and photostats, including some exciting
> new material, and I have at last fathomed the sixteen colours
> of the four winds of the sky, on which the long-haired monks
> with painted eye-lids disputed in the hospice at Jarrow.[16]

By the end of the decade, Bruce Chatwin was at last an acclaimed and prize-winning author. When he was working on his second novel, *The Viceroy of Ouidah*, Bruce rented a house in Ronda for five months. In the afternoon, he usually went to swim in Magouche's pool. When the glowing American reviews for *In Patagonia* arrived, he could not resist sharing them, and would always arrive at lunch, just when there was a captive audience. Then he talked. 'He did see himself as a sort of present to mankind. He'd come with such nice ribbons and wrapping and heaven knows what goodies inside, yet you never did unwrap it,'[17] Jim Lees-Milne wrote. Eventually Xan went off climbing in the Pyrenees in order to escape the younger writer's gloating. 'And so everyone is much more relaxed,' Chatwin wrote.

Xan found it impossible to find a publisher for *Aeolus Displayed*, his book on the winds, so in 1983 he turned to Paddy for advice. Paddy made some changes to the text and then sent it to Elizabeth Sifton, Bruce's American editor. Paddy wrote to his friend a few weeks later:

> *I've been meaning to write for three weeks and now that here I am pen in hand, I can no longer find the letter I wanted, in spite of hunting high and low viz. Elizabeth Sifton's regretful return of the winds. Damn, on both headings! Her drift was that it was a fascinating and well written book, too good in the present state of publishing to be a commercial proposition, – it looked as if she was saying it was too good to publish, though not quite that. The only serious criticism she made is that the book didn't seem to progress, and left the reader pretty well where he started. I must say, this remark went through me like an arrow, and I can't help wondering whether my Florentine advice altering the order of the chapters is to blame for this. I am very surprised at their not taking it on, and would like to give them a good shake. I've just written a letter in which I said that, considering the amount of bilge that is published, it seems extraordinary that a book like the Winds (she freely admits it too, seems soft soap) should have such a hard coming of it.*[18]

It is a measure of Paddy's love for Xan that he should give him such support. The book, like *The Nomadic Alternative*, is virtually unreadable.

Chatwin, meanwhile, had returned to his own great idea. Like Paddy in his younger days, Bruce was very good at finding other people's houses in which to write. In the autumn of 1984, after Paddy decided to swim the Hellespont, Bruce turned up again at Kardamyli. Joan wrote to her friends Michael and Damaris Stewart:

> *The Hellespont was glorious but of course agony for me as I knew he would never give up. 'Tell him to swim faster,' the nice Turk in the boat kept saying to me. 'I can't,' said Paddy, continuing his stately side stroke & being carried past yet another landing place.*
>
> *We've had a working winter, enlivened by the dazzling Bruce Chatwin, who has been staying with us or next door most of the time. He & Paddy go for tremendous walks & he's marvellous in the kitchen.*[19]

The ability to cook always raised someone in Joan's estimation, but her praise was entirely justified. *The Nomadic Alternative*, the book Chatwin was struggling with, at last found form at Kardamyli as *The Songlines*, which was published in 1987 and reviewed by Paddy in the *Spectator*.

Although Bruce found Penelope Betjeman impossibly demanding and almost wilfully eccentric, she had become a sort of second mother to him. Then, two years after John's death in 1984, Penelope died in India. Around ten in the morning, she had called in on her favourite temple. She received the blessing and rode on towards a place called Khanag, and was talking her head off to her Tibetan porter when her head tilted sideways and the talking stopped.

Bruce was shattered; his wife, Elizabeth, said it was the only time she had seen him in tears. He went immediately to Kulu to scatter Penelope's ashes. He wrote to Paddy and Joan:

*Yesterday morning, her friend Kranti Singh and I carried her
ashes in a small brass pot to a rock in the middle of the R[iver]
Beas which was carved all over, in Tibetan, with Om mani
padme hum. He tipped some into a whirlpool and I then threw
the pot with the remainder into the white water. The flowers
– wild tulips, clematis, and a sprig of English oakleaves (from
the Botanical gardens in Manali) vanished at once into the
foam.*[20]

Joan wrote to Billa Harrod saying that she had been reading Penelope's
letters, which was 'agonizing' – 'I regret bitterly not going to Kulu
with her – She was the most extraordinary & wonderful person & I
feel so lucky to have been her friend.'[21]

Joan's own family was also now touched by death. In 1972 her sister
Diana, a widow for many years, sold her farm in Rutland and moved
back to Dumbleton – which was home for her as it was for all the
family – and built a house. She also kept a flat in London and most
years she visited Paddy and Joan in Greece. Although sisters and in
some ways close, as well as physically alike, they had little in
common by way of interests – Diana was conventional and never
approved of Joan's bohemian friends. It had always been her sister
Joan who was smart and glamorous and gained attention, but they
had their memories, their past and family ties – and these mattered.
In 1974 Diana's eldest daughter Anna, who had made the curtains
for Kardamyli, died. She was still only in her early thirties. In the
autumn of 1985, aged seventy-eight, Diana began to lose all energy
and the will to live. Her second daughter, Bridget, who was staying
at Dumbleton, woke her in the morning, went away to fetch her
breakfast and found her dead when she returned. Her heart had
quietly failed. Bridget, whom Joan had once described to Paddy as
'so pretty and gay and having a wonderful life with swarms of young

men' also died only a few years later. Joan never mentioned her family in her letters or her conversation with friends. It was as if she put different areas of her life into different compartments.

Bruce's conjectures about walking and wandering had a less romantic side: they were also an excuse for unlimited sexual cruising. During the course of his many casual encounters he was infected with the HIV virus, which developed into AIDS. After a lingering illness, he died in Nice in January 1989, aged just forty-eight. His ashes were interred under an olive tree close to a ruined Byzantine chapel dedicated to St Nicholas, two miles above Kardamyli. Libations of retsina were poured over the grave and a prayer said in Greek. Then Paddy, Joan and Elizabeth had a picnic, which they thought he would have enjoyed.

Two years later, in August 1991, Xan died in Paris, where he was being treated for cancer. Joan wrote to Janetta:

> *Magouche arrived last night & is being wonderful, much calmer than she sounded on the telephone, & we talked about Xan & his life a lot at dinner in an easy way. It's a horrid, cloudy, hot, damp day for the first time in the morning for ages, just when we wanted it to be perfect for bathing but M at least swam before breakfast & is now reading with a very energetic kitten trying to pull the buttons off her shirt.*[22]

The following year, Magouche had *Aeolus Displayed* published privately.

16

Endings

While staying in Kardamyli in late 1987, Graham began to become very confused. Billa Harrod, who was also there at the time, helped escort him to hospital in London. She wrote to Alan Pryce-Jones to say how worrying the future was for him. It was 'a bad outlook'. Graham was eighty-two. It was the beginning of the dementia with which Graham would live for the rest of his life. Alan's reply to Billa from Newport, Rhode Island, was typically Alan, rather more aesthetic than practical.

I am sorry to get your letter. I simply don't believe how old we are. Graham: but surely he has just left Eton and we are going to meet in Paris next month . . .

Here all is well. Nothing is lovelier than a New England autumn: cold, even snowy, but with brilliant sunlight. If I had a family house to return to I should hurry home, but I haven't. Moreover, I should wish the house to be not less than 150 miles from London in a good estate with ancient servants surviving and a financial background like that of Alec Home's, who used to send to the Estate Office for a stack of bank notes when he needed money, but otherwise let things ride. Yes, and I should like to be a marquis: an Earl like Home is not enough to make

life easy in England. No wonder Stephen Tennant* stayed in
bed, a mere Hon.[1]

Graham was frail but not sick. He could be looked after at home,
but the housekeeper at Graham's London home in Eaton Terrace
was an alcoholic. After she was found collapsed on the floor, it fell
to Joan to take responsibility for her brother. Jochen Voigt, someone
Graham already knew, moved in to look after him, provide compan-
ionship and cook for him. After a couple of years it was decided to
return Graham to Dumbleton, where, as his health declined, he
had round-the-clock care provided by a staff of four, paid for by the
family trust.

As ever, Paddy and Joan came over regularly from Greece. Paddy
found life at Mill House too depressing and went off to make visits
of his own.

I went down to the Mill House for the weekend. No change with
Graham but he seems perfectly happy, poor chap. Joan looked v.
exhausted after 10 days. The worrying thing is that topics last
such a short time – one gets about 50 killed in an hour, like
steeds in battle, as none of them are ever taken up or developed.
I felt rather guilty, sneaking off to the delights of Crichel – end-
less croquet in midsummer weather, glass-in-hand, with pigeons
and rooks overheads, and a pretty well non-stop cuckoo (thanks
to its being May) seldom out of earshot. We went to Cranbrook
which was ravishing – slightly clumsy, moss-grown English
renaissance, v. rare: it would do splendidly for Theseus and

---

* Stephen Tennant (1906–87) was the younger brother of David Tennant. In the
1920s and 30s he had an affair with Siegfried Sassoon. Reputedly he spent the last
seventeen years of his life in bed.

Hippolyta's palace in A Midsummer Night's Dream, *the inhabitants were exceptionally nice.*[2]

Graham Eyres Monsell, second and last Viscount Monsell, died in January 1993 and was buried in Dumbleton churchyard after a funeral at St Peter's Church. Having no male heirs, the title died with him. After she had returned to Kardamyli, Joan wrote thanking Janetta for staying with her at Mill House and coming with her to the service: 'That kind of funeral seems to me totally pointless, much better, if one has to have one, here [in Greece] everyone is wailing & screaming & tearing their hair out, a real catharsis of emotions instead of having to bottle everything up still more. My only dangerous moment was Paddy reading those beautiful verses, the rest of the service I didn't connect with Graham at all & never felt he was in that hideous coffin.'[3]

Joan now inherited a substantial part of the estate, including the Mill House, from her brother. The Mill House was an old farmhouse surrounded by fields of sheep and its own orchard while the deserted mill with its huge rusty wheel standing in a busy mill stream was about thirty yards away. Inside, the house was a mixture of shabby elegance and bohemia. A warren of narrow corridors and stairs led to bedrooms and bathrooms of various vintage, some with far-reaching views of the Worcestershire countryside. On the walls hung ancestral portraits, nineteenth-century seascapes by Bonnington, and twentieth-century artists like Robin Ironside, John Craxton, John Banting and Isabel Rawsthorne – Joan's friends. The dining room was dark red and hung with various Eyres and Monsell pictures. In the morning room, where friends were greeted, there hung a large full-length portrait of Graham – as if to say that nothing much had changed since the house had been handed over, which was how Joan and Paddy wanted it. And when the curtains turned to shreds and the paint began to peel, they were mended and repainted in identical shades so that no one would notice.

JOAN

During the three times a year in which Joan and Paddy returned to England Joan spent every Monday morning with Jonathan Reeves, the land agent, to discuss estate matters and repairs and improvements to Mill House. He found her intelligent and interested, always concerned about the people on the estate and what was happening. At 12.30 they would stop to have a glass of gin or vodka; Paddy would appear and they would walk around the house discussing what might be done. After Reeves's wife began to join them for lunch, Paddy used to insist on a lively game of croquet with the coffee, which he usually won. Reeves beat him one day, and Paddy said this was the first time anyone had ever beaten him – it was the last time they played together.[4]

Joan's life in England had its own set pattern. The cook-housekeeper, Rita Walker, brought her tea and toast in bed at 8.30. When she had finished, she rang the bell – all the rooms had bells – and while she had her bath, the bed was made. Hair was allowed to dry naturally. Joan invariably dressed in corduroy trousers and jumpers. The latter sometimes had holes, but everything was always very clean. She then stayed in her room reading and writing until 11.45, when she came downstairs for a vodka and tonic before lunch. The food was plain. As a starter, she always had a bowl of fresh garden peas with mint, and this was followed by a cheese soufflé, potatoes and a dressed salad. For puddings, she had nursery food: apple crumble, sticky toffee pudding, treacle tart (Joan's favourite). They also ate a lot of game and chicken. Rita once made a pie with shortcrust pastry; a guest at the meal said the pastry was 'shorter than Ronnie Corbett'. Living abroad and having no interest in popular culture, Paddy and Joan had no idea what was meant: the only Ronnie Corbett they knew lived in Greece and was over six foot tall. Sir Michael and Lady Stewart, Maurice and Leonora Cardiff, as well as Charles Hudson and his wife Cressida Connolly from Wick Manor near Pershore, were all regular visitors.

In 1999, while government legislation for the ban on fox hunting was going through parliament, Joan wrote to the *Daily Telegraph*:

Sir,

As an animal lover, I would like to know what the animal welfare people intend to do about foxes if hunting stops. Will they be shot, poisoned or trapped when their population gets too large and farmers, without the protection of the hunts, are forced to start treating them as vermin? Shooting often means wounding and a long and painful death, poisoning can often take days of agony; a vixen caught in a trap will tear her leg off to get back to her cubs.

It is an upsetting fact that no wild animal has a peaceful death in old age. Before hunting started, foxes were kept down by wolves. Perhaps Nature's way of a chase by 'dogs' and a quick death may be the best of a bad job.

Mrs Joan Leigh Fermor, Morea, Greece[5]

However much of her early life she rejected, part of Joan was always an English countrywoman at heart. This must have been the only letter Joan ever published in the newspapers: it was many years now since they had featured Joan as a story.

In the years immediately before Graham's death, and for the rest of her life afterwards, Joan preferred to spend her Christmases at Mill House. Billa Harrod and Coote Lygon always came to stay with her, and when they arrived would squabble cheerfully with one another over which of them was to get the Green Room – the better of the two guest rooms. (Billa, the more forceful of the two friends, usually won.) Paddy preferred to spend Christmas at Chatsworth with Deborah Devonshire, where there were many more seasonal and social entertainments of the kind he enjoyed. Joan and Debo never shared the depth of affection which Paddy and Debo had for one another. When Paddy and Joan were invited for a weekend at Sandringham with the Prince of Wales, the presence of the Duchess of Devonshire – 'as Paddy is tucking up with Debo there doesn't seem much room' – was one of the reasons she gave Billa for not going.[6] She had also long since lost interest in the ceremony of such occasions. She wrote to Janetta:

> *Paddy can't get back earlier as has got going on the book, I hope,*
> *& feel he must get on as much as possible before he has to get*
> *back for his long-fixed date, 10th, when he stays with the P of W*
> *for his Sandringham week-end. Billa fixed this as she is a great*
> *friend & I was asked too but of course have not got three evening*
> *dresses which one has to have &, as you can imagine, couldn't*
> *possibly buy even one. Twenty people sound rather terrifying too,*
> *like a three day cocktail party, & I believe one has to go to*
> *church on Sunday. Otherwise I should like to meet him & I could*
> *do with a bit of the luxury & delicious food promised by Billa.*[7]

'Paddy was 77 yesterday,' Joan wrote in February 1992. 'He has no intimations of mortality & has planned several more books, each taking, I suppose, the usual 5–10 years.'[8] All of these were books Paddy intended to write after he had finished Volume III of his walk across Europe. Six years had passed since the publication of *Between the Woods and the Water*. Several first versions of its intended successor stood among the coloured folders on the window shelves: two yellow files, 'Vol III, early drafts' and 'Vol III fragments'; a yellow file, 'vol III, ms notes'; two black files, 'drafts 2 (Varna to Burgas)' and 'drafts 3 (Wallachian Plain to Varna)'; an orange file, 'False starts to vol III'. Last and latest of all were the pink and blue ring folders, which held the typescripts which eventually saw the light of day as *The Broken Road*, a book which was to end in the middle of a sentence.

Unfortunately, Paddy kept stalling. Joan's letters provide a commentary on his progress or lack of it. In November 1993, she wrote:

When we got back [from London] there was still the drought, no
olives & lots of things dying & then a few days later came
storms, hurricanes, floods, all the precious water of course
pouring into the sea taking all the top soil with it. Our road was
completely destroyed, a rushing river at the bottom & six
crevasses in it, no question of getting the car out. Luckily two
days ago it stopped raining & this morning, with layers of stones
& branches we somehow bounced the car across & now have to
leave it half way up the hill. Now it is pouring again, pitch dark
at 12 noon & water pouring through the ceiling. The electricity
is more off than on & we've had no hot water since we've been
back. But extraordinarily we have been rather happy & all
because, of course, Paddy is really getting on with Vol. 3.

But then Joan added, 'Or so I believe, I haven't seen anything.'[9] In February 1995: 'Paddy is 80 in two days' time. He sits at his desk all day long & I think is getting on a bit. I feel so sorry for him & it's very annoying.'[10] 'Paddy is very well, tremendously busy with everything except his book.'[11] 'Paddy is a bit down, can't get used to old age & spends too long sorting out endless papers & losing them again. We need a secretary, a cook & a chauffeur & wonderful party for P.'[12] When offered a knighthood, which would have cheered him, he turned it down: Joan thought titles absurd and would have hated being Lady Leigh Fermor, and it was always Joan's opinions which mattered.

It is impossible to give a single reason for why Volume III was never completed. Paddy had never found writing easy, and as he aged the weight of expectation and effort required inevitably increased. He also now lacked a Rudi Fischer figure to spur him on and provide him with new ideas. The only equivalent was a retired actress called Mairi Bostanzi who, between 1988 and 2010, wrote Paddy some 500 letters. Paddy referred to her as his 'Theatrical Friend'. Mairi was bilingual in Greek and English and worked as a translator; like Fischer, she became acquainted with Paddy through her translations of his books. She also made suggestions and provided comments on Paddy's translations, going to the Gennadius Library in Athens to do further research for him. The work she carried out on his behalf was scholarly and highly academic. Mairi's letters, however, were also highly singular: she was completely besotted with the man to whom she was writing. While the first paragraphs in each letter are devoted to erudite research and inter-pretation, the rest of the letter would be given over to a sort of star-struck fan mail: 'You are the most handsome man in Greece, etc.' Mairi was far from being a teenager, rather she was an elderly lady who lived alone in Athens with only her cats for company.

Paddy was also still working on his occasional journalism, and was always more than willing to find other tasks to distract him from the book. That he had never kept a proper diary was a great regret: it might have helped him pick up the threads he now found so attenuated.[13] Every day he wrote letters, 'not good for vol. 3 alas', said Joan, and many of his letters were very long indeed.[14] Dick Usborne, a journalist and former member of the SOE, was in charge of getting a P. G. Wodehouse story – 'The Great Sermon Handicap' – trans-lated into dozens of languages, and he asked Paddy to make a translation into modern Greek for him. Paddy said no at first, but then tried it before breakfast one morning, and continued until the work was finished.[15] When Paddy appeared waving his pages Joan was delighted – but it turned out that this great breakthrough was not what she had been hoping for. Some years later, when Paddy's papers were being sorted after his death, a Greek professor examined them and was baffled by the Wodehouse. He enclosed a note with them which he hoped might be of use: 'Mentions a horse-race.

Probably of ecclesiastical or Byzantine origin.' Paddy's draft had queries alongside: 'Old son? A flutter? In the soup?' Unfortunately, Greek scholarship had found the world of Bertie Wooster, Bingo Little and Honoria Glossop incomprehensible.

Peter Levi once wrote that getting to Kardamyli was more difficult than getting to the Hindu Kush. There were new roads now and this was no longer the case, but Joan said that she sometimes wondered what she and Paddy were doing 'in this exile' (as she called Kardamyli), but she could not live in London or for long in the English countryside. This did not prevent her from adding in the same letter that she would 'give anything for a Cordon Bleu cook' and that Paddy was 'trying to get thin as usual'.[16] Good food and good books were two of life's greatest pleasures, and Joan's letters had always had been full of references to them both. Even when things went wrong, such things put life into proportion. As she wrote to Paddy:

A traumatic morning last week. As I was having breakfast, eating a large piece of toast dripping with new honey & reading Macaulay's essay on Warren Hastings & feeling rather happy Lela came in to say the police were here to take off the number plates of the car as we hadn't paid the licence. Can you imagine my horror. In the end, by telephoning to Kalamata, the police agreed if I got it done by Saturday it would be alright. Of course when I got there they were charming and it's all arranged now.[17]

Bad food, on the other hand, was to be excoriated:

Caroline Conran, translating Michel Guérard's Cuisine Gourmande, says that one can use lumpfish roe instead of caviar in some recipe. This seems to me to be the complete explanation of the awfulness of most English cooking.[18]

When guests asked what they might bring when they came to stay, Joan invariably asked for some French or English cheese, which she herself would then offer to pay for (although gifts which just came from the counter at Marks and Spencer were met by undisguised consternation). As she grew older, Joan said herself that wine, books and cheese were the only things she could buy – she had lost interest in shopping for everything else. It was at the supermarket at the other end of the village, however, that Joan met a shop assistant called Gula. Joan recognized the girl's natural intelligence, and paid for her to further her education. Her own education, although a world away in experience, had been so totally inadequate and stultifying that when she saw talent in someone she was determined to help as their patron. In some measure, she was helping someone share the advantages she had herself enjoyed.

John Rayner, Joan's first husband, died in August 1990. Miranda, his third wife, had predeceased him in 1981 and he had married his fourth wife, Heulyn Dunlop, after a twenty-year-long love affair. She had met JR when they worked together in the Foreign Office. Heulyn was brought up in Tangier, where her father was a doctor – Cecil Beaton once made a drawing of her rather than pay her father's bill. She had also known Xan and Daphne when they lived in Tangier. She had already met Paddy and Joan, and as a young woman she had worked in the interior decorating shop run by Jaime Parladé, Janetta's fourth husband. Alan Pryce-Jones, Joan's first boyfriend, died of diabetes in 2000, aged ninety-one. He was buried in Chantilly in France beside his wife, Poppy. In his final years Alan became a close friend and travelling companion of Greta Garbo, although he never wrote about her, for which she was grateful. She kept a copy of his memoirs, *The Bonus of Laughter*, in her Manhattan apartment. His last boyfriend had died of an HIV-related illness shortly before Alan's own death.

Billa and Joan once had a row at Kardamyli about Bruce Chatwin's death from AIDS. Billa had been less than sympathetic, but when she got back to England she wrote to apologize. The best night of her stay, she said, was the last one, when she was in her bedroom sitting in her knickers and Joan came in and they talked as they did in the old days when they were young. Billa said she felt so sorry for the young of today. She herself had taken lovers and slept with a man who was wildly promiscuous without having had to care about the consequences. Joan replied that she did not remember their AIDS talk very much, but did not think Billa could ever be boring. In later years Billa had founded the Norfolk Churches Trust and was an upholder of all things traditional, but together with Coote Lygon – the third member of the trio of friends Paddy called 'the three Musketeers' – they had shared so much of their lives since their debutante days and their wild parties. Billa often mentioned how she had broken the candelabra and come crashing down from the Dumbleton ceiling. They had supported Coote through her family scandals – the disgrace of her father, Coote's late and wretched marriage to Robert Heber-Percy, and the death of her alcoholic sister Mamie (the beautiful Julia of *Brideshead Revisited*): 'What a very very sad family – all the brothers dead & no-one to continue the Lygons who were so interesting. Poor poor Coote – she is brave and wonderful.'[19]

Joan, who was having trouble walking, wrote again:

Is the delay for your cataract op due to the NHS or does the surgeon not think it's ready? If the former please darling have it done privately and I will pay for it. I'm having mine, I think, done at the beginning of Aug. but have to see the surgeon first.

*It would make me feel less privileged if I could help you. I
would love it & it would make me feel really happy. I have so
much unaccustomed money now and long to give most of it
away & why not to friends instead of charities which usually
turn out to be helping missionaries or gun-running. Do agree,
and there's no time to be lost, & don't tell anyone . . .*

*I couldn't face another hip op. at my age so just hope it won't
go wrong again. I go about with morphine in my pocket but
they won't help me to be able to move.*[20]

And when Billa came to Greece, 'A bit of French or English cheese
would be more than welcome (for me to pay for) & please don't
bother about anything else, it's hard enough getting oneself here!'[21]

When old friends wrote they reminisced about their rich mutual
memories. A former debutante like Joan, Celia Paget had briefly
worked for Cyril Connolly on *Horizon* and had received a proposal
from George Orwell after the sudden death of his wife, but her reply
had been equivocal. In a letter to Joan, Celia wrote about her recollections of Dick Wyndham's house at Tickerage, 'the intellectual
treasure hunts (you won one of them), the bluebell wood,' and
about Dick Wyndham himself, 'a very special person, and I miss
him still'.

*Another of my treasured memories is of the day when you and
Paddy turned up in the New Angleterre – delightful name –
when I was staying there. You were off to dine in the Embassy
and invited me into your room to chat while you were dressing,
where I recall the following conversation:*

*J. I can't possibly wear this dress – it's hideous. I knew it was
going to be very hot, so why didn't I bring a single cotton dress?
– that's what interests me.*

P. Joan, this jacket hasn't been cleaned – it's spotted like a leopard.

J. Can you believe it, someone has been into the room and removed the centre of my brooch, it doesn't [look right] without it, and I can't wear this dress without a brooch. Well, we shall go off looking like the Ugly Sisters.

Of course you went off looking as beautiful and immaculate as ever, leaving me [to] roar with laughter at all our doubts, which I suppose is why I remember it so well.[22]

'Biographers are the bane of one's life here as usual,'[23] Celia wrote drily. She lived in Cambridge, where it was difficult to avoid them – from that point of view Kardamyli was easier. Any enquirer turning up at Joan's door uninvited would have been turned away – she could be unforgiving to anyone who even took her photograph without her permission. Occasionally researchers wrote to Joan but she would pass the letter over to Paddy: he was less discreet anyway.

Biographical researchers might not have been welcome, but friends always were. Even if old friends found getting to Kardamyli too difficult, new ones continued to arrive. Among them was Joan's nephew Robert, who came with his wife Bridget and their two young sons, Ben and James. Robert's interests had changed from fossils to ecology and raptors; his work was in preserving the environment in international and local communities, concerns which were sympathetic to Joan's own view of the world. After lunch, Paddy, who had never welcomed children to the house before, used to tell the young boys stories. Near the end of his life he wished he had had children of his own.[24] The impression Joan now made on small children was of someone rather ancient, but loving and motherly. As she walked in her espadrilles around the several layers of the house and its outside corridors, she seemed to belong to a different age from the one they were used to. She wore large, thick-rimmed spectacles wherever she was. In Greece her clothes were more suited to a warmer climate: linen slacks of cream or beige; a vest or blue-and-white-striped T-shirt; in the evening, a thin blue cardigan with wooden buttons. When Paddy talked, she remained gently berating and encouraging: 'Oh Paddy . . .' Her voice had a gentle creak in it, and her accent was rather old-fashioned and upper class, it was such a very long time since she had lived in England permanently. As she grew older Joan avoided cooking, but she always made the bitter orange marmalade which Paddy liked, as well as serving crispbreads spread with roe from scavenged sea-urchins and making her own lemon vodka using lemons from the garden. The tray for adult drinks was beside the door leading into the corridor, and in the evening she watched, drink in hand, while her young great-nephews made their final race to Jellicoe's Leap – a jutting rock from which one could make a highly tricky landing into the sea, a jump supposedly patented by the Jellicoe family. Joan gave the children all the attention they wanted: what they remember most is her kindness.

Joan never shut off her imagination. For years she had kept a blue exercise book for quotations which appealed to her:

Men live in the cosmos like mice in a great house, enjoying splendours not designed for them. (Plotinus)

Truth, like love & sleep, resents
Approaches that are too intense. (WH Auden)

By the early 1990s, Paddy and Joan had already started to think about what might happen to the house after their day. As the house at Kardamyli had been paid for principally by Joan's money, she gave her nephew Robert first refusal.

Dear Robert

    Do you & Bridget really want this house when we are dead, too feeble to cope or in a loony bin, very soon now? We don't want to sell it but always thought it would be a dreadful white elephant for any friends or relations to be responsible for it, only suitable for an elderly writer who would use the books, the things I mind most about. We have thought of leaving it to some Greek institution or charity but now think that wouldn't work though Paddy still has a few more ideas about that. We are worried that until you both retired (& I don't see why you ever should) it would be abandoned & goodness knows what would happen to it then. The bad thing for you is that the death duties might come to £3 or 400,000 as the whole thing has become rather valuable now but perhaps Martin M[itchell] & our lawyer can put that down & there would be more money coming from the Trust I hope.

    I would like you to have it as I think you would love it & look after it well & be a great help here with the ecology & minerals etc, but it would be a great change for you living here.

    Much love to you all

    Joan[25]

After great consideration, Robert reluctantly turned the offer down. His sons were still at school and he wanted them to have a home in England to return to. Greece was too drastic a move.

Among their friends was Jon van Leuven, who came from a Texan oil family of Anglo-Dutch descent and had degrees in Spanish, French and physics from Yale. Half Jon's life was spent in Gothenburg in Sweden, the other half in the Mani where for twenty years he lived in a tiny shepherd's cottage in the village of Holy Wisdom at the very edge of an escarpment high above Kardamyli. (They were connected by a long track leading from one level to another or by a very long and twisting road.) Jon, a tall, lean, gently humorous man, was full of wholly improbable plans which could never be realized – like the enormous, empty hole in the ground he had dug in his garden one summer as a swimming pool – before being distracted by some other plan just as impossible. Like Paddy he was multilingual but with the addition of Scandinavian languages. And like Paddy he could talk for hours on end about anything, for everything in life was potentially fascinating. He was also immensely well read although he drew the line at P. G. Wodehouse. Whenever Paddy insisted on lending him a Bertie Wooster or a Blandings Castle novel, Jon always, as if by accident, forgot to pick it up when he was leaving.

The poet Hamish Robinson, a close friend of one of Magouche's sons-in-law, also arrived in the lives of Joan and Paddy, and often house-sat for them when they returned to Dumbleton for the summer. In his letters, Paddy always referred to Hamish as 'that very nice Wykehamist poet'. When Paddy's eyesight began to fade, Hamish took him swimming, and in the evening Hamish clambered around, retrieving books from higher shelves to look up poems and information and talk across languages and literatures. He also regularly acted as chauffeur, ferrying Paddy and Joan back and forth from Kardamyli to Athens airport, and sometimes from London to Dumbleton: 'Do you want a book for the car – *Mill on the Floss*?' Paddy fussed over Joan. If Hamish accompanied Paddy on the plane, he went armed with a bagful of miniature bottles to get the older man through the flight. Paddy was once stopped from taking a whisky bottle on board, so did his heroic best to down the whisky while all around him cheered. In the inside cover of the Kardamyli visitors' book, Paddy placed one of Hamish's sonnets, called 'Kalamitsi':

The water, limpid in the morning calm
Will beckon you as if it had a mill
To glittering depths open like a till
Brimming with green and gold; without a qualm
The cats sleep on in shadows out of harm
Or toy with things they did not need to kill;
Only the cypress pointing up the hill
Rejects the banished posture of the palm.

This is no paradise for idle hands
The trophies and mementoes on its shelves,
The written books and maps of travelled lands,
All tell of those who raised up for themselves
A habitation built on shifting sands:
These dreams we could not master for ourselves.

Olivia Stewart also became part of Paddy and Joan's intimate circle. Olivia was Paddy's god-daughter – her godmother was Freya Stark. Her father, Sir Michael Stewart, was ambassador in Athens from 1967 to 1971: 'I hadn't, until yesterday, gone even as far as Kalamata. Michael Stewart, who sends his greetings, is here with his nice daughter Olivia, and we went on a picnic to Ithome and Ancient Messenia,'[26] Paddy wrote to Xan in the early 1980s. Olivia made a career in the film industry, in production and then as a script-writer and film consultant. As part of the household, she witnessed the Leigh Fermor domestic choreography. Each morning began with a ceremony; the conversation between Paddy and Joan always commenced, 'Good morning, what book are you reading, would I enjoy it? Shall I give it to you next?' When Joan and Paddy grew older and found it more and more difficult to run the Kardamyli household, Olivia gradually became indispensable. Neither Joan nor Paddy had ever been remotely practical, so Olivia came twice a year to put the house in order: change light bulbs, mend dripping taps, change fuses. When she left again, Joan regretted, the house began to fall to bits, despite daily phone calls.

In her eighties, Joan's health began to fail. Eventually she could no longer get down to the beach to bathe. Then, in April 2002, Joan suffered what Janetta referred to as a 'beastly crash and damaged head . . . how awful you must feel & it's probably hurting & you are probably simply *furious* too, furious with yourself for doing it to your poor self. Oh how *vile* it is being old, & being so horribly aware of one's own idiocy & clumsiness, etc, etc, etc.'[27]

On the morning of 4 June 2003, after Joan had eaten her breakfast, she said to Olivia, 'I really would like to die but who'd look after Paddy?' Olivia answered, flippantly, that she would. A few minutes later, Joan fell in the bathroom, hit her head and died instantly of a brain haemorrhage. Even if she had continued breathing, her wishes were unequivocal; in all the drawers of her desk there were messages saying 'Do not resuscitate'. Joan's body was returned to England. At the funeral at St Peter's, Dumbleton, Jochen Voigt read from Sir Thomas Browne's quest for the secret proof of the existence of God, *The Garden of Cyrus*:

> The huntsmen are up in America, and they are already past their first sleep in Persia. But who can be drowsie at that howr which freed us from everlasting sleep? Or have slumbering thoughts at that time, when sleep itself must end, and as some conjecture, all shall wake again . . .

As Joan had requested, Paddy read from the Apocryphal Book of James, which George Seferis loved so much and which had also been read at Patrick Kinross's funeral:

And behold there were sheep being driven, and they went not

forward but stood still; and the shepherd lifted his hand to smite them with his staff, and his hand remained up. And I looked upon the stream of the river and saw the mouths of the kids upon the water and they drank not.

And all of a sudden all things moved onward in their course.*

The Monsell hymns, 'Oh worship the Lord in the beauty of holiness' and 'Fight the Good Fight', were also sung. Joan was then buried in the churchyard, at Graham's side.

4 November 2003

Dear Robert & Bridget

I'm very apologetic to be only writing now to thank you for your kind and consoling words about Joan. I'd put your letter, & James' & Ben's, in a special clutch to be answered at once – and the reverse happened. They got carried away in a rival tangle of envelopes, &, in spite of prolonged searches, have only just surfaced now, like mountaineers lost in an avalanche & suddenly turning up – thank God not [illegible] but late enough! Please forgive.

Joan's loss wasn't only a loss for us. Letters have been pouring in amain, & from every quarter and period. She really was loved, led by the 8 cats that liked to settle on her counterpane every morning after breakfast, and get in the way, knocking over the chessboard where she had set them out to solve some tremendous problem. When I recline in her place on the sofa to read they gather round me in a recumbent group, but, in a quarter of an hour they have all sloped off. They had realised they were being fobbed off with a fake [. . .] I've got Jochen Voigt, an old friend of both of us, staying at the moment. When

---

* Translated from the Greek by Montague Rhodes James.

*I've got through a few chores I'm going to get down to finishing
Vol III of the books about my youthful trudge across Europe, so
it won't be a misspent winter. It has been a lovely autumn,
Joan's favourite season.*

*I do hope you'll both come and stay next year and in proper
bathing time. (I went in yesterday. It was a bit nippy.) You
remember what fun we all had!*

  Much love to you both
  Paddy[28]

Paddy continued to live at Kardamyli and Dumbleton, and carry on
his life as best he could. Arrangements were made that after his
death the house would be made over to the Benaki Museum in
Athens. In Greece he continued to be looked after by his housekeeper Elpida Beloyannis and in England by Rita Walker.
Encouraged by Olivia he worked on Volume III when he could.
There was as much mail to deal with as ever although his eyesight
– as well as his hearing – was deteriorating. He also continued to
receive visitors and make visits. In the summer of 2006 Joan's gravestone was raised in Dumbleton churchyard at last, which gave him
much pleasure. He wrote to Joan's nephew – Diana's son – Michael
Casey and his wife Joey.

13 September 2006

Dear Michael and Joey,

  *This is a sort of hail and farewell letter – alas. I'm off to
Greece in a few days – but also to send you the snaps that Jeff
has taken of Joan's tombstone, which is in place at last, after
long delays. The rather white-looking Portland stone will
weather a lot in a couple of years. I think it looks very nice, and
that Joan would have approved. I've been longing for it to be in
situ.*

> *The Ancient Greek words at the bottom –* ΚΑΙ ΓΑΙΑΝ ΕΧΟΙ
> ΕΛΑΦΡΑΝ – *'May the earth rest lightly upon her' – were an*
> *ancient saying, often murmured still at rustic funerals.*
> *I've got to dash to Cumbria tomorrow, return and take wing.*
> *Please forgive this wobbly note, and a happy autumn to you*
> *both and love from Paddy.*[29]

Paddy missed her: how could it be otherwise? He kept with him a black and white scarf belonging to Joan, so that her feel and her touch were close by when he needed her presence. Joan was nothing if not complicated – and elusive. From being an awkward little girl standing in the midst of her cousins staring rather resentfully out of a photograph how had she changed? Perhaps in the words of Alan Pryce-Jones many years later 'experience had already taught her to be wary' – when he first got to know her Joan was already pursued by the press for a story. While she knew how to enjoy life, at the same time she called herself 'schizo Joan'. And: 'How I wish I wasn't such a bloody bad-tempered selfish bitch,' she once wrote uncharitably about herself. John Craxton wrote how 'Like all adorable people Joan had something enigmatic about her nature, which combined with her wonderful good looks, made her a very seductive presence. Even in a crowd she maintained a deep and private inner life.' And, he continued, 'it was her elegance, luminous intelligence, curiosity and her unerring high standards that made her such a perfect muse'[30] – to Paddy as well as to many others. Joan indeed had a remarkable life – and a lucky one. She had spent most of it with someone she loved. She had lived where she had wanted and, largely, despite the lack of children, which was her one great, lasting regret, in the way she wanted.

Then, in May 2011, Paddy had a cancerous tumour removed from his throat, but the cancer soon returned. Not long before he died he told his friend Philippa Jellicoe who was staying with him that there was going to be a great tragedy. He returned to hospital where he was looked after by the Kenwards. When he could not speak, he communicated by writing notes on pieces of paper. What was Joan like, he asked James, her great-nephew. Olivia, the Kenwards, Elpida and a nurse managed to get him back to England where, on the morning of 10 June 2011, Paddy died in Dumbleton. When Olivia had asked him what he wanted for his funeral service, 'Same as Joan,' he said.

Sources

Archives in Public Collections

Joan and Patrick Leigh Fermor
John Banting
John Betjeman
Maurice Bowra
Tom Driberg
Lawrence Durrell
Xan Fielding
Francis Guillemard
Wilhelmine Harrod
Patrick Kinross
James Lees-Milne
Alan Pryce-Jones
Isabel Rawsthorne

Merton College, Oxford
Oxford University

Select Bibliography

Annan, Noel, *Our Age: Portrait of a Generation* (Weidenfeld & Nicolson, 1990)
Ayer, A. J., *More of My Life* (Collins, 1984)
Benton, Charlotte, Benton, Tim, and Wood, Ghislaine, *Art Deco 1910–1939* (V&A Publications, 2003)

Betjeman, John, *Letters* volume 1: 1926–1951, ed. Candida Lycett-Green (Methuen, 1994)
—, *Letters* volume 2: 1951–1984, ed. Candida Lycett-Green (Methuen, 1995)
Bloch, Michael, *James Lees-Milne: The Life* (John Murray, 2009)
Boston, Richard, *Osbert: A Portrait of Osbert Lancaster* (Fontana, 1989)
Bowen, Wayne H., *Spain During World War II* (University of Missouri Press, c.2006)
Brooks, Alan, and Pevsner, Nikolaus, *The Buildings of England: Worcestershire* (Yale, 2007)
Byron, Robert, *Letters Home*, ed. Lucy Butler (John Murray, 1991)
Cardiff, Maurice, *Friends Abroad* (Radcliffe Press, 1997)
Cartland, Barbara, *We Danced All Night* (Hutchinson, 1970)
Chatwin, Bruce, *Under the Sun: The Letters of Bruce Chatwin*, eds Elizabeth Chatwin and Nicholas Shakespeare (Jonathan Cape, 2010)
Chester-Lamb, Kate, *Eventful Days, the Centenary History of St James's and the Abbey School, Malvern* (St James's and the Abbey School, 1997)
Clark, Adrian, and Dronfield, Jeremy, *Queer Saint: The Cultured Life of Peter Watson* (John Blake Publishing Ltd, 2015)
Clark, Kenneth, *Another Part of the Wood* (John Murray, 1974)
Collins, Ian, *John Craxton* (Lund Humphries, 2011)
Connolly, Cyril, *The Unquiet Grave, A Word Cycle by Palinurus* (Harper & Brothers Publishers, 1945)
Cooper, Artemis, *Cairo in the War 1939–1945* (Hamish Hamilton, 1989)
—, *Patrick Leigh Fermor: An Adventure* (John Murray, 2012)
Costello, John, *Love, Sex and War, Changing Values 1939–45* (Collins, 1985)
Culme-Seymour, Angela, *Bolter's Grand-daughter* (Bird Island Press, 2001)
De-la-Noy, Michael, *Eddy: The Life of Edward Sackville-West* (Arcadia Books, 1999)
Delmer, Sefton, *Trail Sinister* (Secker & Warburg, 1961)
—, *Black Boomerang* (Secker & Warburg, 1962)
Devonshire, Deborah, *Wait for Me!* (John Murray, 2010)
Devonshire, Deborah, and Leigh Fermor, Patrick, *In Tearing Haste*, letters ed. Charlotte Mosley (John Murray, 2009)
Dinshaw, Minoo, *Outlandish Knight: The Byzantine Life of Steven Runciman* (Allen Lane, 2016)
Eade, Philip, *Evelyn Waugh: A Life Revisited* (Weidenfeld & Nicolson, 2016)
Farson, Daniel, *The Gilded Gutter Life of Francis Bacon* (Vintage, 1993)
Fielding, Daphne, *The Nearest Way Home* (Eyre & Spottiswood, 1970)
Fielding, Xan, *Hide and Seek* (George Mann, 1973)

Fisher, Clive, *Cyril Connolly: A Nostalgic Life* (Collins, 1983)

Fleming, Ann, *The Letters of,* ed. Mark Amory (Collins Harvill, 1985)

Gathorne-Hardy, Jonathan, *Half an Arch: A Memoir* (Timewell Press, 2004)

Green, Martin, *Children of the Sun: A Narrative of Decadence in England after 1918* (Constable, 1977)

Guillemard, F. H. H., *The Cruise of the Marchesa to Kamschatka & New Guinea* (John Murray, 1889)

Hillier, Bevis, *Young Betjeman* (Cardinal, 1989)

—, *John Betjeman, New Fame, New Love* (John Murray, 2002)

Hodges, John Richard, *Dumbleton Hall: The Story of a Victorian Country House* (privately printed, 2014)

Jackson, Major F. G., *The Lure of Unknown Lands* (G. Bell and Sons Ltd, 1935)

Kavanagh, Julie, *Secret Muses: The Life of Frederick Ashton* (Faber, 1996)

Kingsley, N. W., and Hill, Michael, *The Country Houses of Gloucestershire* (Nicholas Kingsley, 1989–2001)

Knox, James, *Robert Byron* (John Murray, 2003)

—, introduction and selection, *Cartoons and Coronets: The Genius of Osbert Lancaster* (Frances Lincoln, 2008)

Lancaster, Osbert, *With an Eye to the Future* (John Murray, 1967)

Laski, Marghanita, preface by Juliet Gardiner, *To Bed with Grand Music* (Persephone, 2009)

Lees-Milne, Alvide, and Moore, Derry, *The Englishman's Room* (Viking, 1986)

Lees-Milne, James, *A Mingled Measure: Diaries 1953–1972* (John Murray, 1994)

—, *Fourteen Friends* (John Murray, 1996)

—, *The Milk of Paradise: Diaries, 1993–1997* (John Murray, 2005)

—, *Diaries 1971–1983,* abridged and introduced by Michael Bloch (John Murray, 2007)

Leigh Fermor, Patrick, *Roumeli: Travels in Northern Greece* (Penguin, 1983)

—, *Mani: Travels in the Southern Peloponnese* (Penguin, 1984)

—, *A Time to Keep Silence* (Penguin, 1988)

—, *Three Letters from the Andes* (John Murray, 1991)

—, *The Traveller's Tree: A Journey through the Caribbean Islands* (John Murray, 2005)

Levi, Peter, *A Bottle in the Shade: a Journey in the Western Peloponnese* (Sinclair Stevenson, 1996)

Lewis, Jeremy, *Cyril Connolly: A Life* (Jonathan Cape, 1997)

MacNiven, Ian, *Lawrence Durrell: A Biography* (Faber & Faber, 1998)

Mitchell, Leslie, *Maurice Bowra: A Life* (Oxford University Press, 2009)

Mitford, Nancy, *The Letters of*, ed. Charlotte Mosley (Sceptre, 1994)

Mitford, Nancy, and Hill, Heywood, *The Bookshop at 10 Curzon Street: Letters between Nancy Mitford and Heywood Hill*, ed. John Saumarez Smith (Frances Lincoln, 2004)

Moorhouse, Paul, *Giacometti, Pure Presence* (National Portrait Gallery, 2015)

Motion, Andrew, *The Lamberts: George, Constant and Kit* (Chatto & Windus, 1986)

Mowl, Timothy, *Stylistic Cold Wars, Betjeman versus Pevsner* (John Murray, 2000)

Norwich, John Julius, 'Costa' in *Ox Travels* (Profile Books, 2011)

Paice, Edward, *Lost Lion of Empire: The Life of 'Cape-to-Cairo' Grogan* (HarperCollins, 2001)

Partridge, Frances, *Diaries 1939–1972* (Phoenix Press, 2001)

Peppiatt, Michael, *Francis Bacon in Your Blood: A Memoir* (Bloomsbury, 2016)

Pryce-Jones, Alan, *The Bonus of Laughter* (Hamish Hamilton, 1987)

—, *Devoid of Shyness: From the Journal 1926–1939*, ed. John Byrne, introduction by David Pryce-Jones (Stone Trough Books, 2015)

Pryce-Jones, David, *Fault Lines* (Criterion, 2016)

Quennell, Peter, *The Marble Foot: An Autobiography, 1905–1938* (Collins, 1976)

—, *The Wanton Chase: An Autobiography from 1939* (Collins, 1980)

Rayner, Heulyn, *John Rayner: A Life* (Alumnia Publishing, 2014)

Rayner, John, *Towards a Dictionary of the County of Southampton, commonly known as Hampshire or Hants* (B. T. Bashford, 1937)

Richards, J. M., ed., *The Bombed Buildings of Britain* (Architectural Press, 1947)

Schindler's Guide to Cairo (Schindler, 1943)

Scott, J. M., *Gino Watkins* (Hodder & Stoughton, 1935)

Shakespeare, Nicholas, *Bruce Chatwin* (Vintage, 1999)

Shelden, Michael, *Friends of Promise: Cyril Connolly and the World of Horizon* (Hamish Hamilton, 1989)

Skelton, Barbara, *Tears Before Bedtime* (Hamish Hamilton, 1987)

—, *Weep No More* (Hamish Hamilton, 1989)

Spalding, Frances, *John Piper, Myfanwy Piper: Lives in Art* (Oxford University Press, 2009)

Stewart, I. McD. G., *The Struggle for Crete 20 May–1 June 1941: A Story of Lost Opportunity* (Oxford University Press, 1966)

Sykes, Christopher, *Four Studies in Loyalty* (Collins, 1946)

Symons, Julian, A. J. A. *Symons: His Life and Speculations* (Eyre & Spottiswoode, 1950)

Tarling, W. J., *Café Royal Cocktail Book* (Pall Mall Ltd, 1936)

Thorpe, D. R., *Alec Douglas-Home* (Sinclair-Stevenson, 1996)

Tinniswood, Adrian, *The Long Weekend: Life in the English Country House between the Wars* (Jonathan Cape, 2016)

Waugh, Evelyn, *Diaries*, ed. Michael Davie (Weidenfeld & Nicolson, 1976)

Waugh, Evelyn and Cooper, Diana, *Mr Wu and Mrs Stitch: the Letters of Evelyn Waugh and Diana Cooper*, ed. Artemis Cooper (Hodder & Stoughton, 1991).

Wheen, Francis, *Tom Driberg: His Life and Indiscretions* (Chatto & Windus, 1990)

Williams, Val, *The Other Observers: Women Photographers 1900 to the Present* (Virago, 1991)

Wishart, Michael, *High Diver: An Autobiography* (Quartet, 1978)

Articles

Hardy, Henry, 'Maurice Bowra on Patrick Leigh Fermor', *Spectator*, 17 December 2011

Hastings, Max, 'Demob Unhappy, the Ex-Officers Left Behind After VE Day', *Spectator*, 16 May 2015

Leigh Fermor, Patrick, 'Observations on a Marine Venus', *Twentieth Century Literature*, Hofstra University, vol. 33, no. 3

Notes

Abbreviations

APJ: Alan Pryce-Jones
GEM: Graham Eyres Monsell
JB: John Betjeman
JLF: Joan Eyres Monsell; Joan Rayner; Joan Leigh Fermor
JR: John Rayner
NLS: National Library of Scotland
PLF: Patrick Leigh Fermor
XF: Xan Fielding

Letters and other documents are dated where possible; 'nd' is used for undated; approximate dates and dates which are inferred from internal evidence are given within square brackets.

Introduction

1   Noel Annan, *Our Age*, p. 3
2   Patrick Leigh Fermor is mentioned among other war heroes on p. 205.
3   JLF to PLF, 24 April [1959]

Chapter 1: The Eyres and the Monsells

1   JLF to PLF, 28 May [1962] (NLS)
2   Information from Joey Casey, February 2016

3 Patrick Leigh Fermor, *Roumeli*, Penguin (1983), pp. 110–14
4 *Leeds Times*, January 1868, quoted in John Richard Hodges, *Dumbleton Hall: The Story of a Victorian Country House* [self-published] (2015), p. 147
5 Family information
6 *Morning Post*, 26 October 1880
7 F. H. H. Guillemard, *The Cruise of the Marchesa to Kamschatka & New Guinea*, John Murray (1889), p. 118
8 Ibid, p. 436
9 Edward Paice, *Lost Lion of Empire: The Life of 'Cape-to-Cairo' Grogan*, HarperCollins (2001), p. 57
10 Ibid, p. 61
11 *Leeds Guardian*, 29 November 1935
12 JLF to Professor Stuart Ball, 11 December [1999]

Chapter 2: Growing Up

1 John Richard Hodges, *Dumbleton Hall*, pp. 156–8
2 Alan Pryce-Jones, *The Bonus of Laughter*, Hamish Hamilton (1987), p. 26
3 D. R. Thorpe, *Alec Douglas-Home*, Sinclair-Stevenson (1996), pp. 23–4
4 Michael Bloch, *James Lees-Milne: The Life*, John Murray (2009), p. 304
5 Quoted in Adrian Clark and Jeremy Dronfield, *Queer Saint*, John Blake Publishing Ltd (2015), p. 25
6 Alan Pryce-Jones, *The Bonus of Laughter*, pp. 28–9
7 Michael Bloch, *James Lees-Milne*, p. 20
8 Martin Green, *Children of the Sun: A Narrative of Decadence in England after 1918*, Constable (1977), pp. 244–5
9 J. M. Scott, *Gino Watkins*, Hodder & Stoughton (1935), p. 2
10 Ibid, p. 171
11 Ibid, p. 310
12 Osbert Lancaster, *With an Eye to the Future*, John Murray (1967), pp. 64–5
13 Ibid, pp. 84–5
14 Quoted in Francis Wheen, *Tom Driberg: His Life and Indiscretions*, Chatto & Windus (1990), p. 40
15 *Gloucestershire Echo*, 24 May 1928
16 Kate Chester-Lamb, *Eventful Days, St James's and the Abbey School, Malvern*, St James's and the Abbey School (1997), p. 54

Chapter 3: Romance

1 Bevis Hillier, *Young Betjeman*, Cardinal (1989), p. 149
2 GEM to APJ, nd [winter 1931] (Yale)
3 JB to Camilla Russell, 2 September 1931, in *John Betjeman: Letters*, vol. 1, 1926–1951, ed. Candida Lycett-Green, Methuen (1994), p. 81
4 GEM to APJ, nd [1932] (Yale)
5 'Our Ladies Letter', *Cheltenham Chronicle*, 7 June 1930
6 Alan Pryce-Jones, *The Bonus of Laughter*, p. 82
7 Ibid, p. 72
8 Ibid, p. 231
9 Bevis Hillier, *Young Betjeman*, p. 374
10 Alan Pryce-Jones, *Devoid of Shyness: From the Journal 1926–1939*, ed. David Byrne, Stone Trough Books (2015), p. 136
11 *Bystander*, 10 February 1932
12 GEM to APJ, 13 November [1932] (Yale)
13 Alan Pryce-Jones, *Devoid of Shyness*, p. 138
14 Ibid
15 Ibid, p. 139
16 Hugo Vickers, *Cecil Beaton: The Authorized Biography*, Weidenfeld & Nicolson (1985), p. 163
17 JLF to APJ, nd [1933] (Yale)
18 JLF to APJ, nd [1933] (Yale)
19 JB to APJ, 18 February 1933, in *John Betjeman: Letters*, vol. 1, p. 117
20 JB to Billa Cresswell, nd [February 1933], ibid, p. 96
21 JLF to Billa Cresswell, nd [February 1933], ibid, p. 96
22 'Obituary of Lady Harrod', *Daily Telegraph*, 12 May 2005
23 GEM to APJ, 5 February [1933] (Yale)
24 GEM to APJ, nd [March 1933] (Yale)
25 JLF to APJ, Hotel Mexen, nd [March 1933]
26 JLF to APJ, nd [April/May 1933] (Yale)
27 Alan Pryce-Jones, *The Bonus of Laughter*, p. 83
28 *Daily Express*, 2 May 1933
29 *Daily Mirror*, 3 May 1933
30 David Pryce-Jones, *Fault Lines*, Criterion Books (2015), p. 62
31 Ibid, p. 26
32 Patrick Balfour to James Lees-Milne, 13 September [1933] (Yale)
33 Court Circular, *The Times*, 24 November 1933

Chapter 4: Earning One's Living

1 *Bystander*, 27 February 1934
2 Clive Fisher, *Cyril Connolly: A Nostalgic Life*, Macmillan (1995), pp. 149–50
3 David Pryce-Jones, *Cyril Connolly: Journal and Memoir*, Collins (1983), p. 254
4 David Pryce-Jones, *Fault Lines*, p. 101
5 Ibid, p. 104
6 Alan Pryce-Jones, *Devoid of Shyness*, p. 159
7 Alan Pryce-Jones, *The Bonus of Laughter*, p. 98
8 Patrick Balfour to James Lees-Milne, 4 September [1934] (Yale)
9 JB to APJ, 6 October 1934, quoted in *John Betjeman: Letters*, vol. 1, p. 146
10 Deborah Devonshire, *Wait for Me!*, John Murray (2010), p. 186
11 JB to Billa Cresswell, 10 December 1936, quoted in *John Betjeman: Letters*, vol. 1, p. 162
12 Conversation with Jochen Voigt, May 2014
13 *Bystander*, 5 July 1933
14 Ibid, 6 September 1933
15 Philip Eade, *Evelyn: A Life Revisited*, Weidenfeld & Nicolson (2016), p. 159
16 GEM to APJ, 22 November [c. 1935] (Yale)
17 Maurice Richardson, 'Portrait of Brian Howard', *Listener*, 18 January 1968
18 Ibid
19 Jonathan Gathorne-Hardy, *Half an Arch: A Memoir*, Timewell Press (2004), p. 18
20 Bevis Hillier, *Young Betjeman*, p. 150
21 Christopher Sykes, *Four Studies in Loyalty*, Collins (1946), p. 83
22 *The Times*, 1 October 1935
23 Robert Byron, *Letters Home*, ed. Lucy Butler, John Murray (1991), p. 238
24 Ibid, 2 November 1935

Chapter 5: Love – and Marriage

1 Billa Cresswell to APJ, nd [1933]
2 *Hull Daily Mail*, 5 August 1936

3   *Cheltenham Chronicle*, 5 September 1936
4   Julie Kavanagh, *Secret Muses: The Life of Frederick Ashton*, Faber (1996), p. 206
5   Billa Harrod to Jaime Parladé. Janetta Parladé to author, May 2017
6   Adrian Tinniswood, *The Long Weekend*, Jonathan Cape (2016), p. 324
7   Osbert Lancaster, *With an Eye to the Future*, p. 120
8   Patrick Balfour, 'Society', *Listener*, 12 June 1935
9   Michael Bloch, *James Lees-Milne: The Life*, p. 81
10 Alan Pryce-Jones, *The Bonus of Laughter*, p. 85
11 Peter Quennell, *The Marble Foot*, Collins (1976), pp. 220–1
12 Jeremy Lewis, *Cyril Connolly: A Life*, Jonathan Cape (1997), pp. 269–70
13 JB to Gerald Berners, 6 September 1936, quoted in *John Betjeman: Letters*, vol. 1, p. 158
14 Heulyn Rayner, *John Rayner: A Life*, Alumnia Publishing (2014), p. 60
15 *Daily Express*, 14 February 1936
16 *Tatler*, 10 March 1937
17 *Daily Express*, 5 March 1937
18 Heulyn Rayner, *John Rayner*, p. 11
19 Peter Quennell, *The Wanton Chase*, Collins (1980), p. 128
20 Cyril Connolly, *The Unquiet Grave*, Harper & Brothers Publishers (1945), p. 101
21 Celia Paget to JLF, 29 September 1985 (priv. coll.)

Chapter 6: Wartime London

1   JLF to Penelope Betjeman, nd [1939] (Victoria)
2   James Lees-Milne, *Fourteen Friends*, John Murray (1996), pp. 112–13
3   Francis Wheen, *Tom Driberg*, p. 139
4   JR to JB, 4 January 1940 (Victoria)
5   JLF to JB, nd [February/March 1940] (Victoria)
6   JLF to Tom Driberg, nd [April 1940] (Christ Church, Oxford)
7   JLF to Heulyn Rayner, 31 May 1993 (priv. coll.)
8   Nancy Mitford to Jessica Treuhaft, 13 April 1945, in *Love from Nancy: The letters of Nancy Mitford*, ed. Charlotte Mosley, Sceptre (1994), p. 80
9   Heulyn Rayner, *John Rayner*, p. 107
10 Julian Symons, *A. J. A. Symons: His Life and Speculations*, Eyre & Spottiswood (1950), p. 37
11 Sefton Delmer, *Trail Sinister*, Secker & Warburg (1960), p. 105

12 Isabel Rawsthorne, unpublished autobiography (Tate)
13 Ibid
14 Heulyn Rayner, *John Rayner*, p. 109
15 Ian Collins, *John Craxton*, Lund Humphries (2011), pp. 38–40
16 JR to Myfanwy Piper, 20 August 1941 (Tate)
17 Adrian Clark and Jeremy Dronfield, *Queer Saint*, p. 177
18 John Costello, *Love, Sex and War*, Collins (1984), pp. 245–6
19 'Obituary of Joan Leigh Fermor' by John Craxton, *Independent*, 10 June 2003
20 Peter Quennell, *The Wanton Chase*, p. 23
21 Quoted in David Pryce-Jones, *Fault Lines*, p. 201
22 Adrian Tinniswood, *The Long Weekend*, p. 373

Chapter 7: Encounter in Cairo

1 Sefton Delmer, *Black Boomerang*, Secker & Warburg (1962), p. 153
2 GEM to JB, 7 August 1942 (Victoria)
3 GEM to APJ, 21 April 1943 (Yale)
4 JLF to JR, 7 October [1943] (priv. coll.)
5 JLF to Heulyn Rayner, 31 May 1993 (priv. coll.)
6 Patrick Kinross to James Lees-Milne, 17 September 1940 (Yale)
7 Patrick Kinross to James Lees-Milne, 22 July 1941 (Yale)
8 Nancy Mitford to Jessica Treuhaft, 13 April 1945, in *Love from Nancy*, p. 176
9 Evelyn Waugh, *Diaries*, ed. Michael Davie, Weidenfeld & Nicolson (1976), p. 575
10 JR to Isabel Delmer, [July/August 1944] (Tate)
11 JR to Isabel Delmer, 12 November 1944 (Tate)
12 PLF, 'The First Ball at Tara' (NLS)
13 PLF to Lord Lloyd of Dolobran, 9 December 1939 (Churchill College, Cambridge)
14 PLF to Lord Lloyd, 28 May 1940 (Churchill College, Cambridge)
15 Information from Chris White, 3 March 2017
16 Artemis Cooper, *Patrick Leigh Fermor: An Adventure*, John Murray (2012), pp. 193–4
17 Denise Menasce to PLF, 29 October 1944 (NLS)
18 Artemis Cooper, *Cairo in the War 1939–1945*, Hamish Hamilton (1989), p. 36

19 Barbara Skelton, *Tears Before Bedtime*, Hamish Hamilton (1959), p. 59
20 JLF to Janetta Parladé, 6 September [?] (priv. coll.)
21 PLF, draft obituary, www.bookride.com/2010/08/eddiegathornehardy.html
22 Denise Menasce to PLF, 10 November 1944 (NLS)
23 Denise Menasce to PLF, 15 November 1944 (NLS)
24 Artemis Cooper, *Paddy Leigh Fermor*, p. 200
25 Denise Menasce to PLF, [January 1945] (NLS)
26 Ian MacNiven, *Lawrence Durrell: A Biography*, Faber & Faber (1998), p. 276
27 Denise Menasce to PLF, 10 February 1945 (NLS)
28 MacNiven, *Lawrence Durrell*, p. 242
29 Denise Menasce to PLF, postmark 26 April 1945 (NLS)
30 Heulyn Rayner, *John Rayner*, p. 140
31 Isabel Rawsthorne, unpublished autobiography (Tate)

Chapter 8: Athenian Adventures

1   James Knox, *Cartoons and Coronets: The Genius of Osbert Lancaster*, Frances Lincoln (2008), p. 48
2   Maurice Cardiff, *Friends Abroad*, Radcliffe Press (1997), pp. 1–2
3   Ibid, p. 5
4   JLF to Patrick Kinross, 10 November [1945] (Huntington)
5   Nancy Mitford to Mark Ogilvie-Grant, 8 February 1947, in *Love from Nancy*, p. 159
6   Artemis Cooper, *Patrick Leigh Fermor*, p. 208
7   Maurice Cardiff, *Friends Abroad*, p. 17
8   XF to PLF, 25 November 1945 (NLS)
9   Xan Fielding archives (NLS)
10 Max Hastings, 'Demob Unhappy', *Spectator*, 16 May 2015
11 Patrick Leigh Fermor, 'Observations on a Marine Venus', *Twentieth Century Literature*, Hofstra University, vol. 33, no. 3
12 JLF to Lawrence Durrell, 10 November 1946 (South Illinois)
13 PLF to Lawrence Durrell, 18 October 1946 (South Illinois)
14 Tom Driberg to JLF, nd (Christ Church, Oxford)

Chapter 9: From Curzon Street to the Caribbean

1   JLF to Penelope Betjeman, nd [1947] (Victoria)
2   JR to Tom Driberg, 29 March 1947 (Christ Church, Oxford)
3   Ibid
4   Juliet Gardiner, 'Preface', in Marghanita Laski, *To Bed with Grand Music*, Persephone (2009), p. xiv
5   Maurice Bowra to XF, 3 April 1947 (Fielding archive, NLS)
6   *Times* obituary, 6 May 1955
7   *Horizon*, September 1946, pp. 140–75
8   JLF to PLF, nd (NLS)
9   JLF to PLF, postmark 28 May 1950 (NLS)
10 Lawrence Durrell to XF, nd (Fielding archive, NLS)
11 JLF to Penelope Betjeman, nd [1947] (Victoria)
12 Patrick Leigh Fermor, *The Traveller's Tree*, Penguin (2005), p. xi
13 Ibid, pp. 16–17
14 Ibid, pp. 105–6
15 JLF to JR, 31 March [1948] (priv. coll.)
16 Ibid (priv. coll.)
17 Quoted in Jeremy Lewis, *Cyril Connolly: A Life*, p. 416
18 Ian Fleming, *Sunday Times*, 23 May 1948
19 JLF to JR, 3 August [1948] (priv. coll.)
20 JLF to JR, [December 1949] (priv. coll.)
21 Michael Shelden, *Friends of Promise: Cyril Connolly and the World of Horizon*, Hamish Hamilton (1989), p. 198
22 PLF and JLF always refer to the village as 'Gadencourt'; this seems to be a variant of the more usual 'Gadancourt'.
23 JLF to PLF, nd [August 1948] (NLS)
24 JLF to PLF, nd [August 1948] (NLS)
25 Jeremy Lewis, *Cyril Connolly*, op. cit. pp. 418–19
26 Ibid

Chapter 10: Separation

1   Patrick Leigh Fermor, *A Time to Keep Silence*, Penguin (1988), p. 41
2   Ibid, p. 10
3   PLF to JLF, Wednesday [September] 1948 (NLS)

4 PLF to JLF, [30 September 1948] (NLS), Adam Sisman, *The Letters of Patrick Leigh Fermor*, John Murray (2016), pp. 34–5
5 JLF to PLF, Wednesday [October 1948] (NLS)
6 PLF to JLF, [October 1948] (NLS)
7 PLF to JLF, 13 October 1948 (NLS)
8 Patrick Leigh Fermor, *A Time to Keep Silence*, pp. 46–7
9 PLF to JLF, 2 December 1948 (Huntington)
10 Artemis Cooper, *Patrick Leigh Fermor*, p. 234
11 PLF to JLF, Sunday night [December] (NLS)
12 JLF to PLF, [December] (NLS)
13 Ibid, p. 79
14 JLF to PLF, [December] (NLS)

Chapter 11: Family Affairs

1 Patrick Leigh Fermor, *A Time to Keep Silence*, p. 79
2 JLF to PLF, 26 January [1950] (NLS)
3 Harold Nicolson, *Observer*, 10 December 1950
4 JLF to PLF, 21 January [1951] (NLS)
5 JLF to PLF, nd [October 1949] (NLS)
6 JLF to PLF, nd [January 1951] (NLS)
7 PLF to JLF, nd [January 1951] (NLS)
8 JLF to PLF, 10 January 1951 (NLS)
9 JLF to PLF, nd (NLS)
10 Michael Peppiatt, *Francis Bacon in Your Blood*, Bloomsbury (2016), p. 96
11 JLF to PLF, nd [c. May 1949] (NLS)
12 PLF, notebook [NLS]
13 Quoted in Andrew Motion, *The Lamberts: George, Constant and Kit*, Chatto & Windus (1986), p. 240
14 JLF to PLF, 3 February [?] (NLS)
15 Michael Wishart, *High Diver: An Autobiography*, Quartet (1978), p. 149
16 Barbara Skelton, *Tears Before Bedtime*, p. 83
17 JLF to PLF, 26 January [1951] (NLS)
18 PLF to JLF, 28 February 1951 (NLS)
19 Barbara Skelton, *Tears Before Bedtime*, pp. 181–2
20 PLF to the *Spectator*, 16 April 2014
21 PLF to Patrick Kinross, 17 February 1952 (Huntington)
22 JLF to PLF, 18 February 1952 (NLS)

23 PLF, Lismore Castle, Ireland, to JLF, 28 April 1963 (NLS)

24 Family archive

25 GEM to APJ, 4 March 1948 (Yale)

26 JLF to PLF, nd [postmark 28 May 1950] (NLS)

27 JLF to PLF, 6 March 1951 (NLS)

28 JLF to PLF, [postmark 29 November 1954] (NLS)

29 JLF to PLF, [January 1955] (NLS)

30 JLF to PLF, 19 January 1956 (NLS)

31 JLF to PLF, 24 April [1959] (NLS)

32 Adam Sisman, *The Letters of Patrick Leigh Fermor*, p. 185

Chapter 12: In Love with Greece

1   PLF, Greek diary, 'September 1950' (NLS)

2   PLF, Gadencourt diary, 'December 1951' (NLS)

3   PLF, Greek diary, 'September 1950' (NLS)

4   PLF, undated diary [early 1950s] (NLS)

5   Xan Fielding archive (NLS)

6   Charlotte Mosley (ed.), *In Tearing Haste: Letters between Deborah Devonshire and Patrick Leigh Fermor*, John Murray (2009), p. 12

7   Conversation with Janetta Parladé, May 2014

8   Daphne Fielding, *The Nearest Way Home*, Eyre & Spottiswood (1970), p. 10

9   JLF to PLF, 28 November 1954 (NLS)

10 Adam Sisman, *The Letters of Patrick Leigh Fermor*, pp. 93–4

11 Leslie Mitchell, *Maurice Bowra: A Life*, Oxford University Press (2011), pp. 89–90

12 Mark Amory (ed.), *The Letters of Ann Fleming*, Collins Harvill (1985), pp. 138–9

13 PLF to Lawrence Durrell, 24 November 1954 (South Illinois)

14 Mark Amory (ed.), *The Letters of Ann Fleming*, p. 139

15 Conversation with Janetta Parladé, May 2014

16 Leslie Mitchell, *Maurice Bowra*, p. 146

17 JLF to PLF, 9 January [1952?] (NLS)

18 Leslie Mitchell, *Maurice Bowra*, p. 138

19 Charlotte Mosley (ed.), *In Tearing Haste*, pp. 366–7

20 Henry Hardy, 'Maurice Bowra on Patrick Leigh Fermor', *Spectator*, 17 December 2011

21 Patrick Leigh Fermor, *Mani: Travels in the Southern Peloponnese*, Penguin (1983), pp. 9–11
22 JLF to PLF, 21 April [c. 1962] (NLS)

Chapter 13: Kardamyli

1 I. McD. G. Stewart, *The Struggle for Crete 20 May–1 June 1941: A Story of Lost Opportunity*, Oxford University Press (1966), pp. 18–19
2 JLF to PLF, 21 April [c. 1961]
3 PLF to JLF, nd [1962] (NLS)
4 PLF to JLF, nd [1962] (NLS)
5 Charlotte Mosley (ed.), *In Tearing Haste*, p. 109
6 JLF to Maurice Bowra, 16 November [1963?] (Wadham College, Oxford)
7 JLF to Patrick Kinross, [December 1966] (Huntington)
8 JLF to John Banting, 6 January 1968 (Tate)
9 PLF to Patrick Kinross, 8 March 1968 (Huntington)
10 Conversation with Janetta Parladé, May 2017
11 Draft letter, PLF to XF [1960] (NLS). Square brackets in text.
12 Ian Collins, *John Craxton*, p. 132

Chapter 14: Friendship and Loss

1 PLF to Balasha Cantacuzene, 10 November 1971 (NLS)
2 GEM to APJ, 30 November 1961 (Yale)
3 James Lees-Milne, *Diaries 1971–1983*, abridged and introduced by Michael Bloch, John Murray (2007), p. 176
4 JLF to John Banting, 6 April [1960s] (Tate)
5 JLF kept a copy of the letter among her papers (priv. coll)
6 PLF to Balasha Cantacuzene, 10 November 1971 (NLS)
7 Mark Amory (ed.), *The Letters of Ann Fleming*, pp. 395–7
8 PLF to James Lees-Milne, 5 July 1981 (Yale)
9 JLF to XF, 28 August [early 1970s], (NLS)
10 JLF to John Banting, 3 June [1971] (Tate)
11 Conversation with Janetta Parladé, May 2014
12 JLF to Janetta Parladé, nd (priv. coll.)

13 JLF to Janetta Parladé, 14 December [1960s] (priv. coll.)

14 PLF to Robert and Bridget Kenward, 21 December 2004 (priv. coll.)

15 JLF to Patrick Kinross, 14 October [1971] (Huntington)

16 John Saumarez Smith (ed.), *The Bookshop at 10 Curzon Street: Letters between Nancy Mitford and Heywood Hill*, Frances Lincoln (2004), p. 154

17 JLF to Janetta Parladé, 3 October [1973] (priv. coll.)

18 Heywood Hill to Robin Fedden, nd [c. 1978] (NLS)

19 Draft obituary of Edward Gathorne-Hardy (d. 1978) by Patrick Leigh Fermor, www.bookride.com/2010/08/eddie.gathorne.hardy.html

20 Alvilde Lees-Milne and Derry Moore, *The Englishman's Room*, Viking (1986), p. 92

21 JB to PLF, 20 September 1969 (NLS)

22 JB to JLF, 20 September 1969, in *John Betjeman: Letters*, vol. 2, 1951–1984, ed. Candida Lycett-Green, Methuen (1995), pp. 389–90

23 JB to Wayland Kennet, 19 September 1969, ibid, p. 390

24 John Banting to JLF, nd [c. January 1958] (NLS)

25 JLF to PLF, 3 November [1974] (NLS)

26 *John Betjeman: Letters*, vol. 2, p. 450

27 Barbara Skelton, *Weep No More*, Hamish Hamilton (1989), p. 150

28 Stephen Spender, *New Selected Journals*, Faber (2012), pp. 388–9

29 Notebook (NLS)

30 John Banting to JLF, nd [10 May 1971] (NLS)

31 Frances Partridge, *Diaries 1939–1972*, Phoenix Press (2001), p. 322

32 *The Times*, 12 August 1976

33 JLF to JR, 13 October 1976 (priv. arch.)

34 JB to Ena Driberg, 1 October 1976, in *John Betjeman: Letters*, vol. 2, p. 520

35 JLF to Janetta Parladé, nd [November 1976] (private archive)

36 JLF to JR, 15 July 1977 (private archive)

Chapter 15: A Time of Gifts

1 JLF to Sir Michael Stewart, 1 October 1988 (private archive)

2 Conversation with Janetta Parladé, May 2014

3 JLF to Janetta Parladé, 25 November 1967 (private archive)

4 JLF to Patrick Kinross, 29 January 1970 (Huntington)

5 PLF to Janetta Parladé, March 1976 (private archive)

6   Correspondence between author and Michael O'Sullivan, September–December 2016

7   Patrick Leigh Fermor, *Three Letters from the Andes*, John Murray (1991), p. 3

8   JLF to PLF, nd [1971] (NLS)

9   *John Betjeman: Letters*, vol. 2, p. 374

10 JLF to Janetta Parladé, 20 June 1976 (private archive)

11 *John Betjeman: Letters*, vol. 2, p. 450

12 JB to JLF and PLF, 15 February 1979, ibid, pp. 559–60

13 JB to JLF, 18 June 1969, ibid, p. 386

14 James Lees-Milne, *A Mingled Measure: Diaries 1951–1972*, John Murray (1994), pp. 135–6

15 Bruce Chatwin to Elizabeth Chatwin, 30 August 1970, in *Under the Sun: The Letters of Bruce Chatwin*, eds Elizabeth Chatwin and Nicholas Shakespeare, Jonathan Cape (2016), p. 158

16 XF to PLF, 27 April 1980 (NLS)

17 Nicholas Shakespeare, *Bruce Chatwin*, Vintage (2000), p. 566

18 PLF to XF, 12 April 1983 (Fielding archive, NLS)

19 JLF to Michael and Damaris Stewart, nd [1985] (priv. coll.)

20 Bruce Chatwin to JLF and PLF, 24 April 1986, *Under the Sun*, p. 456

21 JLF to Billa Harrod, 9 May [1986] (Norfolk County Records Office)

22 JLF to Janetta Parladé, nd (priv. coll.)

Chapter 16: Endings

1   APJ to Billa Harrod, nd [postmark 3 December 1987]

2   PLF to Janetta Parladé, 15 May 1990 (priv. coll.)

3   JLF to Janetta Parladé, 6 January 1993 (priv. coll.)

4   Jonathan Reeves to author, 10 October 2016

5   JLF to *Daily Telegraph*, 16 July 1999

6   JLF to Billa Harrod, 12 February [1992] (Norfolk County Records Office)

7   JLF to Janetta Parladé, 19 February [1992] (Norfolk County Records Office)

8   JLF to Billa Harrod, 12 February [1992] (Norfolk County Records Office)

9   JLF to Janetta Parladé, 28 November [postmark 1993] (priv. coll.)

10 JLF to Janetta Parladé, nd [13 February 1995] (priv. coll.)

11 JLF to Janetta Parladé, 22 February [nd] (priv. coll.)

12 JLF to Janetta Parladé, 25 February [nd] (priv. coll.)

13 James Lees-Milne, *The Milk of Paradise: Diaries 1993–1997*, John Murray (2005), pp. 142–3

14 JLF to Janetta Parladé, 12 February [198?] (priv. coll.)

15 PLF to XF, 12 April 1983 (Fielding archive, NLS)

16 JLF to Janetta Parladé, nd (priv. coll.)

17 JLF to PLF, Friday [nd] (NLS)

18 JLF to Janetta Parladé, 15 January [?] (priv. coll.)

19 Billa Harrod to JLF, 28 September [1982] (NLS)

20 JLF to Billa Harrod, 4 July [c. 1999] (Norfolk Records Office)

21 JLF to Billa Harrod, 24 September [?] (Norfolk Records Office)

22 Celia Paget to JLF, 29 September 1985 (priv. coll.)

23 Celia Paget to JLF, 28 October 1998 (priv. coll.)

24 Conversation with Janetta Parladé, 27 July 2017

25 JLF to Robert Kenward [1990s] (priv. coll.)

26 PLF to XF, 12 April 1983 (Fielding archive, NLS)

27 Janetta Parladé to JLF, 2 May 2002 (NLS)

28 PLF to Robert and Bridget Kenward, 4 November 2003 (priv. coll.)

29 PLF to Michael and Joey Casey, 13 September 2006 (priv. coll.)

30 'Obituary of Joan Leigh Fermor' by John Craxton, *Independent*, 10 June 2003

Index

C

F

J

I

K

M